2399

# FOOD AND BEVERAGE

# MANAGEMENT

Prentice
Hall

We work with leading authors to develop the
strongest educational materials in hospitality management,
bringing cutting-edge thinking and best
learning practice to a global market.

Under a range of well-known imprints, including
Prentice Hall, we craft high quality print and
electronic publications which help readers to understand
and apply their content, whether studying or at work.

To find out more about the complete range of our
publishing please visit us on the World Wide Web at:
www.pearsoneduc.com

Pearson
Education

# FOOD AND BEVERAGE MANAGEMENT

Second Edition

## JOHN COUSINS, DAVID FOSKETT AND CAILEIN GILLESPIE

THE FOOD AND BEVERAGE TRAINING COMPANY,
THE LONDON SCHOOL OF TOURISM, HOSPITALITY AND LEISURE,
AND THE SCOTTISH HOTEL SCHOOL

Prentice
Hall

An imprint of **Pearson Education**

Harlow, England · London · New York · Reading, Massachusetts · San Francisco · Toronto · Don Mills, Ontario · Sydney
Tokyo · Singapore · Hong Kong · Seoul · Taipei · Cape Town · Madrid · Mexico City · Amsterdam · Munich · Paris · Milan

PEARSON EDUCATION LIMITED
Edinburgh Gate
Harlow
Essex CM20 2JE
England

and Associated Companies around the world
*Visit us on the World Wide Web at*
www.pearsoneduc.com

First published 2002

ISBN 0 582 45271 6

*British Library Cataloguing-in-Publication Data*
A CIP catalogue record for this book can be obtained from the British Library

*Library of Congress Cataloging-in-Publication Data*
A catalog record for this book can be obtained from the Library of Congress

10 9 8 7 6 5 4 3 2 1
06 05 04 03 02

Typeset by 35 in 9.5/13pt Gilliard
Printed in Great Britain by Henry Ling Ltd,
at the Dorset Press, Dorchester, Dorset.

# CONTENTS

# PREFACE

The aim of this book is to provide supporting information for those involved or likely to be involved in a variety of levels of food and beverage management. This is an introductory text for students and practitioners, which also provides a framework on which to develop further knowledge and skill.

In revising this second edition we have taken into account the various changes in examining and awarding body syllabuses and in particular the British National Vocational Qualification (NVQ) standards. The book is specifically intended to cover the underpinning knowledge and skill required by those wishing to be assessed up to level 4. However, the book is also constructed to meet the broader study requirements of a range of other programmes including Higher National Diploma (HND), HCIMA and foundation and undergraduate degree programmes.

The book covers aspects of the management of food and beverage (or foodservice) operations, which are applicable to a wide variety of sectors. We have also assumed that those using this text will have already acquired knowledge and skills in food and beverage operations.

One of the key changes we have made, in addition to updating and revising the material generally, is to set the consideration of the management of food and beverage operations within a broader business framework. Operations are not an end in themselves, and food and beverage management is as much about the management of the business as it is about specific aspects of the food and beverage product. Although this is reflected throughout the book, more consideration is given, for example, to the business environment, in Chapter 1, and to appraising the whole operation and strategic decision-making in Chapter 7.

The other key change is to do with supporting learning. The objectives for each of the chapters have been revised so that they now indicate the learning outcomes that may be achieved. These objectives can also be mapped against the learning outcome requirements of different in-college or in-company courses, as well as being mapped against the underpinning knowledge requirements of the level 4 NVQs (SVQs). To support this approach, a complete listing of all the learning outcomes of the book is given in Appendix A, at the end of the text. Other appendices are provided which detail particular approaches, such as the listing and explanation of operational and financial ratios in Appendix D. Support is also available as a downloadable supplement which provides figures and tables from the text, along with other information about the second edition. A link will also be provided from John Cousins' website: www.food-and-beverage-training.co.uk.

Modern-day food and beverage (or foodservice) operations are continuing to improve in the quality of food, beverages and the service on offer. Professionalism is increasing, through better training and development, and there is a much greater understanding of customer needs, with the quality of service now becoming a key differentiating factor when customers are choosing between similar establishments. It is to provide further support for these approaches that this text has been revised. Our view still remains that successful food and beverage operations are those that have a clear understanding of their customers' needs, which they continually seek to meet.

The content of this book is intended to be reflective of current industrial practice but this does not mean that it should be seen as a prescriptive book. It provides information and viewpoints on a variety of aspects of food and beverage management and considers various approaches which students and the food and beverage manager may find useful.

John Cousins, David Foskett and Cailein Gillespie
*March 2001*

# ACKNOWLEDGEMENTS

The preparation of this text has drawn upon a variety of research and experience. We would like to express our grateful thanks to all the organisations and individuals who gave us assistance and support and especially those who have provided feedback on the first edition.

In particular we would like to thank: Councillor Lloyd Adison, Norfolk County Council; Matthew Alexander, Food and Beverage Manager, The Scottish Hotel School; Denise Bober, Director of Human Resources, The Breakers Resort, West Palm Beach, Florida; Joanna Brynes, Licensing Solicitor, Harper Macleod Solicitors, Glasgow; Richard Congreve, IS (Information Systems) Manager, Scotland, Justerini and Brooks, Edinburgh; Croner's Catering, Croner Publications, London; Andrew Durkan, independent food and wine consultant and lecturer, and a well-known author and wine expert; George Fong, Partner and Vice-President Engineering and Construction, Forresthills Hotels and Resorts, Dallas, Texas; The Hotel and Catering Training Company, London; The Hotel and Catering International Management Association (HCIMA), London; IFS Publications, Bedford; Dennis Lillicrap, consultant, author and trainer in food and beverage service; Andrew Morgan, Food and Beverage Services Manager, Sheraton Park Tower, Knightsbridge, London; Christopher Rawstron, General Manager, Gatwick Hilton Hotel, Gatwick; Robert Smith, Head of Food and Beverage Service at the Birmingham College of Food and Tourism and Creative Studies; Wilfried N. Wagner, Senior Vice-President Project Development, EIH Limited, Delhi, India; Kevin Walters, Vice-President, Food and Beverage, The Breakers Resort, West Palm Beach, Florida, and Thames Valley University, London (for permission to adapt material, previously developed by John Cousins in 1999 from the university's undergraduate distance learning workbook *Strategic Hospitality Management*).

And a very special thank you to David Shortt, catering consultant and co-author of the first edition of *Food and Beverage Management*.

Images on the cover have been used with the kind permission of Bass Hotels and Resorts UK.

## PUBLISHER'S ACKNOWLEDGEMENTS

We are grateful to the following for permission to reproduce copyright material:

Figure 1.4 and Figure 1.5 adapted with the permission of The Free Press, a Division of Simon & Schuster, Inc., from *Competitive Advantage: Creating and Sustaining Superior Performance* by Michael E. Porter, copyright © 1985, 1998 by Michael E. Porter (Porter,

M. 1985); Figure 1.6 adapted from *Excellence Model*, © EFQM, the EFQM Excellence Model is a registered trademark (EFQM, 1999); Figure 2.4, adapted, reprinted by permission of Elsevier Science from 'Defining what quality service is for you' by W. Martin *The Cornell Hotel and Restaurant Administration Quarterly*, Vol. 27, No. 1, pp. 32–8, copyright 1986 by Cornell University (Martin, W. 1986); Figure 7.2 adapted from *Menu Engineering: A Practical Guide to Menu Analysis*, Hospitality Publications, Inc., Okemos, Michigan (Kasavana, M. and Smith, D. 1999); Figure 7.9 and Figure 7.10 adapted from *Exploring Corporate Strategy: Text and Cases*, Fifth Edition, Pearson Education Ltd (Johnson, G. and Scholes, K. 1999).

Whilst every effort has been made to trace the owners of copyright material, in a few cases this has proved impossible and we take this opportunity to offer apologies to any copyright holders whose rights we may have unwittingly infringed.

# CHAPTER ONE

# FOOD AND BEVERAGE OPERATIONS AND MANAGEMENT

## AIM

This chapter aims to set the scene for the rest of the text.

## OBJECTIVES

This chapter is intended to support you in:

- setting the contents of this book in context
- identifying and applying a systems approach to foodservice operations
- developing ways of categorising the industry sectors
- exploring the nature of the foodservice product
- identifying the nature of customer demand
- analysing the business environment in order to identify factors which may affect the success of a foodservice organisation
- identifying the legal framework in which the foodservice industry operates
- setting organisational goals and objectives
- gaining an insight into service quality and quality management issues
- setting standards for food and beverage operations
- balancing customers' service requirements with resource productivity
- developing an integrated approach to service quality management.

## FOOD AND BEVERAGE OPERATIONS

Food and beverage (or foodservice) operations are concerned with the provision of food and a variety of beverages within business. The various elements that comprise food and beverage operations can be summarised in the catering cycle shown in Figure 1.1. Food and beverage operations are therefore concerned with:

1 The markets served by the various sectors of the foodservice industry and consumer needs.

2 The range and formulation of policies and business goals and objectives of the various operations and how these affect the methods adopted.

3 The interpretation of demand and decisions to be made on the food and beverages to be provided as well as the other services.

4 The planning and design to create a convergence of facilities required for food and beverage operations and making decisions about the plant and equipment required.

5 The development of appropriate provisioning methods to meet the needs of the production and service methods used within given operational settings.

6 Operational knowledge of technical methods and processes and ability in the production and service processes and methods available to the foodservice operator, understanding the varying resource requirements (including staffing) for their operation, as well as decision-making on the appropriateness of the various processes and methods to meet operational requirements.

7 Controlling the costs of materials as well as the costs associated with the operation of production and service, and controlling the revenue.

8 The monitoring of customer satisfaction.

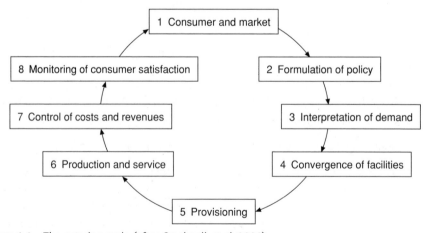

**Figure 1.1** The catering cycle (after Cracknell *et al.* 2000)

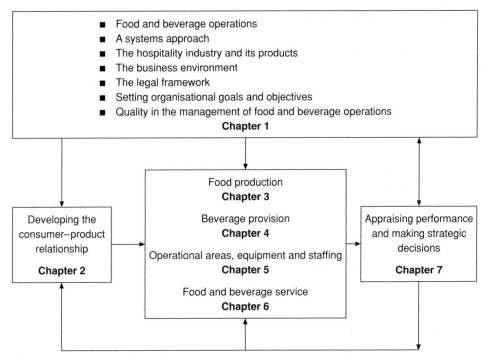

**Figure 1.2** Representation of the catering cycle for the structure of this book

The catering cycle is not just a statement of what food and beverage operations are con-cerned with, but also a dynamic model in the sense that difficulties in one area of the cycle will cause difficulties in the elements of the cycle that follow. Thus, for instance, difficulties with purchasing affect production and service, and control. Similarly, difficulties experienced under one element of the cycle will have their causes in preceding elements.

The catering cycle, and the systematic approach it encourages, has been used to form the basis for the structure of this book. This is indicated by the re-presentation of the catering cycle given in Figure 1.2.

Although presented in this form, which is predominately linear, the actual management of food and beverage operations is organic. The structure of the book given in Figure 1.2 therefore also attempts to indicate the nature of the interrelationship that exists between the various components.

Thus all the issues that are raised in Chapter 1 have an impact on all the other issues that are considered in the rest of the book. Consequently, any consideration of the customer, the methods used in food production and those used in food and beverage service must be carried out taking account of, for instance, the systems approach, the business environ-ment, the nature of demand being met, and approaches to quality management. Equally, any review of the performance of the operation, as discussed in Chapter 7, must also take account of these aspects. Additionally, any operational decisions are as dependent on the outcome of appraising the performance of the operation as they are on appraising the trends in the business environment.

Food and beverage management, then, is the management of all the stages of the catering cycle. It is also systematic and organic; quantitative and qualitative; academic and pragmatic, and also both serious and fun. This is its fascination.

## A SYSTEMS APPROACH

The underlying thinking behind much of this text relies on the application of a systems approach to the management of food and beverage operations. There are two dimensions to a systems approach:

- The first dimension is concerned with being systematic in the design, planning and control of a food and beverage operation.
- The second dimension is concerned with the management of the operating systems within a food and beverage operation.

This systems approach varies considerably from the traditional approaches to service management. The differences are summarised and contrasted by the comparisons presented in Table 1.1.

**Table 1.1 Comparison of traditional and system approaches**

| Traditional approach | Systems approach |
| --- | --- |
| Based on assumptions of linearity in the marketplace | Sensitive to changes in business conditions |
| Depends on the experience of key people | Depends on staff experience and good data |
| Information not readily available | Information available as needed |
| Intuitive | Quantitative |
| Reactive in nature | Proactive in nature |
| Service driven | Cost and service driven |
| Vulnerable to turnover of key people | Less vulnerable to turnover of key people |
| Weak in accountability | Strong in accountability |

*Source*: Records and Glennie (1991)

The application of systems thinking has also led to a different view being taken of the operating systems that exist within a food and beverage operation. Traditionally, a food and beverage operation, and therefore food and beverage management, was seen as being concerned with the management of an operation as a whole. In systems terms this could easily have been seen as the management of two basic systems: a system for food production and a system for food and beverage service. In this view, which was still the traditional view, food and beverage service was seen primarily as a delivery system. This in itself has problems, as the customer was seen largely as a passive recipient of the service rather than, as now more widely recognised, a participant in the service process. Fortunately, the application of operations management approaches, and the systems thinking associated with it, leads to a different view of the management of food and beverage operations.

Up until the late 1980s there was much discussion about differences between the production of goods and the provision of services. Most of the operations literature at the time was concerned with exploring the supposed differences between production operations management and service operations management. However, Morris and Johnston (1987) settled much of this argument by taking a more holistic view. They put forward the argument that operations management, and therefore the management of any operation, is concerned with the management of three elements:

- the management of materials
- the management of information
- the management of people (customers).

By linking this thinking in the general operations management field together with re-considering the management of food and beverage operations, Cousins (1988) identified that there are in fact three distinct systems operating within a single food and beverage operation. These are:

- the system for *food production*
- the system for delivery or the *service sequence*
- the system for customer management or the *customer process*.

These three systems are tangible systems whose properties are known and can be defined. Figure 1.3 presents a generic diagram for a foodservice operation, which summarises the three systems and the relationship between them.

The three systems identified in Figure 1.3 interlink to form the whole operation. In turn each of the three systems can be further broken down into their component parts, or separate subsystems, for example, 'purchasing'. The systems approach can be further clarified by reference to the operations hierarchy in Table 1.2 (this book is concerned primarily with the management of methods and operations under the definitions given in Table 1.2).

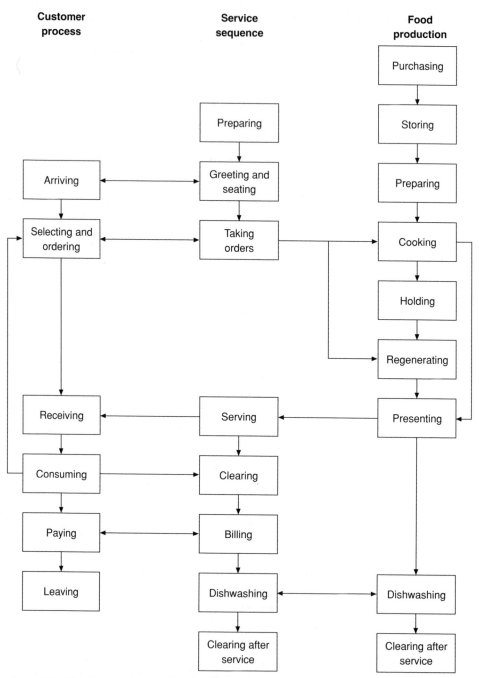

**Figure 1.3** The three systems of food and beverage operations and their interrelationship (after Cousins 1988 and Lockwood 1994)

**Table 1.2** Operations hierarchy

| Element of operation | Description |
| --- | --- |
| Skills and knowledge | Knowledge of food accompaniments, handling a spoon and fork |
| Task | Group of skills, e.g. glasswashing |
| Duty | Group of tasks, e.g. preparing bar for service |
| Method | Group of duties combined to achieve a particular service, e.g. silver service |
| Operation | Combination of various methods, e.g. production, service, billing, thus creating a complete system for the provision of food and beverages within a specific type of outlet |
| Sector | Business environment in which the operation exists |

For a foodservice operation, *food production* may be seen as a 'hard' system, which is expected to behave predictably. The *customer process*, however, may be seen as a 'soft' system because it involves emotional reactions, personal values and attitudes and shifting expectations, which are personal rather than technical in construction. However, the *service sequence* contains characteristics of both 'hard' and 'soft' systems. It is 'hard' in the technical and procedural aspects of service and 'soft' because there are aspects of it that are to do with interactions between staff and customers.

Food and beverage management, therefore, is concerned with the management of an operation, which is constructed from three identifiable operating systems that are interlinked: and each of these three systems is made up from a variety of subsystems. Thinking in this way can be useful. Johns and Jones (2000), amongst others, support this view. For food and beverage managers, understanding the characteristics of systems and the ways in which systems behave can help in the control of resources (systems inputs), efficient and effective operation (systems processes), and assure the achievement of the required objectives (systems outputs).

## THE HOSPITALITY INDUSTRY AND ITS PRODUCTS

The hospitality industry is usually identified by its output of products which satisfy the demand for food, drink and accommodation away from home. The industry is often split into the accommodation and foodservice industries.

Over the years there has been much discussion, reminiscent of the discussion in the operations management field, about possible differences between goods and services. The approach of this book is to follow the lead of many in talking only about products.

Knowles (1996) confirms that there is in fact no such thing as a 'pure product'. Products which are produced and sold have production and delivery elements although these may be separated by distance or time, or both, as in the production of cars which is separated from the selling of cars in showrooms. All products, then, have some form of tangible (or physical) element and all products have some intangible (or non-physical) element. In the hospitality industry these two are operating side by side, as part of the product.

Knowles (1996) also proposes that as well as the four Ps of marketing (product, price, promotion and place) there are seven particular dimensions of the hospitality industry's product that should be taken into account. These are:

- *Intangibility* – referring to the nature of the service element of the product. The accommodation and food and beverages can be described and defined but the service element is potentially variable both in the process and in the way it is carried out.

- *Perishability* – the inability to sell tomorrow the rooms and restaurant seats which were not occupied today.

- *Simultaneous production and consumption* – the product (from the customer's perspective) is not created until the customer requests it.

- *Ease of duplication* – the core (food, drink and accommodation) of the product is the most easily duplicated. The procedural aspects of service are less so, and the convivial aspects (the way the procedures are carried out by staff) the least easy to duplicate.

- *Heterogeneity* – the potential for highly variable procedural execution and conviviality.

- *Variability of output* – demand for the hospitality product varies dramatically throughout the day, week, month, year and over a period. Sustaining consistency of the product within these fluctuations is a major challenge for the hospitality operator.

- *Difficulty of comparison* – the intangible elements of the service product make direct comparison of the service product difficult. Knowles also suggests three comparators that customers use when purchasing. These are:
  - search qualities – attributes that can be identified before purchase
  - experienced qualities – attributes that can be identified only after consumption
  - credence qualities – attributes which customers may find impossible to evaluate because of a lack of experience, knowledge or evaluative skills.

Hospitality-related purchase decisions tend to derive from experience and credence decisions. Consequently, customers tend to rely more on personal sources of information than they might for other products. This may explain the phenomenal demand for reviews and guidebooks.

## Sectors of the foodservice industry

There are many types of eating-out premises, but differing premises do not necessarily indicate the nature of the demand being met. For instance, a cafeteria may be found in industrial catering, motorway service stations, hospitals and retail operations. For marketing purposes, sectors are better identified based upon the nature of customer demand being met and not on the type of operation. The list of the sectors given in Table 1.3 (both in UK and US terminology) is based upon identifying the purpose of the sector, i.e. the nature of demand being met by foodservice operations. This method of classification

**Table 1.3   Sectors of the foodservice industry (including UK and US terminology comparison)**

| Industry sector – UK terminology | Purpose of the foodservice operation | Industry sector – US terminology |
|---|---|---|
| **Hotels and other tourist accommodation** | Provision of food and drink together with accommodation services | **Hotel, motel and other tourist accommodation** Often referred to as the **lodging industry** |
| **Restaurants** including conventional and specialist operations | Provision of food and drink generally at high price with high levels of service | |
| **Popular catering** including cafés, pizza, grills, specialist coffee shops, roadside restaurants and steakhouses | Provision of food and drink generally at low/medium price with limited levels of service | **Separate eating and drinking places** Categories usually defined by reference to three criteria: |
| **Fast food** including McDonald's and Burger King | Provision of food and drink in highly specialised environment characterised by high investment, high labour costs and vast customer throughput | ▪ level of service, e.g. quick service to full service or fine dining ▪ extent of menu, e.g. limited to full ▪ price range, e.g. low to high |
| **Takeaway** including ethnic, spuds, KFC, snacks, fish and chips, sandwich bars, kiosks | Provision of food and drink quickly | |

**Table 1.3**   *(cont'd)*

| Industry sector – UK terminology | Purpose of the foodservice operation | Industry sector – US terminology |
| --- | --- | --- |
| **Retail stores** | Provision of food and drink as adjunct to retail provision | **Retail market** |
| **Banqueting/ conferencing/ exhibitions** | Provision of large scale food and drink alongside services such as conferencing | **Leisure and special event market** |
| **Leisure attractions** such as theme parks, galleries, theatres, airline terminals | Provision of food and drink to people engaged in another pursuit | |
| **Motorway service stations** | Provision of food and drink together with petrol and other retail services often in isolated locations | **Highway (interstate)** |
| **Industrial catering** either in-house operations or through catering contractors | Provision of food and drink to people at work | **Business and industry markets** |
| **Welfare catering** | Provision of food and drink to people in colleges, universities, the forces and to people through established social need | **Social caterer Student, Healthcare, Institutional** and **Military** |
| **Licensed trade** including public houses, wine bars, licensed clubs and members' clubs | Provision of food and drink in an environment dominated by licensing requirements | **Separate drinking places** But also some units included in Separate Eating and Drinking Places above |
| **Transport catering** including railways, airlines and marine | Provision of food and drink to people on the move | **Transportation market** |
| **Outdoor catering** (or off-premises catering or event catering) | Provision of food and drink away from home base and suppliers, usually associated with a major event | **Catering market** |

*Source*:  based on Lillicrap *et al.* (1998)

of sectors by purpose provides for either the small company to identify its immediate competitors, or for the larger company – which may be operating in a number of markets – to identify immediate competitors within a specific sector. It also provides for the identification of other sectors where competition might exist for the sector under consideration, i.e. alternatives (hotels, popular catering, fast food) may attract the same customers at different times or as alternatives.

The foodservice industry is often also separated into two sets of sectors: the profit-orientated sectors and the cost provision sectors (for example, welfare catering). In the profit sectors, marketing is aimed at meeting customer demand, usually in competition with other organisations, for profit. Although the profit motivation does not appear in the cost-provision sectors, the need to satisfy customer demand does, albeit within the constraints of a given budget. It is generally recognised, for instance, that better-fed workers work better, and better-satisfied patients recover more quickly.

## The nature of demand

There are many different kinds of food and beverage or foodservice operation, designed to meet a wide range of types of demand. It is perhaps important, though, to recognise that these different operations are designed for the needs people have at the time, rather than for the type of people they are. The same person may be a business customer during the week, but a member of a family at the weekend; they may want a quick lunch on one occasion, a snack whilst travelling on another or a meal for the family at yet another. Additionally, the same person may be booking a wedding or organising some other special occasion. Clearly there are numerous reasons for eating out, other examples being: to do something different, to try different foods, or for sheer convenience because one is already away from the home, out shopping, at the cinema, a conference or an exhibition.

The reasons for eating out vary and, with this, the types of operation that may be appropriate at the time. Differing establishments offer different service, in both the extent of the menu and the price as well as varying service levels. Also the choice offered may be restricted or wide. Basically there are three types of market in which operations may be meeting demand. These are:

- *Captive markets* where the customer has no choice, for example hospital patients or people in prison.
- *Non-captive markets*, for example those people who have a free choice of establishments.
- *Semi-captive markets* where there is some restriction, for example people travelling by air who have a choice of airline but once the choice is made, are restricted to the food and drink on offer. This category also applies, for instance, to railways, some inclusive-term holidays and people travelling on motorways.

Identifying what business a foodservice operation is in, then, is not simply about what sector it is in or what type of operation: it is also about identifying the range of types of demand that are being met by the operation. This will help with identifying the direct or indirect competition that might exist.

## The nature of the foodservice product

To every product (and the foodservice product is no exception) there are two dimensions: features and benefits. Features are the physical characteristics of the product but marketers tend to stress benefits because of the realisation that products are bought for the satisfaction they provide.

The foodservice industry's products may be defined as the set of satisfactions or dissatisfactions which a customer receives from a foodservice experience. The satisfaction may be physiological, economic, social or psychological or convenience as follows:

- Physiological needs, for example to satisfy hunger and thirst, or to satisfy the need for special foods.
- Economic needs, for example staying within a certain budget, wanting good value, a convenient location or fast service.
- Social needs, for example being out with friends, business colleagues or attending special functions such as weddings.
- Psychological needs, for example responding to advertising, wanting to try something new, fulfilling lifestyle needs or satisfying or fulfilling the need for self-esteem.
- Convenience needs, for example it may not be possible to return home or the desire may be there for someone else to prepare, serve and wash up.

Dissatisfaction falls into two categories:

- Controllable by the establishment, for example scruffy, unhelpful staff, cramped conditions.
- Uncontrollable, for example behaviour of other customers, the weather, transport problems.

Customers may be wanting to satisfy all or some of these needs and it is important to recognise that it is the reason behind wanting or having to eat out, rather than the food and drink by themselves, that will play an important part in determining the resulting satisfaction or dissatisfaction with the experience. It is quite possible that the motivation to eat out is not to satisfy basic physiological needs at all.

## Product augmentation

Sometimes the product delivered to the customer is different from that received by the customer. In other words, the reason for the customer's buying the product (for example, out with friends), and not the product itself, may determine the satisfaction.

.s are often drawn between the core, tangible and augmented concepts of
'or example:

..ic *core* of the product is the food and drink provision itself.

- The *tangible elements* of the product are the methods of delivery (silver service restaurant
  or vending machine) or portions of a certain size.
- *Augmentation* of the product takes into account the complete package.

Differing sectors of the foodservice industry are in essence meeting similar customer
demands, i.e. offering the same core product. However, this can be modified and enhanced
in cost-effective ways to make the product more attractive. Competition within specific sectors
takes place largely at the augmented level. In the foodservice industry this augmentation
might include:

- speed of service
- ordering/booking convenience
- reliability
- provision of special foods
- cooking to order
- home deliveries
- availability of non-menu items
- entertainment
- privacy/discretion
- acceptance of credit cards
- availability of account facilities.

These various elements are often drawn together with the core and tangible elements
under the heading the 'meal experience' concept (Jones 1988).

## The meal experience

If people have decided to eat out then it follows that there has been a conscious choice
to do this in preference to some other course of action. In other words, the foodservice
operator has attracted the customer to buy their product as against some other product,
for example theatre, cinema or simply staying at home. The reasons for eating out may be
summarised under seven headings:

- *Convenience*, for example being unable to return home as in the case of shoppers or
  people at work or involved in some leisure activity.
- *Variety*, for example trying new experiences or as a break from home cooking.

- *Labour*, for example getting someone else to prepare, serve food and wash ._____.....ply the impracticality of housing special events at home.

- *Status*, for example business lunches or people eating out because others of their socio-economic group do so.

- *Culture/tradition*, for example special events or simply because it is a way of getting to know people.

- *Impulse*, for example simply spur-of-the-moment buying.

- *No choice*, for example those in welfare, hospitals or other forms of semi- or captive markets.

People are, however, a collection of different types, as any demographic breakdown will show. Whilst it is true that some types of foodservice operation might attract certain types of customer, this is by no means true all the time; for example, McDonald's is marketed to the whole population, and customers are attracted depending on their needs at the time.

The decision to eat out may also be split into two parts: first, the decision to do so for the reasons given above, and then the decision as to what type of experience is to be sought. It is generally agreed that there are a number of factors influencing this latter decision. These factors extend the core, tangible and augmented distinctions drawn earlier. The factors that affect the meal experience may be summarised as follows:

- *Food and drink on offer*   This covers the range of foods, choice, availability, flexibility for special orders and the quality of the food and drink.

- *Level of service*   Depending on the needs people have at the time, the level of service sought should be appropriate to these needs. For example, a romantic night out may call for a quiet table in a top-end restaurant, whereas a group of young friends might be seeking more informal service. This factor also takes into account services such as booking and account facilities, acceptance of credit cards and also the reliability of the operation's product.

- *Level of cleanliness and hygiene*   This relates to the premises, equipment and staff. Over the past decade this factor has increased in importance in the customers' minds. The recent media focus on food production and the risks involved in buying food have heightened awareness of health and hygiene aspects.

- *Perceived value for money and price*   Customers have perceptions of the amount they are prepared to spend and relate these to differing types of establishment and operation. However, many people will spend more if the value gained is perceived to be greater than that obtained by spending slightly less. (Also see the notes on price, cost, worth and value in Chapter 2, page 40.)

- *Atmosphere of the establishment*   This is difficult to quantify, as it is an intangible concept. However, it is composed of a number of factors such as: design, decor, lighting, heating, furnishings, acoustics and noise levels, the other customers, the staff and the attitude of the staff.

Identifying the factors above is important because it considers the product from the point of view of the customer. All too often, foodservice operators can get caught up in the provision of food and drink, spend several thousands on design, decor and equipment, but ignore the actual experience the customer might have. Untrained service staff are a good example of this problem. Operations can tend to concentrate on the core product and forget the total package. A better understanding of the customer's viewpoint or the nature of customer demand leads to a better product being developed to meet it. The meal experience factors are discussed further in Chapter 2, pages 46–55.

## THE BUSINESS ENVIRONMENT

Any foodservice business operates within the hospitality industry environment and this in turn operates within the wider business or macro-environment. The macro-environment and the industry environment are interrelated. Although the split is not totally clean, it can be convenient to consider them as separate parts of the business environment before looking at the links between them. Clearly, changes in the macro-environment can have an impact on the hospitality industry itself and then on the current and future competitors of any operation. These impacts can also be reciprocated.

## The macro-environment

The macro-environment is the broader environment outside the immediate environment of a particular foodservice business and the hospitality industry.

PEST, STEP, PETS, PESTEL, STEEPL and PESTLE are all variations of the acronym that might be used to refer to the relevant factors when carrying out an analysis of the macro-environment. The influences they stand for are:

P   Political

E   Economic

S   Socio-cultural

T   Technological

L   Legal

E   Ecological.

The value of whichever version of the acronym is chosen (and here we use PESTLE) is that it offers a simple mechanism for grouping related factors, although this might hide the interrelationships.

There are many possible influences which can be identified, such as:

■ The changing age profile of the population and how it will affect markets in ten years' time, when a relatively well-off, retired population may offer better prospects than a smaller, younger generation with limited spending power.

■ Government policies on privatisation or ecological issues, especially through the impact of European legislation, because of the influence of Germany and the Scandinavian countries.

■ The effect of changes in exchange rates and domestic interest rates which can seriously affect financial performance, especially with globally operating hospitality businesses.

■ The advances in technology, which include the innumerable developments in computing and telecommunications.

It may be difficult to detect the impact of many of the factors on the foodservice industry. There is also a danger of sterility in using a formal approach to PESTLE analysis. At worst, it can become a ritual listing of all possible influences. This has three possible dangers:

■ Data overload.

■ Failure to try to assess the potential impact of an environmental change, however unlikely it may seem.

■ Failure to recognise the combined impact of a number of influences.

So, looking outwards means also having to look inwards at the organisation to answer question such as:

■ Why are we, or how can we be, successful?

■ Is it because there is a growing market out there?

■ Is it going to keep growing?

■ Will customers still buy our products?

■ Is it because our products are affordable?

■ If so, what are the major influences on our costs?

■ What changes of policy or price are we vulnerable to?

■ How can the product life cycle be extended?

### Interactions between PESTLE elements

It can be an instructive and creative exercise to look out for interactions between the PESTLE elements. This is well illustrated by the all-important environmental factor: the ecological movement.

Technology has produced damaging effects on the environment. These have led to social concerns, which have manifested themselves in political action and eventually legislation, especially at the European level. This has in turn spurred companies on to seek out technological developments to cope with the problem and gain competitive advantage.

Thus foodservice operations are having to respond to, for instance, consumer mistrust of genetically modified foods, with some firms making specific marketing claims based on not using such foods. As regards ecologically friendly products, Germany is pressing for European legislation not only to reflect the concerns of its electorate, but also to create potential markets for its companies which have been forced to be at the forefront of product development in this field.

### Identifying changes in the PESTLE elements

It is important also to keep a close watch on influences that are unlikely to occur but, if they did, could have a major impact on an organisation.

Many organisations are, or should be, aware of the main external influences that affect them at present. These could include factors that are fairly easy to identify and to monitor, such as the weather, government legislation, changes in the local business environment, changes in fashion, and developments in technology in directly related areas. Examples of these could be:

- The closure of a local manufacturing plant, which is a major source of local employment, directly affecting both business and leisure-based demand for hotel and catering services and leading to a decline in the area generally.
- The opening of a major tourist attraction which offers an opportunity for local food-service operations but may also encourage new businesses into the area and therefore increased competition.
- The introduction of parking restrictions around a restaurant which might seriously reduce direct access and therefore business.

Other areas are less easy to grasp. These include:

- Developments that are so new or unknown that most people have not realised they may be important and virtually nobody has any knowledge of the impact they might have. Examples of new developments have been microcomputers in business, Teflon® (using technology originally developed for space exploration) in cooking utensils, and the life-saving use of a simple and cheap sugar–salt solution for dehydrated children in areas suffering famine.
- Developments that seem extremely unlikely but may have a massive impact on a food-service business if they do occur. Unlikely developments might be Germany's leaving the European Union, the oil industry's being nationalised in the Gulf states, or a massive migration to the north of people caught in an extensive drought in Africa.

There is no simple way of recognising and selecting developments. It can, however, be useful to try to identify reasons for the current success of an operation and the factors that might affect these reasons. It is also worth considering what developments might give a foodservice organisation the opportunity to build on its strengths.

The most difficult of all to pull together are those influences which, taken separately, seem insignificant, but taken together can constitute a significant influence. It might not be recognisable by any one person or department because of the complex interlinking across many aspects of the organisation. Once again, this illustrates the need for cross-functional/cross-departmental creative forums to examine the interlinking of potential influences. This requires much more than a sterile listing of influences or naming of parts.

Most books on strategic management provide coverage of the macro-environment. Kotler *et al.* (1999) discuss it as one component of a marketing audit and Johnson and Scholes (1999) and Knowles (1996) link together the macro-environment with industry analysis. All cover the material summarised here in much more depth.

## Industry environment

Of all the business gurus since 1980, Michael Porter has probably been the most acclaimed and possibly the most influential. Porter proposed that competitiveness within an industry can be determined by reference to five forces.

The famous five forces model is shown in Figure 1.4. He has developed the model further in his books *Competitive Strategy* (1980) and *Competitive Advantage* (1985).

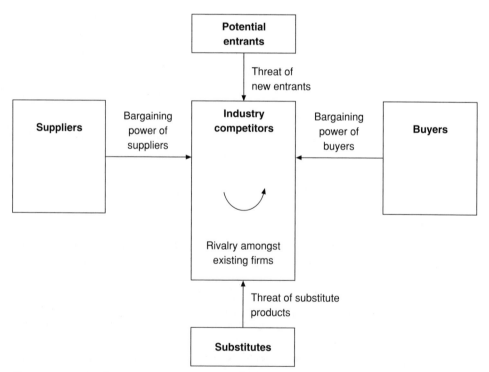

**Figure 1.4**   The five competitive forces (Adapted with the permission of The Free Press, a Division of Simon & Schuster, Inc., from *Competitive Advantage: Creating and Sustaining Superior Performance* by Michael E. Porter. Copyright © 1985, 1998 by Michael E. Porter)

The central force is the *rivalry amongst existing firms* in the industry. But the strength of the model is that it includes other competitive forces that influence the attractiveness and profitability of the industry. These are:

- The threat of *new entrants* and how easily they can break into the market.
- The bargaining power that can be exerted on the industry by its *buyers*.
- The bargaining power that can be exerted on the industry by its *suppliers*.
- The extent to which *substitute products* can take over from the existing industry.

These forces represent the industry environment, and the extent and strength of these forces determine the attractiveness of the industry. Of crucial importance is the fact that not only competitors but also the nature and strength of competitive forces change with time, and sometimes very suddenly. These changes can be provoked by, amongst others, changes in the PESTLE factors.

### Using the five forces model

The use of the five forces model provides for the systematic review of the organisation's competitive position at both the corporate and the business level. What the model does is to help focus attention not only on direct competitors but also on substitutes. For example, better transport systems, which directly reduce the demand for overnight accommodation, are a clear, but not immediately obvious, example of a substitute for accommodation services.

Porter's full diagram of the five forces is shown in Figure 1.5. Here he adds practical determinants of the relative power of each of the five forces.

From this version of Porter's model it can be seen that many of the determinants are themselves determined either by PEST factors or, importantly, by factors that the organisation can itself directly influence by changing its strategies at business or operational level.

The *industry competitors* are those organisations that a foodservice business identifies as being in direct competition and the *rivalry amongst existing firms* is the level of competition that exists between the existing operations.

*Potential entrants* are the new organisations which may threaten the business of existing organisations within the market. The *barriers to entry* into the market are the factors that might deter new operations. These include:

- capital cost of entry (for example plant and equipment)
- cost disadvantages such as licence requirements or adverse government policy
- entrenched customer loyalty to existing organisations
- economies of scale achieved by existing large businesses.

*Buyers* are the customers of the foodservice operation. Buyers can have varying degrees of power. A strong *bargaining power of buyers* will make it easier for buyers to attempt to force down prices whilst at the same time demanding better quality. Buyers will also tend

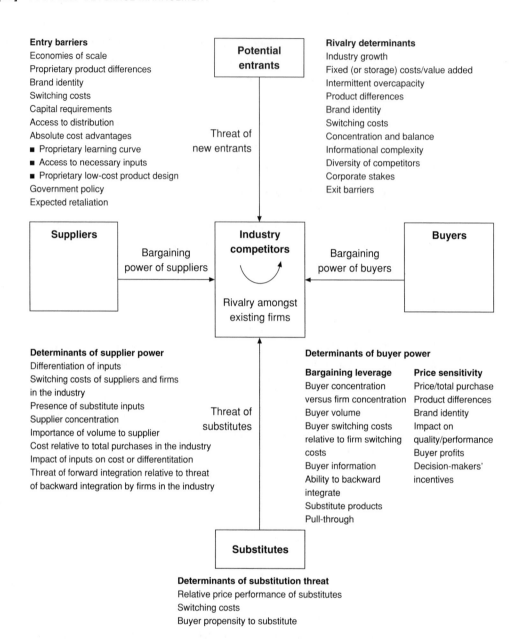

**Entry barriers**
Economies of scale
Proprietary product differences
Brand identity
Switching costs
Capital requirements
Access to distribution
Absolute cost advantages
■ Proprietary learning curve
■ Access to necessary inputs
■ Proprietary low-cost product design
Government policy
Expected retaliation

**Potential entrants**

Threat of new entrants

**Rivalry determinants**
Industry growth
Fixed (or storage) costs/value added
Intermittent overcapacity
Product differences
Brand identity
Switching costs
Concentration and balance
Informational complexity
Diversity of competitors
Corporate stakes
Exit barriers

**Suppliers**

Bargaining power of suppliers

**Industry competitors**

Rivalry amongst existing firms

Bargaining power of buyers

**Buyers**

**Determinants of supplier power**
Differentiation of inputs
Switching costs of suppliers and firms
in the industry
Presence of substitute inputs
Supplier concentration
Importance of volume to supplier
Cost relative to total purchases in the industry
Impact of inputs on cost or differentitation
Threat of forward integration relative to threat
of backward integration by firms in the industry

Threat of substitutes

**Determinants of buyer power**

| **Bargaining leverage** | **Price sensitivity** |
|---|---|
| Buyer concentration versus firm concentration | Price/total purchase |
| | Product differences |
| Buyer volume | Brand identity |
| Buyer switching costs relative to firm switching costs | Impact on quality/performance |
| Buyer information | Buyer profits |
| Ability to backward integrate | Decision-makers' incentives |
| Substitute products | |
| Pull-through | |

**Substitutes**

**Determinants of substitution threat**
Relative price performance of substitutes
Switching costs
Buyer propensity to substitute

**Figure 1.5** Porter's five forces model (Adapted with the permission of The Free Press, a Division of Simon & Schuster, Inc., from *Competitive Advantage: Creating and Sustaining Superior Performance* by Michael E. Porter. Copyright © 1985, 1998 by Michael E. Porter)

to play off different foodservice operations against each other. The influence of buyers is greater if, for instance, they are large in terms of volume of business or spend or if the market is highly competitive.

*Suppliers* provide the materials and other stocks for the business. The *bargaining power of suppliers* tends to be powerful where, for instance:

- they are integrated – operate as a cartel
- they are suppliers of small organisations with essential materials
- their groups of products are integrated, for example a brewer who is also a wine merchant
- they integrate forwards, for example, a wine supplier which also operates wine bars.

*Substitutes* are those alternative products which the buyers might choose instead of the foodservice operation's product. This is complex. For a foodservice operation, the nature of demand being met will be a key *determinant of the substitution threat.* Foodservice operations that are linked to another activity, such as retail or leisure, will be highly dependent on the customer's carrying out the first activity. There are many alternative or substitute activities that the customer might choose instead of retail or leisure pursuits. This will then affect demand for the foodservice product. Even where this is not the case, substitutes for foodservice operations are also other types of foodservice operation that might not be seen initially as in direct competition: customers choosing a McDonald's rather than a fine dining restaurant for instance.

Organisations need also to be constantly aware that existing or potential competitors will also be modifying their strategies in an attempt to be more competitive. In turn, many of these possible changes to strategy, or changes to the relative competitiveness of an industry, are caused by changes to PESTLE factors.

Gaining an understanding of the macro-industry environment and the competitiveness within an industry can inform a foodservice organisation about how its strategies can be managed successfully. We return to further consideration of making strategic decisions for a foodservice organisation in Chapter 7, page 267.

## THE LEGAL FRAMEWORK

Part of considering the business environment is also about considering the legal framework in which the foodservice organisation has to operate. For foodservice operations there are many situations that are subject to legal regulation. These are highlighted below. It should, however, be borne in mind that these are summarised guidelines and that many of the issues highlighted are affected by the particular circumstances at the time.

## Provision of services

Foodservice operations are under no obligation to provide services unless the operation is an establishment covered by the Hotel Proprietors Act 1956 and the customers seeking services are classed as bona fide travellers. Establishments may refuse to serve people who do not meet the dress requirements of the establishment, for example the wearing of jackets or the disallowance of beachwear. Additionally, licensed establishments may refuse to serve people who are drunk or quarrelsome.

Establishments are, however, under the obligation to ensure that they do not breach the Sex Discrimination Act 1975, the Race Relations Act 1976 and the Disability Discrimination Act 1995. These Acts, amongst other things, legislate against discrimination on the grounds of disability, sex, race, creed or colour. Under these Acts, establishments may not refuse services, provide inferior services or set unreasonable conditions on the basis of these characteristics.

## Describing services

Under the Sale of Goods Act 1979, as amended by the Sale and Supply of Goods Act, 1994, the customer can refuse to pay for a meal or demand a replacement if:

- The goods supplied do not correspond to the description.
- A displayed item is not what it seems: for example, a sweet where the cream which would reasonably be expected to be fresh is in fact artificial.
- The food is inedible or the drink undrinkable.

Additionally, the Trades Description Acts 1968/1972 make it a criminal offence to misdescribe goods or services. There are also offences under the Food Safety Act 1990.

## Customer payment

If the customer is without the means to pay and this is a pure mistake, then the operation can seek proof of identity and take a name and address. However, if fraud is suspected, then the police may be called in. The operation may not take personal items as security unless the customer is staying in a hotel covered by the Hotel Proprietors Act 1956. In this case the proprietor has the right to lien; in other words, luggage may be taken pending payment.

## The customer and their property

If an establishment is covered by the Hotel Proprietors Act 1956, then it is liable for customers' property while they are staying there. Other than this, there is no automatic liability unless the damage to, or loss of, the customer's property has resulted from negligence on behalf of the establishment, which would have to be proved. Under the health and safety legislation (1974 and other) there is a duty on the part of the establishment to care for all lawful visitors, and negligence is a criminal offence. Establishments are, therefore, legally bound to look after the customers' (and all the lawful visitors') health and safety while they are on their premises.

The health and safety issues are of particular importance within foodservice operations. The Food Safety Act 1990 is a piece of wide-ranging legislation designed to ensure that all food (and in this context it includes beverages) produced and offered by sale is safe to eat and is not misleadingly advertised or presented.

## Price lists, service and minimum charges

Foodservice operations are required to display food and drink priced (Price Marketing Order 1979) so customers can see them before entering the premises or, in the case of a complex, before entering the dining area. If service and cover charges are stated on menus and price lists, then they should normally be paid unless, in the case of service charges, the customer considers that the service has been poor.

Part III of the Consumer Protection Act 1987 came into force in 1989. This part of the Act deals with misleading prices, and amongst the provisions it states that it is an offence to give misleading price information. It recommends that, where the customer has to pay a non-optional charge, it should be incorporated into the total price or should not be charged at all. It also states that cover charges and minimum charges should be prominently displayed. Compliance with these provisions is not obligatory, but failure to do so could be used as evidence by the Office of Fair Trading that an offence has been committed.

## Health and safety

Following from the Health and Safety at Work Act 1974 and the considerable amount of subsequent legislation, there is a continuous need for establishments to ensure the health and safety of all employees and all lawful visitors. The range of regulations is far-reaching and establishments are well advised to seek guidance from the local environmental health officers.

Other legal issues are considered in this book under the appropriate chapter (licensing, in Chapter 4 for example). For further information see, for instance, *Croner's Catering* (1999) and Pannett and Boella's *Principles of Hospitality Law* (1996).

## SETTING ORGANISATIONAL GOALS AND OBJECTIVES

Understanding the business environment leads to greater confidence in determining appropriate goals and objectives for a foodservice organisation. This is important, as the setting of goals and objectives will play a crucial role in the determination of the direction of a particular foodservice organisation and its likely success.

Goals, or aims, are the broad intentions of an organisation. Objectives are the measurable outcomes, which will indicate the progress being made by an organisation towards meeting its specific goals.

Objectives are important: as the old adage says, if you have no idea of where you are going then you won't know if you are ever going to get there.

The orientation of organisational objectives can be classified under three broad headings as:

- economic
- managerial
- social responsibility.

## Economic objectives

Economic objectives assume that the sole purpose of an organisation is to maximise profit for its owners. This approach tends to be predominant where the foodservice operation is owner-managed and provides a single product, or a limited range of products, under near-perfect market conditions. It is also likely to operate most successfully under the assumption of a unitarist perspective, that is, where everyone within the organisation shares the same objectives.

There are, however, some problems when objectives are based purely on the economic theory of the firm. It can be difficult to define exactly what is meant by profit maximisation. Does it mean profit in absolute terms or profit expressed as return on capital employed, return on equity or profit margin (that is, profit as a percentage of sales) or some other measure of profit? The other dimension which needs to be determined is the timescale over which this is to be achieved: short-term profits, one, two, three years, or a much longer period?

Creating economic objectives also relies on the assumption that the achievement of profitability can be measured in a meaningful and consistent way. It also assumes that customers make their purchasing choices solely on economic grounds.

Moreover, it is easy to argue that such an approach ignores the reality of organisational life in today's complex organisations. Clearly, many organisations have non-economic goals, especially but not exclusively those in the public and charitable sectors. There are also likely to be circumstances under which the interests and objectives of the organisation's owners and its managers may be in conflict.

## Managerial objectives

The maximisation of profit for the owners of a foodservice organisation may not always be perceived to be a desirable objective for the managers. For example, food and beverage managers may seek to:

- Maximise revenue through a high market share, thereby increasing their own prestige in their industry.

- Increase the assets of the organisation (for example, by acquisition), thereby increasing their own power and personal reward.

- Empire-build inside the organisation, again increasing their own status, salary and associated perks.

- Increase the technical sophistication and complexity of the organisation (for example, in products and processes) thereby achieving growth, increasing managerial independence and providing fresh challenges.

The existence of these types of managerial objective is widespread, especially in the private sector.

On the other hand, it can also be argued that the best interests of a firm are served by its managers. Managers may be more interested, for instance, in the long-term success of the organisation than are its owners, whose interest may be transitory as they can sell the business or their shares in it.

The complexities of organisational life mean that managers are often faced with conflicting objectives. These may arise from their personal objectives, those of the owners, customers, suppliers, different groups of employees, the government and possibly other interested stakeholders. Under such conditions they may seek a compromise that satisfies every party to some extent. Such behaviour is termed 'satisficing'.

## Social responsibility objectives

Social responsibility objectives stress the ethical aspects of a foodservice organisation's objectives. These can include:

- safety of products
- working conditions
- honesty, for example not offering or accepting bribes or other inducements
- equal opportunities
- pollution and other environmental concerns.

For many organisations, a code of business and social ethics is seen as good for business. Also, for many public, charitable and voluntary sector organisations, the organisation's *raison d'être* is allied to particular social or ethical objectives. However, the issues raised in the preceding section on managerial objectives can also apply in the cost provision sectors.

It is also sometimes worth speculating whether social and ethical concerns amongst a profit-seeking organisation's managers and owners derive from genuinely held beliefs or whether they exist merely to satisfy the concerns of external stakeholders such as pressure groups, governments or society at large.

## Summarising the need to set objectives

Generally, objectives for an enterprise tend to be a mixture of economic, management and social responsibility factors. In all cases, though:

- The goals of a foodservice organisation are bound to affect the strategic options that it will consider appropriate and the particular objectives that will be set.

- Organisational objectives have an implicit impact on planning when strategic choices are being considered.

- Setting objectives for a foodservice organisation provides a basis for making choices about the policies and plans to be adopted in order to achieve the goals of the organisation.

- Having agreed objectives which are also made explicit means that there is something to measure the performance of the organisation against.

- The agreed objectives may also be the criteria which are used when making future strategic choices and determining the resulting policies and plans.

### QUALITY IN THE MANAGEMENT OF FOOD AND BEVERAGE OPERATIONS

The term 'quality' is currently used in a variety of ways to mean a variety of things. To support the approach of this book, the term 'quality' relies primarily on the approach of the British Standard Quality Award BS EN ISO 9002:1994, on an assessment: 'in the fitness for purpose and safe in use sense: is the service provided or product designed and constructed to satisfy the customer's needs'.

This process, however, does not include some external measure of the customer's satisfaction with a particular operation. It is concerned primarily with evidence of systematic processes, which are employed within an operation and which can demonstrate that there is a link between customer demand and the services and products on offer. In this respect, the catering cycle (page 2) can provide a useful model on which to base this approach.

## European Foundation for Quality Management excellence model

The various approaches to quality management all support the systems approaches, and are intended to achieve total quality management within an organisation. This is summarised by the European Foundation for Quality Management (EFQM) excellence model (1999) shown diagrammatically in Figure 1.6.

The EFQM excellence model is a non-prescriptive framework which recognises that there are many approaches to achieving sustainable excellence in all aspects of performance. The model is based on nine criteria. In essence the model tells us that *results* for *customers*, *people* (employees) and *society* are achieved through *leadership* driving *policy and strategy*,

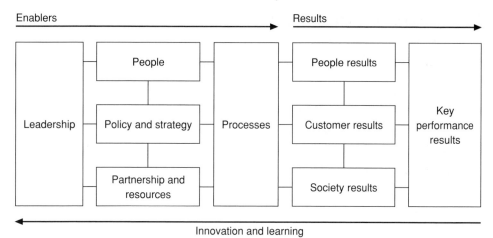

**Figure 1.6**   European Foundation for Quality Management excellence model (Adapted from EFQM, 1999)

*people management, partnership and resources* and *processes,* leading ultimately to *key performance* (business) *results.*

Each of the nine elements shown in the model is a criterion that can be used to appraise an organisation's progress towards total quality management. The four *results* criteria are concerned with what the organisation has achieved and is achieving. The five *enablers* criteria are concerned with how results are being achieved. The arrows shown in Figure 1.6 are intended to emphasise the dynamic nature of the model. They indicate that *innovation and learning* help to improve *enablers* and that this in turn leads to improved *results.*

The overall objective of a comprehensive self-appraisal and self-improvement programme is to regularly review each of these nine criteria and, thereafter, to adopt relevant improvement strategies.

## British Standard EN ISO 9002:1994

The British Standard scheme was introduced in 1979 with the aim of providing one methodology for organisations to assess the suitability of their suppliers' products. The scheme aimed to rationalise many schemes of supplier assessment by various purchasing firms and organisations. BS 5750 was amended in May 1987 to bring it into line with the international ISO 9000 series and then assimilated in 1994.

BS EN ISO 9002 identifies the systems, procedures and criteria that ensure that a product or service meets a customer's requirements. The key elements in quality management for most organisations in the hospitality industry include:

- Management responsibility – policy, objectives, identification of key personnel.
- Quality system procedures – all functions must be covered.

■ Auditing the system – it must be audited internally.

■ Quality in marketing – honest promotional activities.

■ Material control and traceability – supplies must be traceable.

■ Non-conformity – ensuring that faulty products/service do not reach the customer.

■ Corrective action – identifying reasons for faults, measures taken to correct them and records to be kept.

■ After-sales service – procedures for monitoring quality of after-sales service.

■ Documentation and records – records of checks and inspections, action taken, audit reports.

■ Personnel and training – identification of needs, provision and verification of training.

■ Product safety and liability – procedures for handling, storing and processing materials, for example foods.

BS EN ISO 9002 can be important to foodservice operations for two reasons. First, when purchasing goods and services, BS EN ISO 9002 indicates that a supplier operates a quality system of a high standard. Secondly, foodservice operators, such as contract caterers, may find that they will not be considered as potential tenderers if they have not achieved BS EN ISO 9002. Additionally, BS EN ISO 9002 may even provide useful evidence that due diligence had been exercised, for example in the event of a foodservice operation's being prosecuted under the Food Safety Act 1990.

In an increasingly competitive marketplace, and with increasing uniformity between operations, the level of service provided and its quality become ever more important. It is the front-line members of staff that offer this service: hence their training and development are crucial to the successful running of an operation. Total quality management offers a framework by which members of staff are given the scope to treat guests as individuals, and thereby offer superior service.

However, the costs involved in attaining the standard can be high, and therefore the introduction of BS EN ISO 9002 needs to be carefully assessed before implementation takes place. On the other hand, the reviews from many of the organisations moving towards BS EN ISO 9002 have suggested that it is cost-effective.

Further information on quality matters can be obtained from:

European Foundation for Quality Management
Brussels Representative Office
Avenue des Pleiades, 15
1200 Brussels
Belgium
http://www.efqm.org

The complete documents on BS EN ISO 9002:1994 are available from:

British Standards Institution
Linford Wood
Milton Keynes
MK14 6LE

Also see *Managing Quality in the Catering Industry* (East 1993) and HCIMA Technical Brief no. 20/98, 'BS EN ISO 9002: 1994' (HCIMA, 1998).

## Standards in foodservice operations

Within foodservice operations, standards may be categorised under two broad headings: technical standards and service standards.

- *Technical standards* refer to the items on offer, the portion size or measure, the cooking method, the degree of cooking, the method of presentation, the cover, accompaniments, the cleanliness of items, and so on.
- *Service standards* refer to two aspects: first, the procedures for service, and second, the way in which the procedures are carried out. Procedures include meeting and greeting, order-taking, seeking customer comment, dealing with complaints, payment, special needs of customers. The method in which the service is carried out includes paying attention to the attitude of staff attentiveness, tone of voice, body language, and so on.

Accepting that any standard must be achievable and measurable then this is quite possible with technical standards and with some aspects of service standards. However, it becomes increasingly difficult to set standards for the way that the service should be carried out.

Below are a number of possible aims for the service to achieve but is it arguable whether all of these are in fact standards or simply intentions:

- The supervisor should be visible in the room.
- The supervisor will visit all tables at least once during the customers' meal.
- Service employees should have positive attitudes.
- Servers should be noticeably comfortable in their respective roles.
- Cooperation between staff should be noticeable.
- Regular customers should be addressed by name.
- All customers should be addressed by name at least once during the meal.
- Customers' needs will be met.
- Ninety per cent of customer requests will be met.
- Menu items can be substituted or combined.

The other difficulty is that the intentions may not suit all customers all the time and therefore the service staff in endeavouring to meet these intentions may not be providing good service when considered from the customer's perspective.

An alternative to this approach is first to recognise that the product is the totality of what the customer receives. The customer makes no real distinction between the physical product and the intangible aspects of service. It is probable in this context that the manager should also view the product as a whole, setting standards only where the standards are actually achievable and measurable.

## Customer service and resource productivity

On the one hand, a foodservice operation is designed to provide customer service, and on the other, the achievement of profit is determined largely by the efficiency of the use of resources. Customer service can be defined as being a combination of five characteristics. These are:

- *Service level* – the intensity of or limitations in, the individual personal attention given to customers.

- *Availability of service* – for example the opening times, variations in the menus and drinks lists on offer.

- *Level of standards* – for example food quality, decor, equipment cost, staffing professionalism.

- *Reliability of the service* – the extent to which the product is intended to be consistent in practice.

- *Flexibility of the service* – the provision of alternatives, variations in the standard product on offer.

The resources used in foodservice operations are:

- *Materials* – commodities and equipment.
- *Labour* – staffing costs.
- *Facilities* – basically, the premises and the volume of business which the premises are able to support.

This can be seen as a model, as shown in Figure 1.7. The management of the operation must therefore take account of the effect that the level of business has on the ability of the operation to maintain the service whilst at the same time ensuring a high productivity in all the resources being used. (This application of this model is discussed further in Chapter 6, pages 196–7).

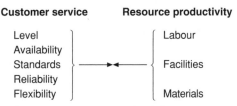

**Figure 1.7** Customer service versus resource productivity

## An integrated approach to quality management and service standards

Total quality management (TQM) has had a controversial existence. Burill and Ledolter (1999) identify that the concept has, on the one hand, been praised by those who have successfully interwoven the TQM concepts into their organisational culture and, on the other hand, been panned by those organisations that have had problems with it.

There can be a tendency for quality management to be applied as a highly structured approach, which becomes internalised in the organisation, and as such is often supported by a weighty bureaucracy. Orientation to quality customer service is seen as a strategic dominant competitive tool, but, any strategy taking on board service quality must also consider the human element both within and external to the organisation. The customer can be too easily lost sight of in the highly regulated system of operating a business. In many ways the aim of management has been to reduce the aggregate cost of quality, and so the cost of failure is likely to be reduced. Also, businesses have often spent more money on prevention strategies, whereas the more prudent strategy is one of getting the job done correctly the first time.

### Identifying the question of balance

The question, then, is how can highly structured and systematised approaches to quality really allow personnel to contribute from the heart – the very essence of genuine good service? Product quality (in terms of technical standards) and service quality (in terms of service standards) are, by their very nature, different. Technical standards can be identified, measured and compared. Service, though, is highly varied. This is its distinguishing feature, and the essence of it is individuality.

However, it is possible to create an expectation that helps the customer to both perceive consistency and to recognise the variable factors that make that service what it is. There is a need, then, to develop a culture which views quality as a natural part of what everyone is doing. Standards, manuals and auditing are appropriate as part of the process but it can only really ever work if everyone in the organisation is focused on real quality as viewed by the customer. There needs to be cohesion in moving towards ensuring emotional added value for the customer (doing the things your customers like – but genuinely).

Overall the extent to which customers appreciate a foodservice enterprise and its people is a function of the emotional value that has been added to the relationship, the product and the core design. When no emotional value exists in this relationship, there is, in essence, no relationship. How can a foodservice operation blame customers for moving on to another business, when that other business recognises the importance of, and can support, rich, rewarding, physical and emotional relationships with its clientele? The level to which customers can appreciate a foodservice business and its people clearly has a critical impact on the success of the business. Consequently the benefits of true service quality probably come from giving service staff more freedom to do what they feel is in the best interests of their customers within a loose strategic framework.

### *Towards an integrated approach*

Taking account of the various thoughts on quality management, the place of standards within it and ensuring that there is scope for developing a relationship between the organisation and the customer, then it is possible to bring these various ideas together and to develop an integrated approach to service quality management. It is also very necessary, as the food and beverage manager is having to manage the relationship between the service sequence (or service delivery system) and the customer process (see Figure 1.3).

The first stage of the integrated approach to service quality management is to draw up a customer service specification, using the five meal experience factors (identified on page 13) and the five customer service factors identified in Figure 1.7 above. The important exercise here is to define technical and procedural standards where they can be defined (and achieved, measured and compared) and then also to describe what the customer experience should be like from the customer's perspective. The next step is to check that this customer service specification can be achieved and supported over time by the physical

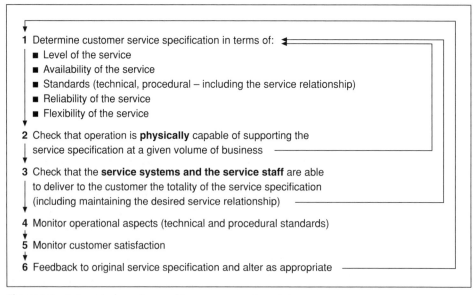

**1** Determine customer service specification in terms of:
- Level of the service
- Availability of the service
- Standards (technical, procedural – including the service relationship)
- Reliability of the service
- Flexibility of the service

**2** Check that operation is **physically** capable of supporting the service specification at a given volume of business

**3** Check that the **service systems and the service staff** are able to deliver to the customer the totality of the service specification (including maintaining the desired service relationship)

**4** Monitor operational aspects (technical and procedural standards)

**5** Monitor customer satisfaction

**6** Feedback to original service specification and alter as appropriate

**Figure 1.8**   Integrated service quality management model

capabilities of the operation. Following this it is important to check that the customer service specification can be delivered through the service system (including being supported by the service staff). This can be seen as an *integrated service quality management model*. It is a six-stage process and is summarised in Figure 1.8.

This integrated approach to quality management ties in with the systems approach to operations and also follows from the philosophy of the various approaches to quality management.

## SUMMARY

This chapter has provided information as a foundation for the remainder of the text. The catering cycle is identified as providing a tool for the systematic examination of foodservice operations, and the relationship between the cycle and the content and structure of this book has been explored. The nature of the foodservice industry has been examined and sectors identified, as well as the range of differences between customers' needs and the range of operations designed to meet their needs. Tools to explore the business environment have been described together with examples of how these can interlink. The subsequent need for the creation of goals and objectives for an organisation has been reinforced. Quality management approaches have been briefly examined as being relevant to the management of foodservice operations. Customer service issues have then been highlighted, including the possible trade-off between the maintenance of customer service and the efficient management of resources. Finally an integrated service quality management model, which includes the development of a customer service specification, has been detailed and this draws together the systems approach to operations and also follows the philosophy of the various approaches to quality management.

## REFERENCES

Burill, C. W. and Ledolter, J. (1999) *Achieving Quality through Continual Improvement*, New York: Wiley.

Cousins, J. (1988) 'Curriculum development in operational management teaching in catering education' in *The Management of Service Operations*, Johnson, R. (ed.), Bedford: IFS Publications, pp.437–59.

Cracknell, H. L., Kaufman, R. J. and Nobis, C. (2000) *Practical Professional Catering Management,* London: Macmillan.

*Croner's Catering* (1999). Updating service from Croner Publications, London.

East, J. (1993) *Managing Quality in the Catering Industry*, London: Croner Publications.

European Foundation for Quality Management (EFQM) (1999) *Excellence Model*, Brussels: Belgium.

HCIMA (1998) 'BS EN ISO 9002: 1994', HCIMA Technical Brief No. 20/98, London: HCIMA.

Johns, N. and Jones, P. (2000) 'Systems and management: understanding the real world' *The Hospitality Review*, January. This was one of a series of three articles presented in *The Hospitality Review* by Nick Johns and Peter Jones which examine the systems concept (general systems theory) and its application to the hospitality industry. The articles are presented under the general heading 'Systems and management', with individual titles as 'Mind over matter', (July 1999), which introduces key systems concepts, 'The principles of performance' (October 1999), which applies seven systems principles, and 'Understanding the real world' (January 2000), which integrates the concepts and principles.

Johnson, G. and Scholes, K. (1999) *Exploring Corporate Strategy*, 5th edition, Hemel Hempstead: Prentice Hall.

Jones, P. (1988) *Food Service Operations*, London: Cassell.

Knowles, T. (1996) *Corporate Strategy for Hospitality*, Harlow: Longman.

Kotler, P., Bowen, J. and Making, J. (1999) *Marketing for Hospitality and Tourism*, 2nd edition, Hemel Hempstead: Prentice Hall.

Lillicrap, D., Cousins, J. and Smith, R. (1998) *Food and Beverage Service*, London: Hodder and Stoughton.

Lockwood, A. (1994) 'Developing operating standards' in *The Management of Foodservice Operations*, Jones, P. and Merricks, P. (eds), London: Cassell.

Morris, B. and Johnston, R. (1987) 'Dealing with the inherent variability – the difference between manufacturing and service'. Paper given at the Operations Management Association International Conference, University of Warwick.

Pannett, A. and Boella, M. (1996) *Principles of Hospitality Law*, London: Cassell.

Porter, M. (1980) *Competitive Strategy*, New York: Free Press.

Porter, M. (1985) *Competitive Advantage*, New York: Free Press.

Records, H. and Glennie, M. (1991) 'Service management and quality assurance' *The Cornell HRA Quarterly* **32** (1) pp.26–35.

# CHAPTER TWO

# DEVELOPING THE CONSUMER–PRODUCT RELATIONSHIP

**AIM**

This chapter aims to further explore the nature of demand for food and beverage products through the application of a systematic approach to the development of the consumer–product relationship.

**OBJECTIVES**

This chapter is intended to support you in:

- adopting a systematic approach to the development of a consumer–product relationship

- further identifying and appraising key issues associated with the nature of demand for food and beverage products

- identifying key stages of product development

- identifying and applying various approaches to the development of a consumer–product relationship

- determining the usefulness and limitations of various techniques and their application to the development of the consumer–product relationship

- developing the consumer–product relationship as a dynamic process.

## FRAMEWORK FOR DEVELOPING A CONSUMER–PRODUCT RELATIONSHIP

In Chapter 1 we introduced issues regarding the nature of products (page 7), sectors of the industry (page 9), the nature of demand (page 11) and the nature of the foodservice product (page 12). This chapter extends this material and proposes that in order to be effective in identifying the key issues which shape the nature of demand for food and beverage products and create the consumer–product relationship, a systematic approach needs to be adopted.

Literature concerning consumers and markets is readily available, much of which applies specifically to food and beverage operations. The literature explores the nature of demand for products from different viewpoints. These viewpoints include marketing, psychology, anthropology, economics, sociology, geography and social psychology. Other points of view or subjects appear as these sciences develop into new disciplines, i.e. consumer behaviour.

## Considering the product

The key issues concerning the nature of demand for food and beverage products are identified using a well-validated, if somewhat oversimplified list of questions:

■ Who are the consumers of the food and beverage product?
■ What food and beverage product do they want?
■ Why do they want a food and beverage product?
■ When do they want a food and beverage product?
■ Where do they want a food and beverage product?
■ How do they obtain a food and beverage product?

These questions can be explored individually, but only one is crucial: what products do consumers want? Who, why, where, when and how are all part of the product and are inherent in answering the question as to the nature of the products that consumers want. The first important issue in the framework is therefore centred on the product.

## Considering the consumer

Consumers of food and beverage products are increasingly sophisticated, complex and dynamic. Psychology, sociology, social psychology, geography and anthropology identify the behaviour of individuals and groups in an attempt to understand the human condition, and relate to the consumer through the examination of human needs, wants, demands, goals and values. Economics focuses on the examination of the human condition as it relates to the commercial and business world through the examination of the allocation of scarce resources and the link between supply and demand. Marketing focuses on the human condition as it relates to products, i.e. the study of the consumer. Kotler *et al.* (1999) argue that: 'Marketing attempts to serve as a link between society's needs and its pattern of industrial response.' The consumer is the link. Without the consumer there is no link between the human needs and food and beverage products. A product is simply a consumer's satisfied need.

People who do not consume are not consumers. However obvious or trite this statement might appear it does eliminate the possible confusion between a consumer and a non-consumer. For example, families who eat four times a year in a motorway service area are consumers of the motorway service area food and beverage product, even if they consume relatively little of this product. They are potential consumers of many existing and future food and beverage products but at present are consumers of only one product from a vast range available, but are not consumers of the rest. They are at the same time consumers of many other products but are consumers of only one food and beverage product. They may have an unsatisfied food and beverage need, but a product is unavailable to them as yet which may satisfy this need.

When 'consumers' are discussed they are often addressed as large groups comprising millions of people, which they are when added together. But when they are examined in detail they are certainly not homogeneous, because they consume, or do not consume, millions of products in a very dynamic and rapidly changing way. They are individuals who group together to form a market for a particular product. This market grouping may range from 300 people, as in a small, rural, exclusive restaurant, up to and beyond 300 million people for world-branded products like McDonald's. The question for food and beverage managers is: who do we want our consumers to be?

Managers may say that their consumers are the same as the consumers they want them to be, i.e. 'We have achieved our objective of creating a consumer that fits our product.' However, even if such a desirable state exists, the nature of the consumer is continually changing and, as such, managers need to understand not only their consumers but also how changes which affect consumers are taking place. It is a clear argument for the establishment of a customer-orientated business. The second key issue in the framework is therefore centred on consumers.

## Being systematic in developing the consumer–product relationship

The two key issues – product and consumer – can be examined by expanding them to identify their component parts. This expansion is illustrated in Figure 2.1. The component parts represent tasks listed chronologically, both culminating in a product–consumer relationship.

These various component parts of the *product* and the *consumer* may then be merged to form a framework (Figure 2.2), which then provides for a systematic approach to the development of a consumer–product relationship. Although this framework can give the

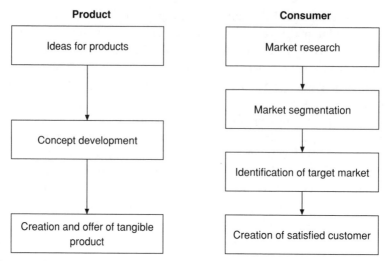

**Figure 2.1**   Product and consumer issues

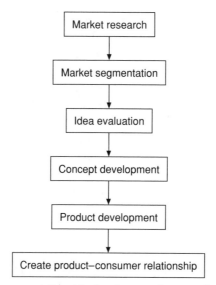

**Figure 2.2**   Product–consumer relationship development framework

impression that it is a list of tasks which are performed chronologically, in practice many of these tasks will be performed simultaneously. Additionally, this is not a one-off process. It is a dynamic and organic process in which any food and beverage operation is continuously engaged.

**MARKET RESEARCH**

Researching into the food and beverage market can be performed at various levels. Large food and beverage businesses may invest considerable resources in acquiring market information. Marketing departments will use consumer panels, questionnaires, interviews, sales analyses, market information from specialist publications, specifically commissioned market information and other generally available data. Small food and beverage businesses do not usually have a marketing department and in these instances the unit manager or owner-operator will perform the market research function. In all types of operation the focus of market research is on human needs, wants, demands, goals and values.

## The nature of needs

From Chapter 1 (page 12) we saw that food and beverage needs arise as a consequence of the desire to satisfy a range of needs. Both Kotler *et al.* (1999) and Buttle (1996) point out that these needs are inherent in human biology and the human condition and as such are not created by society or by marketers.

Food and beverage needs are basic needs for satisfactions but these needs do not arise independently. They are associated with other basic needs such as those for shelter, safety, belonging and esteem, as well as food and beverage. Food and beverage wants are desires for satisfiers of this complex set of needs. A hamburger can be a want for food *and* a want for belonging and esteem. Seven-year-old children may want to go to McDonald's to satisfy their need for belonging to their peer group, to satisfy their need for esteem within their peer group and to satisfy their need for food and drink. Wanting to satisfy their belonging and esteem needs may outweigh their food and drink needs. A food and beverage product may therefore satisfy needs not initially stimulated by hunger and thirst.

## The nature of demand

We saw from Chapter 1 (page 11) that it is important to recognise that it is the needs people have at the time, rather than the type of people they are, that different operations are designed for. The Pizza Hut product may be demanded and purchased by customers wanting, at that time, to satisfy their need for belonging to their peer group, to satisfy their need for esteem within their peer group and to satisfy their need for food and drink.

Food and beverage demands are wants for specific food and beverage products, but the level of demand is also affected by the capability of the consumer to buy them and to meet the other costs which may be involved. Food and beverage operators should try, then, to influence demand by making their product desirable, valuable, available and affordable. In essence this is following the 4Ps of the marketing mix: product, price, promotion and place (location and availability); see, for instance, Buttle 1996.

Consumers have a variety of goals when they decide to choose a food and beverage product. These goals can include esteem, belonging, status, attention, entertainment, privilege, relaxation, intimacy, romance, convenience, physiological and psychological comfort, and satisfying hunger and thirst. Again, satisfying hunger and thirst are not always goals needing to be achieved. The collection of goals that an individual has when choosing a food and beverage product may be referred to as the *goal set*. Each food and beverage product has the capacity to satisfy different goal sets. Accordingly, a consumer may perceive a takeaway as providing greater convenience and as being less expensive than an up-market à la carte restaurant, but the restaurant may be perceived as providing greater attention (level of service) and a higher level of esteem and status. The consumer will make a choice as to which is the most satisfying product for their particular goal set at the time.

Value is identified by Kotler *et al.* (1999), as 'the consumer's estimate of a product's capacity to satisfy a set of goals'. If a consumer's goal set is prioritised as food, convenience and variety, different food and beverage products may satisfy them in different ways. A consumer with this goal set may satisfy these goals with a fish and chip shop product, whereas another consumer may satisfy the same goal set with a public house meal product. This has important implications, as the direct competitors for a food service operation are not only those operations that are similar but also those that the consumer may choose simply as an alternative option. This can be, for instance, where the consumer is making a choice motivated primarily by the desire to save money or reduce travel time.

Individual consumers will have different priorities depending on their needs at the time. An individual may prioritise convenience when purchasing coffee and croissants on the way to work in the morning, low price at lunchtime when purchasing a meal in the workplace restaurant, and high levels of service and entertainment when purchasing a celebration meal in the evening. These priorities will also change during an individual's life cycle as their needs, wants and demands also change in relation to their circumstances. Individuals may desire a nightclub product in their youth, a fast food restaurant when they have young children and a reduced price product as a pensioner in their old age. Additionally, consumers may give differing importance to the same product or parts of a product. One individual may value silver service because it is perceived as increasing the status of the occasion, while others may not value silver service because it makes them feel uncomfortable in an unusual situation.

## Price, cost, value and worth

Although values are attached to various products because of the perception of the needs it can satisfy, the ability to realise those goals is dependent on the ability to pay. But payment is not just about having the required amount of money. Choices are also made by considering the relationship between price, cost, worth and value:

- *Price* is the amount of money required to purchase the product.

- *Cost* includes, as well as price, the cost of not going somewhere else, the cost of transport and time, the cost of potential embarrassment, the cost of having to look and behave in a required manner and the cost in terms of effort at work to earn the money to pay the required price.

- *Worth* is a perception of the desirability of a particular product over another in order to satisfy a set of established goals.

- *Value* is not only the personal estimate of a product's capacity to satisfy a set of goals but also a perception of the balance between worth and cost.

Good value for a food and beverage operation, indeed any operation, is where the worth is perceived as greater than the costs, and poor value where the costs are perceived as greater than the worth.

## MARKET SEGMENTATION

Researching the market will facilitate the identification of consumers' needs, wants, demands, goals and values as they relate to food and beverage products. Having identified these it is possible to group them using a mix of criteria. These groupings are termed *market segments*.

There are many different ways to segment a market. Food and beverage operators will try different segmentation variables in the attempt to identify the needs, wants and demands of possible market groupings. These variables are most usually grouped using four sets of criteria:

- geographic segmentation
- demographic segmentation
- psychographic segmentation
- behavioural segmentation.

*Geographic segmentation* involves dividing the market into geographical areas such as nations, regions, cities, districts and neighbourhoods. Food and beverage products such as Forte's Harvester and Whitbread's Beefeater target regions of the UK's food and beverage market. My Kinda Town restaurants target European capital cities. Up-market restaurants may target a district, and a fish and chip shop may target only a neighbourhood.

A food and beverage product may operate in areas with different geographical needs, satisfying these different needs by making alterations to their product mix. Menu items vary between the My Kinda Town restaurants in different European cities. Well-known fast food restaurants operate discriminatory pricing by applying a different price to the same product in relation to location, for example higher prices at airports than on high streets, and different prices in relation to different countries. The reason this is done is because the needs, wants and demands vary by geographical location, and the product/marketing mix will be altered in an attempt to exploit and/or accommodate the differences.

*Demographic segmentation* will involve dividing the market into groups using such variables as age, sex, stage in the family life cycle, income, occupation, education, religion, race and nationality. A public house may segment its markets into, for instance, single, 25–35-year-old men with average incomes, whose education finished at 16, and who are employed in manual skilled and semi-skilled professions. Another public house, however, may segment its market in a similar way but substitute married couples with two small children for the 25–35-year-old single males. The first public house could be located in a city centre, and the second in a seaside holiday resort. The needs, wants and demands of these two segments are very different and this will have implications for the nature of the food and beverage product being required and offered.

*Psychographic segmentation* is a stage further on from demographic grouping and identifies the social class, lifestyle and personality characteristics of a consumer. Social class exists in all areas of our society with various individuals forming into sets whose patterns of behaviour and attitudes vary widely. Food and beverage consumers may be segmented as to their social class with products designed specifically to satisfy their demands. Some social groupings will prefer seclusion and formality when consuming a food and beverage product while another group may prefer informal and crowded atmospheres.

Further social groupings can be distinguished as captive and semi-captive markets, such as those in hospital or on board a cross-Channel ferry (see page 11). Different social groupings exhibit preferences for particular food and beverage products.

Lifestyle segmentation can be seen in the development of food and beverage products such as TGI Friday, appealing to consumers who see themselves as young, fashionable, informal and adventurous. Personality segmentation is used to develop beverage products such as beers, appealing to consumers who see themselves as sharp and quick-witted (Harp lager), or discerning traditionalists (real ale).

*Behavioural segmentation* divides the market into groups depending on the way in which customers use the product. The food and beverage product may be used as a place to meet others, or as a place of anonymity. The behaviour exhibited will relate to consumer needs which the product must try to satisfy, i.e. lots of open areas in the former, and booths in the latter.

Behavioural segmentation also includes identifying the position of consumers in the hierarchy of usage, from having never used the product through regular users to ex-users. Consumers who have never used the product before may need to be made psychologically comfortable by a genuinely friendly welcome and an informative introduction to the food and beverage product. Some steakhouse chains ask customers if it is their first visit to the brand as standard practice, with different procedures depending on the customer's response, yes or no.

Attracting first-time buyers necessitates the identification of how first-time buyers behave. How often the product is consumed is another behavioural variable. A consumer may use a bar every day, a takeaway once a week, a pizza restaurant once a month or go to a dinner dance twice a year. Identifying the usage rate enables the identification of the needs, wants and demands of that segment, and will contribute to product design. Consumers may perceive a dinner dance as a special occasion and they must therefore be made to feel special, with personalised attention from senior staff. A bar may be perceived as a place to rest and unwind after work and may therefore be designed to be peaceful and comfortable.

Loyalty is another behavioural variable that applies to food and beverage products. Loyalty is measured as the ratio of consumption levels of a range of products. If a customer eats in only one restaurant then they are 100 per cent loyal to that restaurant. If a customer eats in a mix of six restaurants, they may be 50 per cent loyal to one, and 10 per cent loyal to the rest. The consumer's needs, wants and demands may be different at different loyalty levels.

Using segmentation variables allow for a more objective view of food and beverage consumers, and adopting this approach assists in the identification of consumers with similar needs, wants and demands. New groups are continually forming and old groups dying, therefore the need to make this identification is also continual.

The identified groupings or market segments must be the focus of the food and beverage operator's business. Choosing which segments the product will target will then depend on the financial, technological, material and human resources available. Food and beverage management is the manipulation of these resources to achieve customer satisfaction, organisational efficiency and effectiveness, and ultimately profitability.

## IDEA EVALUATION

How market segments are chosen, shaped, reached, targeted and satisfied by the operation begins by generating ideas. Ideas can be generated using a variety of techniques and sources.

Ideas can come from examining how existing food and beverage products are meeting the demands of various segments. Researching how well one's own and the competition's products satisfy customers' demands may stimulate ideas and identify key factors for success. Other methods of generating ideas include management and staff brainstorming sessions, and asking customers, with the focus for these approaches always being clearly on establishing customers' needs, wants and demands.

The generation of many ideas, which will then need to be considered, enables a more objective appraisal to be made. It is a sad situation that many new food and beverage operations fail because only one idea has been generated and alternatives have not been considered. Idea generation should be sought from all the stakeholders of the operation in an open and supportive atmosphere. If one idea is criticised, other ideas may not be forthcoming for fear of ridicule. Food and beverage operators can also benefit by formalising the idea-generation process and by giving their employees information about segmentation variables. This would lead to a continuous flow of good new ideas to meet customer needs.

A flow of product ideas focused on consumers' needs, wants and demands should be screened. Screening out ideas and progressing the remainder into the next stage of concept development can be achieved by setting up processes through which the idea must pass successfully. Screening processes will be drawn up by the stakeholder(s) and applied accordingly. An example idea-screening process is as follows:

- Does the idea meet consumers' needs?
- Is the group of consumers with these needs large enough to make the idea worthwhile?
- Does the food and beverage operator or potential operator have the necessary resources available to deliver the idea?
- Will the idea generate customer satisfaction?
- Will the idea generate a benefit to the operation, economically, managerially and socially?

This idea-screening process asks questions which may be difficult, and sometimes impossible, to answer, but trying to answer them will give indications of what will be needed to make the idea worth investing in further. This approach to idea screening should reduce the amount of ideas considerably, but is by no means a foolproof system. Good ideas may still be discarded and poor ones adopted no matter how sophisticated the screening processes are.

These approaches to market research, market segmentation and idea generation and screening apply to all situations where new products are being developed. A brand new restaurant concept like Planet Hollywood will have gone through this development process, as will a change in the opening times, service methods and decor of an existing food and beverage product. All ideas need to be screened according to the stakeholders' objectives and resources. Screening processes should be individually tailored to suit the objectives of the business. It is also necessary to review the screening process periodically as business objectives may change. If a successful food and beverage operation decides to expand and open other operations, the idea-screening process may need to be changed to accommodate product branding, continuity and consistency issues.

## CONCEPT DEVELOPMENT

It is helpful to consider the ideas which pass a screening process in terms of how they might be conceptualised as products or parts of products. For example, an idea to introduce a self-service buffet operation could be conceptualised as:

- An informal, continental-style, all-day restaurant.
- A family meal occasion to satisfy all appetites.
- An inexpensive, value-for-money, eat-as-much-as-you-like concept.

Turning the ideas into concepts allows for the identification and consideration of the potential market as well as the potential competition if the concept was converted into a product.

Evaluating the competition using, for example, a relative strengths and weaknesses analysis, will help position the new product. The position of the product is related to key consumer needs variables. These variables will be directly related to a particular market segment and should be clearly focused on customers' needs. Product positioning draws a map of the food and beverage market and places the various products in relation to each other. For example, if speed of service and convenience are identified as key consumer needs for a particular target market, the perceptions of various products might be placed relative to each other as shown in Figure 2.3.

Other variables, which may also be used to position a concept/product, include price, flexibility, availability, reliability, amount of choice, quantity, consumers' quality perceptions and the likely amount of product usage. It is also possible to set up a three-dimensional model using three customer needs variables.

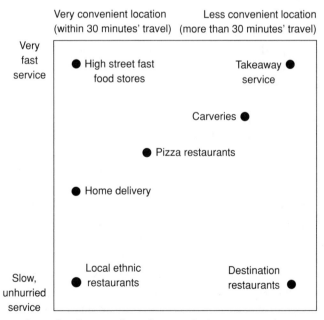

**Figure 2.3**  Perceptions of various products for a particular target market

Once the idea has been converted into a concept it should be tested in the identified market segment by asking consumers and potential consumers questions about the concept. These questions might include:

- How they view the concept in relation to the competition.
- If they would purchase the product and how frequently, and what price might they be prepared to pay.
- What they see as the benefits of the product.
- What improvements to the product could be made.

Asking these sorts of question can help to position the new concept more accurately.

Testing new product concepts is essential. Even if performed badly it is probably better than not testing at all. Large operations will test their new concepts thoroughly using consumer panels or sometimes by creating the real product and testing consumer reaction in selected areas. Smaller operations with fewer resources to test the concept can still be thorough by talking, and most importantly, listening, to existing customers and likely competitors' customers. Well-structured interviews relating to a product's benefits and image will produce valuable data to inform the development of the new concept. Well-tested food and beverage concepts have a reduced risk of failure.

## PRODUCT DEVELOPMENT

This stage of developing a consumer–product relationship considers the nature of a food and beverage product, and the questions and decisions which need to be addressed in order to turn a consumer focus (the abstract concept that consumers purchase) into an operational focus.

Customers may view a food and beverage product as a quick snack, a night out, a celebration, an indulgent extravagance or an absolute necessity. These concepts are what customers purchase, but the food and beverage product is what operators construct and provide.

Marketers will identify the product as: a central consumer concept known as the core concept; a surrounding layer of tangible features; and an outer layer of augmentation (also see page 12). Placing the framework on a food and beverage product might show that the core product is a wedding celebration, the tangible product is a full wedding banquet, and the augmented product includes the opportunity to pay in instalments. It is helpful to apply this product framework to the development of concepts. This is where concepts such as the *meal experience* concept can be useful. The meal experience concept, which was introduced in Chapter 1 (page 13), comprises five elements: the food and beverage itself, the level of service, the cleanliness and hygiene, the price, and the atmosphere.

As there are five elements to consider, the inevitable question arises as to which one should be addressed first. Most food and beverage operators immediately explore the food

**Table 2.1** Possible factor ranking for different meal experiences

| Core concept | Possible factor ranking |
|---|---|
| Night out | Atmosphere<br>Food and drink<br>Service<br>Price<br>Cleanliness and hygiene |
| Gourmet event | Food and drink<br>Service<br>Atmosphere<br>Cleanliness and hygiene<br>Price |
| Cheap meal | Price<br>Food and drink<br>Cleanliness and hygiene<br>Service<br>Atmosphere |
| State banquet | Service<br>Atmosphere<br>Food and drink<br>Cleanliness and hygiene<br>Price |

and beverages, with the construction of a menu and beverage list being given the highest priority. However, it might be more appropriate to explore the price first, or the style and level of service that will be provided, the level of cleanliness and hygiene, or the atmosphere and ambience to be created. The intended core, tangible and augmented concepts of the product, considered in the form of benefits to the consumer will guide an operator when ranking the meal experience factors in order of priority to the consumer. Table 2.1 gives some examples of how differing core concepts might change the ranking of the meal experience factors.

When setting out to design a tangible product it is therefore appropriate to consider the core concept in order to establish the weighting of the meal experience elements and the priority given to them by the customer so that the operation can develop the product from this perspective.

The other dimension which this approach is demonstrating is that limitations in the operation in one part of the *meal experience* provision will create stronger expectations in the customers' minds from the other parts. For instance, a limited menu operation will find that customers are more concerned with value for money and speed of service than they would be in an operation where the menu offered greater choice. In all cases, then, although the meal experience elements can be identified in all operations, the intended product will determine the emphasis or limitations placed on them. This in turn will affect the intended customer's expectations of them and in turn should determine the priorities for operational development of the product.

## Exploring the meal experience further

In order to continue to explore product development more fully it can be useful to consider each of the five meal experience elements separately. The five elements are:

1 food and drink

2 level of serivce

3 cleanliness and hygiene

4 price and value for money

5 atmosphere.

Each of these factors is considered below as if they were the element with the highest priority.

### Food and drink

The food and drink itself, usually in the form of a menu and beverage lists must clearly focus on the needs and demands of the consumer. Operators must ask themselves what food and drinks do market segments want. The permutations of range, tastes, textures and presentations of food and beverages are almost endless. However, the menu and beverage offerings are a list from which customers construct a package to suit their own needs, and therefore the range of food and beverages offered should be considered in this light. There may be vegetarians, dieters, customers who are hungry and ones who are not, ones who like seafood and those who do not, ones who like steaks and not much else, all part of any intended market segment. However, if there is a very wide variety of demands in the intended market segment it may be appropriate to consider further market segmentation. Trying to satisfy everyone can lead to satisfying no one.

Many operators are identified by the types of food and beverage that they offer. Food can include a wide range of styles and cuisines. These can be by country, for example traditional British or Italian, by type of cuisine, for example oriental, or aiming for a particular speciality such as fish, vegetarian or health food. These operations can all be identified by their cuisine. Other operations can be identified principally by the beverage provisions, for example pubs, wine bars and clubs. The food and beverage offering, therefore, will play a considerable part in influencing the customers' perceptions and expectations of the product, and consideration of the market's needs, wants and demands in terms of the food and beverages is important. Ideas can be generated and tested on consumer panels to identify these demands more specifically rather than relying on instinct and a propensity to deliver what the operator knows how to deliver as opposed to what the customer wants.

### Level of service

Service is a part of the product and may be considered the human (usually) interface between the product and the consumer. The exception is vending operations, where the machine is the interface. Food and beverage operators usually identify service as different service methods, such as silver service, buffet service, cafeteria service and so on, from which can be selected the most appropriate service method to meet the demands of their customers: quick service when the customer is in a hurry, slower service for an intimate dinner, and stylish service for customers who want to be entertained, are examples of service methods meeting demand.

However, service also involves a personal interaction between customers and service personnel. This interaction can deliver benefits to the customer, such as feeling valued, and should therefore be designed into the product; the operator should not just hope that these benefits will be delivered. William Martin (1986) identified two factors which shape food and beverage service. One factor is 'procedural', which includes how timely, consistent and organised the service is, and the second is 'conviviality', which includes the friendliness and attitude of the staff. These two factors can be used to construct a framework into which service styles can be placed. Figure 2.4 shows what consumers may think and say about particular styles of service.

It is hoped that all operators would wish to be in the vicinity of 'we care and we deliver'. However, the two factors are interdependent and if the procedural element of the service is poorly designed and delivered, resulting in overworked and poorly motivated staff, it

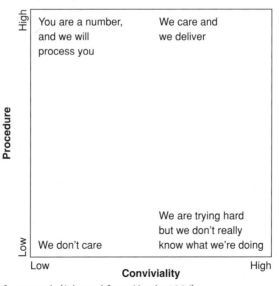

**Figure 2.4** Service framework (Adapted from Martin 1986)

is more likely that conviviality will deteriorate. A food and beverage operator must ensure that both elements are addressed and design them into the product. Training and feedback concerning service performance should also be built into the product to ensure the standards required by consumers are delivered.

The level of service can also be affected by the standards being achieved. The level of service should not be confused with standards. Low levels of service, such as in a fast food operation, are often achieved with very high standards, which are consistent over time. On the other hand, an operation offering a high level of service, such as silver service, can be poorly regulated and standards can be low and variable.

The level of service provided can also be augmented, and this can have a considerable influence on the success of a foodservice operation. Being able to reserve a table, pay by credit card, vary portion size, access health information and availability of highchairs, for example, will be factors that will influence consumer choice. They may be factors which particular market segments value highly and should be researched, and, if thought worthwhile, introduced.

### Cleanliness and hygiene

Cleanliness and hygiene issues are relevant to the premises, equipment and staff. The significance of this factor has increased substantially in recent years. The media focus on food hygiene and the risks involved in buying food have heightened awareness of health and hygiene aspects. Customers are now far more aware of, and prepared to complain about, issues of cleanliness and hygiene. Operations should be concerned about assuring the proper levels of cleanliness and hygiene all the time as a normal part of working practice, rather than following the required practices and procedures in order to avoid being caught out.

As well as ensuring that food and beverage product is prepared in hygienic conditions and that customers are provided with a clean environment in which to consume the product, there is also the need to reinforce the perception of the foodservice operation as being clean and hygienic. Tidy premises, smart uniforms and the use of protective gloves, for instance, can all have a positive effect on this perception. Negative impressions can be created by, for instance, scruffy staff, fiddling with hair, eating, or holding equipment badly (for example, holding cups and glassware by the rim rather than the handle or the base), poor standards of personal hygiene amongst staff, poorly presented food items or food not being served at the right temperature.

### Price

Price is that element of the meal experience that also relates to value. Price is also directly related to profitability. However, price is also very flexible and can be changed relatively easily, thereby changing value perceptions and possibly changing profitability. Chapter 7 on food and beverage operations appraisal covers profitability in more detail. Earlier we saw that good value is where the worth is perceived as greater than the cost (page 40), and therefore a successful operator must add value for the consumer into the product.

Prices should also be set in relation to the quality and value perception that operators want consumers to have. A high-priced product might be perceived as either good quality or a rip-off, and a low-priced product as poor quality or good value, indicating that it is more than just the absolute price which determines value, but rather price and other costs relative to worth. Price is also used to stimulate demand by using special offers and happy hours, and to attract custom from the competition.

When developing, changing or supporting a product concept it is good practice to establish a price range within which the consumer will be prepared to pay. Another price range can be established within which the operator is prepared to offer the product. The overlap is the range available to the operator. Setting prices within ranges which the consumers will pay should be accomplished with reference to the particular market segment and the core concept. Market research can determine a range within which families travelling on motorways are prepared to stop and pay for food and drink, and will also be able to determine a price range for a particular menu item. This can be achieved through setting up consumer panels and asking them about price and product. The information to be gained from researching customers' attitudes and behaviour towards price will reveal that lowest price is far from always the main consideration, as Table 2.1 showed.

Pricing methods used by operators vary in their appropriateness and sophistication. The various pricing methods include the following:

*Cost-plus*   Cost-plus is the most common method. The ingredient cost is established – not always very accurately – and the required profit (referred to as gross profit) is added. The result is a selling price that gives the operator the required profit for that dish (although it should be noted that this required profit is realised only when that dish is sold). This method is attractive because of its simplicity but it ignores price sensitivity of demand (price is a determinant of demand) and that value for money must be factored into the pricing decision. It also makes the assumption that the required profit can be established by making it a set percentage of the selling price (often between 65 and 75 per cent), fails to account for different restaurant types and different menu categories and does not take into account that each dish or beverage is only part of a collection of items purchased to produce the meal experience. Where this method is applied, differentiated percentages are used so that low-cost starter items earn proportionately more gross profit than higher-cost main course items.

*Prime costing methods*   Prime costing methods attempt to factor in the labour cost of a dish, and *actual* cost pricing attempts to include fixed and variable costs as well as labour. These additional costs are also established as a percentage of the final selling price (for example, labour at 25 per cent and variable costs at 10 per cent). These methods are flawed in the same way as cost-plus: labour is a factor related to the time needed to prepare a dish, not to the value of the ingredients used to prepare it; no account is taken of volume of business or item popularity in assessing the labour content of a dish, therefore not taking into account economies and diseconomies of scale; and allocating fixed and variable costs to each menu item should at least be related to the volume of each dish sold rather than a fixed percentage figure to be used for each menu item.

*Backward pricing*    Backward pricing attempts to match costs to a price previously established for a desired potential market. This market-driven approach – which is not really backwards – is a good starting point in new product development but it is still difficult to establish the necessary gross profit, ingredient and labour costs, and care must be taken to avoid the problems of using percentages. However, identifying what the customer is prepared to pay for a particular product and investigating whether the operation can provide the product, profitably, at that price may avoid an operation being created that was never going to be profitable anyway.

*Rate of return pricing*    Rate of return pricing tries to establish price based on a forecast of sales and costs and may be used to produce a break-even matrix for the operation. This approach may help give a guide to the price range but will not in itself establish individual selling prices.

*Profit-per-customer pricing*    Profit-per-customer pricing establishes the total profit required and allocates this to a forecast demand resulting in an average profit per customer. This 'profit' is then added to the material and other costs to produce a selling price for each dish. Again this may be used to produce a break-even matrix, but caution should be exercised because profit is a factor of demand, which is a factor of price, which is a factor of demand, and so on. However, as with backwards pricing, relating the required profitability of an operation to a given level of demand and within a price range that the customer is likely to pay can be used in determining if the operation can ever be successful.

*Elasticity pricing*    Elasticity pricing asks how sensitive a market is to price changes. In order to determine menu prices the operator will try to determine the effect that a price change may have on demand. It should be remembered that it is possible to increase demand and profitability through price decreases. However, it is very difficult to predict market responses to price changes, but considering elasticity may inform the pricing decisions.

*Competition pricing*    Competition pricing means copying the competitors' price. However, there is no guarantee that the cost structure of any competitor offering a similar product will be similar, so a particular market price may produce higher or lower profits than the competitor is earning. Copying the competition may also take the form of discounting, premium promotions, happy hours, special meals, free wine and children's toys, all short-term tactics, which can lead to increasing costs and fierce price-based competition.

There are more menu pricing methods including: marginal analysis (see Buttle 1996); break-even analysis (see Miller 1980; Greenburg 1986; Jones and Lockwood 1989; Buttle 1996); cost margin analysis (Pavesic 1985); individual menu item profit and loss (Hayes and Huffman 1985); and frequency distribution pricing (Miller 1988). Whichever methods are used, an operator should always have a clear pricing policy or objective in mind. Some of these pricing objectives might include:

- Sales volume maximisation, where the pricing objective is to achieve the highest sales possible.
- Profit maximisation, where the pricing objective is to achieve the highest profit possible.
- Market penetration, where the pricing objective is to move from a position of a zero or low market share to a significant market share.

Once a clear pricing objective is established, the pricing methods most suitable to that particular objective can be drawn from the various methods available, often being a combination of a range of pricing methods. (The nature of and the relationship between revenue, costs and profits is explored in Chapter 7).

### Atmosphere

Atmosphere development leads to the creation of emotions. It is created through the combination of a number of factors such as: design, decor, lighting, heating, furnishings, acoustics and noise levels, the other customers, the staff and the attitude of the staff. There are happy atmospheres, gloomy, stressful, joyful, cheerful, angry, bustling, sedate, calming, invigorating, indulgent, peaceful, comfortable, uncomfortable, boring and inviting atmospheres. All of these different types of atmosphere can be created, and examples abound. The bright, young, clean atmosphere of McDonald's; the farmhouse atmosphere of Forte's Harvester, the luxurious atmosphere in the Princess Grill on the *QE2*, the cosy and informal atmosphere of a local French bistro, are all created. With so much control available, food and beverage operators clearly have opportunities to match the atmosphere with the concept.

Atmosphere is sensed through sight, sound, touch, taste and smell. Food and beverage operators' use:

- The sense of sight through furniture and textures, colours, employees, shapes, spaces and their own customers.
- The sense of sound through acoustics, the use of materials and shapes, which alter sound, and the use of music and operational sounds including speech.
- The sense of touch through, for instance, the quality of the air and the fabrics and equipment with which customers come into contact, the texture of the foods and the touching of other people.
- The sense of taste, which has great volumes of documentation dedicated to it through recipe and wine books and the variations are almost infinite.
- The sense of smell, which is used by many food and beverage operators to attract customers through coffee, bread, roast meat and any other aromas which may be associated with the core consumer concept.

Atmosphere is also created through the attitude of the staff. A pleasing environment soon becomes an unbearable one if staff are unhelpful, lacking in competence, unresponsive and rude. Conversely, a potentially poor environment can be enhanced through genuine interest in customer needs, competence and good interpersonal skills.

Other customers have an impact on atmosphere. There is a range of customer-related factors that operations need to consider which can affect the atmosphere. The proximity of other customers through the spacing of tables in a restaurant, for instance, will affect the feeling of privacy or otherwise. Additionally, operations need to make decisions about policies for:

- customer dress requirements
- smoking/non-smoking
- mobile phone usage
- maximum group size
- accepting children
- alcohol overconsumption
- minimum levels of acceptable guest behaviour.

Having policies for these factors means that the policies have also to be reinforced. Procedures for dealing with this need to be developed so that the consistency in the application of the policies is maintained, and the potential for customer relations problems minimised. (See also the section on customer relations in Chapter 6, pages 197–9.)

There are always structural and cost constraints to atmosphere creation, but operators should invest in atmosphere to their best ability. If the right atmosphere is not created, in the hope that business success will finance further atmosphere development, success might not come at all. It might be better to consider targeting a different market for which atmosphere creation is less expensive, and then moving on to the original target market when the atmosphere-creation funds are available.

Some consumers want hot, sweaty, noisy, dark, vibrant and exciting atmospheres, whilst others will prefer quiet, comfortable, light, relaxing atmospheres. Specialist designers are available to construct an atmosphere for a food and beverage operation, and some large businesses employ their own design teams. These designs can be used to test the concept further by showing them to consumer panels and recording the reaction. At whatever level a food and beverage operation is resourced, investing in a part of the product which so heavily influences the customers' perception of the product should be a priority.

## Developing the customer service specification

The five meal experience factors identified above are interdependent and should be examined together in order to consider the potential operation as a whole. This provides the basis for the creation of the customer service specification, which then also takes account of the service level, availability, standards, reliability and flexibility, and also the resources required in terms of materials, labour and facilities. This follows the approach to integrated service quality management, which was first identified in Chapter 1, page 31. The *integrated service quality management model* (detailed in Figure 1.8) also identifies that there are two specific checks to be made. For any customer service specification to be achieved successfully an operation must have examined:

■ the extent to which the customer service specification can be achieved and supported over time by the physical capabilities of the operation, and

■ the extent to which the customer service specification can be delivered through the service system (including examining capabilities of the staff).

This examination will lead to changes being made to the physical capabilities of the operation, or changes in the service system (and staff requirements), or changes being made to the customer service specification. Often it is a combination of all three. Unless the specification, physical capabilities and service system are in harmony then quality in the operation will never be achieved.

## CREATING THE PRODUCT–CONSUMER RELATIONSHIP

Once products to satisfy particular market segments have been designed it is necessary to identify the steps to be taken to create the product–consumer relationship. This final element in the process may be viewed as a four-stage sequence.

**1** determine promotional channels

**2** estimate profitability

**3** plan product launch

**4** offer product and appraise performance.

### Determining promotional channels

Determining promotional channels is important because it will identify how consumers will be reached and attracted to the product. Food and beverage operators should identify and monitor consumers in order to be informed as to which promotional channels are best for their product.

When choosing promotional channels the target market segment variables are considered in relation to the product message and the medium through which it may be delivered. The message to be delivered should relate to the consumer's needs, wants and demands, and be delivered through a medium used by the target consumers, reflecting their lifestyles and self-images. Table 2.2 shows possible messages and media for different food and beverage products.

Choosing the message and the medium is a critical element in promoting the product. Large businesses will spend millions of pounds promoting their product through national television, radio, press and billboards. Small operations may spend only hundreds of pounds

**Table 2.2 Possible message and media for food and beverage products**

| Product | Message | Media |
|---|---|---|
| Branded pizza restaurant | Meet friends and have fun | Television, local radio and press, mailshots |
| New Year's Eve dinner dance | Celebrate in style and spoil yourself | Local radio and press, in-house literature, direct suggestive selling to existing customer base |
| Local bistro | A touch of continental style | Word of mouth |
| Public house | Traditional British hospitality | Word of mouth, local press, *Good Food Guide* |

but the criterion is the same: is it effective? Regular reviewing of promotional activity and spending and how it relates to increased sales and profits will enable effective evaluation of the process to take place. Consumers' responses to promotional activities should be researched.

### Estimating profitability

Estimating profitability is a case of budgeting costs and sales. How these budgets might be set is addressed in Chapter 7 (pages 221–3), but when launching new products and changing existing ones, the art of predicting outcomes is extremely indefinite. Methods used can, however, be very sophisticated. Some operators will measure the size of their selected target and segmented market, apply usage or uptake measures between competing products and multiply the resultant number of customers for their product by an estimated average spend per head. This may be performed for each hour, day and month to produce the sales budget. Applying a 'profitability on sales percentage' approach will determine the budgeted profit. However, the measures used cannot be guaranteed correct, and therefore a best and worst scenario should be considered. This may take the form of a break-even chart to show an operator what the profitability levels are for various levels of demand or numbers of customers.

Having said this, outcomes are usually different from those expected. Estimating profitability will at least give some indication as to what might happen, and progress after launch can be evaluated against the estimates.

### Planning the product launch

Planning the product launch is an operational as well as a promotional issue. Operationally, the new food and beverage product will need testing. This will involve staff scheduling and training, specifying and sourcing the necessary ingredients and equipment and, if possible, testing full-scale production. If a full-scale test production run is not possible, perhaps owing to cost restraints, a reduced-scale test should be performed. There will always be elements of the product that will not work entirely as planned, and finding out about these before the product launch enables these elements to be rectified. Not being able to deliver the product as promoted will result in consumers' expectations not being met, and this could negatively affect the market segment's uptake of the product. It is also worth remembering that customers seem to remember bad experiences more than good ones.

The launch of a new product gives rise to promotional opportunities. Special sessions can be organised by offering the product free, or at reduced prices, to selected groups on a one-off basis, thus gaining good public relations exposure. This would also be a good operational test of the product without the repercussions of not meeting customers' expectations. Special offers can also be introduced to attract customers to the product, such as two items for the price of one, or a free bottle of wine with a meal. However, special consideration must be given to the market segment's perception of the promotion, as free offers or reduced prices may not project the required image.

The timing of the product launch is also an important consideration. There are two issues regarding timing: one is getting the time right, and the other is having enough time available to get the product right. Getting the time right involves choosing a launch date that provides the best advantage to the operator. This will mean investigating the possibility of other events which are going on at the same time and which may detract from or enhance the product launch. If demand is expected to fluctuate, and demand for food and beverage products does fluctuate between time of day, week, month and year, the planned launch time should be set to take this into account. It may be appropriate to launch the product before a busy period, in order to be able to build up to full capacity. Operations which do not give themselves enough time to develop and launch their product can find themselves offering products which are not successful, and the time available to develop a product may often be seen as insufficient. However, if the product is not ready to be introduced in time, it is probably worth considering delaying the launch rather than offering a substandard product.

### *Offering the product and appraising performance*

Offering the product and appraising performance are about putting the plan into action and monitoring the result. Chapter 7 details approaches to operations performance appraisal (pages 220–52) and to product performance appraisal (pages 252–9).

## THE CONSUMER–PRODUCT RELATIONSHIP AS A DYNAMIC PROCESS

Although presented here primarily as a sequence, the process of developing a consumer–product relationship is a dynamic and organic one which is also continuous. As consumers' needs, wants and demands change, and as the competition increases and technology offers new opportunities, managing the process of creating a consumer–product relationship is also about managing change.

This chapter has explored the issues surrounding the consumer–product relationship, and has suggested some frameworks to help evaluate and develop the relationship. These frameworks may be viewed as tools to be applied when required, but they are also tools that will need to be applied continuously. Food and beverage operations will engage in different stages of developing a consumer–product relationship at the same time. Market research should be an ongoing commitment; generating ideas and concepts should be built into the management of an operation; and searches for new and developing market segments is a major management responsibility. With so many variables changing all the time, including the operator's own personal and business objectives, it can be seen how promoting the status quo and relying on consumers to remain fixed over time is a dangerous assumption. As product life cycles continue to shrink, the importance of managing these changes in order to defend against threats and respond to opportunities, is increased.

Managing change effectively and profitably in a food and beverage environment is as complex and as difficult as in any other type of business. In order to embrace change there must be a management vision of where it wants the business to be. The focus of this vision will be satisfying the consumers of the food and beverage product. Managers' first commitment is to communicate this vision to their staff, for without members of staff who are convinced of the need to change, and of the need to do things differently, the vision will not happen. Managing relationships within food and beverage operations, between groups of personnel, will play an ever-increasing role for management in the successful development and adaptation of the consumer–product relationship.

## SUMMARY

This chapter has further explored the nature of demand for food and beverage products through the application of a systematic approach to the development of the consumer–product relationship. The importance of satisfying consumers' needs, wants and demands, and understanding their goals and values, has been addressed. Component parts of the consumer–product development process have been identified and explored, and the usefulness and limitations of various techniques and their application have been considered alongside the needs to determine promotional channels, estimate profitability, offer product and appraise performance. Finally the need to view the consumer–product relationship as a dynamic process has been identified, with the management of change being seen as key management skill.

## REFERENCES

Buttle, F. (1996) *Hotel and Food Service Marketing – A Managerial Approach*, London: Cassell.

Greenburg, C. (1986) 'Analyzing restaurant performance, relating cost and volume to profit' *The Cornell Hotel and Restaurant Administration Quarterly* **27** (1) pp.6–11.

Hayes, D. K. and Huffman, L. (1985) 'Menu analysis, a better way' *Cornell Hotel and Restaurant Administration Quarterly* **25** (4) pp.64–9.

Jones, P. and Lockwood, A. (1989) *The Management of Hotel Operations*, London: Cassell.

Kotler, P., Bowen, J. and Making, J. (1999) *Marketing for Hospitality and Tourism*, 2nd edition, Hemel Hempstead: Prentice Hall.

Martin, W. (1986) 'Defining what quality service is for you' *The Cornell Hotel and Restaurant Administration Quarterly* **27** (1) pp.32–8.

Miller, J. (1980) *Menu Pricing and Strategy*, New York: Van Nostrand Reinhold.

Miller, S. C. (1988) 'Fine tuning your menu with frequency distributions' *Cornell Hotel and Restaurant Administration Quarterly* **29** (3) pp.86–92.

Pavesic, D. V. (1985) 'Prime numbers, finding your menu's strengths' *Cornell Hotel and Restaurant Administration Quarterly* **26** (3) pp.56–7.

# CHAPTER THREE

# FOOD PRODUCTION

**AIM**

This chapter aims to demonstrate the importance of sound menu planning and emphasise its importance in the planning, implementation and management of food production systems.

**OBJECTIVES**

This chapter is intended to support you in:

■ planning menus

■ ensuring that hygiene management is an implicit function in the food production process

■ managing food production as an operating system

■ knowing details of the main centralised production systems available to the food-service operator and the advantages and disadvantages of each

■ managing volume within food production systems

■ developing and managing the purchasing function and its relationship with the total operational process

■ developing and applying operational control procedures.

## MENU PLANNING

The menu is often considered to be the prime selling tool of a foodservice operation and therefore it should be written to inform and sell. The menu, or bill of fare, is a means of communication, informing the customer of what the establishment has to offer. The compiling of the menu is one of the foodservice operator's most important jobs, whether it is for establishments in the profit sector, or for those working to a budget, such as hospitals, schools or other, similar institutions. The menu is a central management document that directs and controls the foodservice operation. It establishes what is going to be purchased, the cost, what staff and other resources are required and the types of service needed. In addition, the beverage offer, the decor, atmosphere, theme or logo and service system all revolve around the provision of the menu.

## Developing a menu policy

When compiling the menu for an operation it is necessary to consider the creation of a menu policy which will govern the approach to the composition of the menu. This policy will determine the methods the operation will take to:

- Establishing the essential and social needs of the customer.
- Accurately predicting what the customer is likely to buy and how much they are going to spend.
- Ensuring a means of communication with customers.
- Purchasing and preparing raw materials to pre-set standards in accordance with purchasing specifications and forecasted demand.
- Portioning and costing the product in order to keep within company profitability objectives.
- Effectively controling the complete operation from purchase to service on the plate.

## Food and restaurant styles

Over recent years a number of terms have been adopted to signify differing types of food and establishment styles. Examples of these are given in Table 3.1.

## Types of menu

There are several types of menu:

- *Table d'hôte*  A set menu forming a complete meal at a set price. A choice of dishes may be offered at all courses; the choice and number of courses will usually be limited to two, three or four.

**Table 3.1** Examples of cuisine and restaurant styles

| Cuisine or restaurant style | Description |
| --- | --- |
| Bistro | Often a smaller establishment, with checked tablecloths, bentwood chairs, cluttered decor and friendly, informal staff. Honest, basic and robust cooking, possibly including coarse pâtés, thick soups, casseroles served in large portions |
| Brasserie | This is often a large, styled room, with long bar, normally serving one-plate items rather than formal meals (though some offer both). Often it is possible just to have a drink, or coffee, or just a small amount to eat. Traditional dishes include charcuterie, moules marinières, steak frites. Service often by waiters in traditional style of long aprons and black waistcoats |
| Farmhouse cooking | Simply cooked with generous portions of basic, home-produced fare using good, local ingredients |
| Country house hotel cooking | Varies from establishment to establishment but food is often modern British style with some influence from classic or even farmhouse style. Often the home of top-end destination restaurants |
| Classic/haute cuisine | Classical style of cooking evolved through many centuries, best chronicled by Escoffier. Greater depth of flavour. Style does not necessarily mean the most expensive ingredients – can include simply poached and boiled dishes such as chicken, tongue and offal. Classical presentation of food with table, guéridon or plated service |
| Ethnic | Indian, Oriental, Asian, Spanish, Greek, Italian, Creole and Cajun are just some of the many types of ethnic cuisine available, with establishments tending to reflect ethnic origin. Many of the standard dishes are now appearing within a range of other menu types |
| Health food and vegetarian | Increasing specialisation of operations into vegetarianism and/or health foods (though vegetarian food is not necessarily healthy) meeting the needs of lifestyle as well as dietary requirements |
| Popular catering and fast foods | Developed from teashops and cafés through to steakhouses, and then incorporating takeaways and cafeterias, on to modern-day burger, chicken and fish concepts with ethnic foods also being incorporated. Meeting the needs of all-day meal-taking ('grazing') and especially meeting leisure, industrial and travelling market requirements |
| New/modern British/French | Cuisine drawn from the classical style but with new-style saucing and the better aspects of nouvelle presentation. Plated in the kitchen, allowing the chef the final responsibility for presentation |
| Fusion/eclectic cuisine | As the world is getting 'smaller' through efficient transport and tourism, modern cuisine uses a variety of ingredients from all over the world. This has led to an inter-mix of cuisine cultures, for example a 'fusion' of particularly western and eastern styles. May also be described as eclectic cuisine |

- *A la carte* A menu with all the dishes individually priced. The customers can therefore compile their own menu. A true à la carte dish should be cooked to order and the customer should be prepared to wait for this service.

- *Special party or function menus* These are set menus for banquets or functions of all kinds.

- *Ethnic or speciality menus* These can be both table d'hôte or à la carte menus specialising in the food (or religion) of the country or in a specialised food itself.

- *Hospital menus* These usually take the form of a menu card given to the patient the day before service so that their preferences can be ticked. Both National Health Service and private hospitals cater for vegetarians and also for religious requirements. In many cases a dietician is involved in menu compilation to ensure nothing is given to the patients that would be detrimental to their health. Usually, hospital meals are of two or three courses.

- *Menus for people at work* These are menus that are served to people at their place of work. Such menus vary in standard and extent from one employer to another.

- *Menus for children* These should emphasise healthy eating through a balanced diet. Those areas with children of various cultural and religious backgrounds should also have menus that reflect this cultural diversity.

### Cyclical menus

Cyclical menus are menus compiled to cover a given period of time, for example one month or three months. They consist of a number of set menus for a particular establishment, perhaps industrial restaurant, cafeteria, canteen, directors' dining room, hospital or college refectory. At the end of each period the menus can be used over again, thus limiting the need to keep compiling new ones. The length of the cycle is determined by management policy, by the time of the year and by different foods available. These menus need to be monitored carefully to take account of changes in customer requirements and any variations in weather conditions which are likely to affect demand for certain dishes. If cyclical menus are designed to remain in operation for long periods of time, then they must be carefully compiled in order that they do not have to be changed too drastically during operation if, for instance, stock availability changes.

Advantages of cyclical menus are:

- They save time by removing the daily or weekly task of compiling menus, although they may require slight alterations for the next period.

- When used in association with cook–freeze operations, it is possible to produce the entire number of portions of each item to last the whole cycle, having determined that the standardised recipes are correct.

- They give greater efficiency in time and labour.

- They can cut down on the number of commodities held in stock and can assist in planning storage requirements.

Disadvantages are:

- When used in establishments with a captive clientele, then the cycle has to be long enough so that customers do not get bored with the repetition of dishes.
- The foodservice operator cannot easily take advantage of 'good buys' offered by suppliers on a daily or weekly basis unless such items are required for the cyclical menu.

### Preplanned and predesigned menus

Preplanned menus are often found in, for instance, banquet or function operations. Before selecting dishes the foodservice operator is able to consider what the customer likes and the effect of these dishes upon the meal as a whole.

Advantages of preplanned menus are:

- They enable the foodservice operator to ensure that good menu planning is practised.
- The menu construction can be well balanced in terms of texture, colour ingredients, temperature and structure.
- Menus which are planned and costed in advance allow banqueting managers to quote prices instantly to a customer.
- Menus can be planned taking into account the availability of kitchen and service equipment and the capability of the service staff, without placing unnecessary strain upon any of these.
- The quality of food is likely to be higher if kitchen staff are preparing dishes that they are familiar with and have prepared a number of times before.

Disadvantages are:

- Preplanned and predesigned menus may be too limited to appeal to a wide range of customers.
- They may reduce job satisfaction for staff who have to prepare and serve the same menu repetitively.
- They may limit the chef's creativity and originality.

## Essential considerations in menu planning

Prior to compiling menus there are a number of essential considerations. These include:

- *Location of an establishment*  This location should allow easy access to both customers and suppliers. A difficult journey can be offputting no matter how good the quality of food on offer and can affect repeat business and profitability. If the establishment is in an area noted for regional speciality foods or dishes, the inclusion of a selection of these on the menu can give extra menu appeal.

■ *Competition in the locality*  It is important to be aware of what is offered by competitors, including their prices and particularly their quality. Knowing this information enables an establishment to make decisions about how to compete with local competition.

■ *Suitability of a particular establishment to a particular area*  A self-service restaurant situated in an affluent residential district, or a very expensive seafood restaurant in a rundown inner-city area may not be very successful. Anticipating and analysing the nature of demand that the operation is planning to appeal to will contribute to ensuring that the menu will be developed to satisfy, for example, office workers in the city, with a fast lunch service. Also, opportunities may exist for outdoor catering.

■ *The spending power of the customer*  A most important consideration is how much the potential customer is able and willing to pay. (Pricing methods are also considered in more detail in Chapter 2, page 50).

■ *Customer requirements*  It is the customer, not the foodservice operator, who selects their menu, so the analysis of dish popularity is necessary and those dishes that are not popular should not stay on the menu. Customer demand must be considered, and traditional dishes and modern trends in food fashions need to be taken into account.

■ *Number of items and price range of menus*  It is essential to determine the range of dishes and whether a table d'hôte or an à la carte type of menu is to be offered. Decisions regarding the range of prices have to be made. A table d'hôte menu may be considered with an extra charge or supplement for more expensive dishes, or more than one table d'hôte menu of different prices may be more suitable.

■ *Throughput*  If space is limited, or there are many customers (and control of the time the customer occupies the seat is needed) then the menu can be adjusted to increase turnover, for example more self-service items or quick-preparation items, or separate service for beverages.

■ *Space and equipment in the kitchen*  Both of these will influence the composition of the menu and production of dishes. The menu-writer must be aware of any shortcomings or deficiencies in equipment and may be wary of offering dishes that are difficult to produce. Also, certain items of equipment, such as steamers and fritures (deep fat fryers), should not be overloaded by the menu requirements.

■ *Amount, availability and capability of labour*  The availability and capability of both the preparation and service staff must be considered when planning a menu. Enough able and willing staff, both in the kitchen and the restaurant, are necessary to achieve customer satisfaction with any menu.

■ *Supplies and storage*  Menu-planning is dependent upon availability of supplies, that is frequency of deliveries of the required amounts. Storage space and seasonal availability of foods need to be taken into account when planning menus.

- *Cost factor* When an establishment is run for profit, the menu is a crucial consideration; but, even when working to a budget, the menu is no less crucial. Costing is the crux of the success of compiling any menu.

- *Food allergies* The most common food allergies are to milk, eggs, fish, shellfish and nuts. Menu items often contain allergens and these must be identified on the menu. Staff should be trained so that they know how to respond when asked about ingredients. An incorrect answer could have fatal consequences for the customer.

- *Food Labelling (Amendment) Regulations 1999* These regulations apply to pubs, restaurants, hotels, cafés and takeaways including all food outlets. These regulations apply to genetically modified (GM) foods. Menu items and products containing genetically modified soya and/or maize must be clearly labelled. There is, however, no requirement to label genetically modified food additives and flavouring substances.

- *Genetically modified organisms (GMOs)* Modern methods of biotechnology are being used increasingly by the farming and food manufacturing industry to produce foods and ingredients. Genetic modification is a major development and affects all foodservice operators. Common GM foods are maize and soya, and 15 per cent of worldwide production of soya is now genetically modified. Together these derivatives are found in up to 60 per cent of all processed foods including cakes, biscuits, meat substitutes, bread, peanut butter and chocolate. Tomato purée may be made from GM tomatoes. There is considerable public concern over health and environmental safety and it is probable that all consumers are likely to encounter GM foods. There is also the continual potential for considerable adverse customer reaction to foodservice operations that use these products.

## Menu copy

Items or groups of items should bear names that people recognise and understand. If a name does not give the right connotation, additional descriptive copy may be necessary.

Mistakes in approaches to menu copy can include:

- Descriptive copy is left out when it is required.
- The wrong emphasis is given.
- Emphasis is lost because print size and style are not correctly used.
- The menu lacks creativity.

Carefully devised descriptions can help to promote the individual dish, the menu generally and, in turn, the establishment. However, descriptions should describe the item realistically and not mislead the customer. The Trades Description Acts 1968/1972 make it a criminal offence to mis-describe goods or services. There are also offences under the Food Safety Act 1990. Care should therefore be taken in the use of terms such as fresh, British, organic, and also cooking terms such as fried or roasted. The description should always be a true one. (In the case of organic it is only the food item that can be described as organic, and even then the establishment should be recognised by the UK Register of Organic Food Standards or one of its approved bodies such as the Soil Association.)

Interesting descriptive copy is a skill; a good menu designer is able to illuminate menu terms or specific culinary terms and in doing so is able to draw attention to them. Simplicity in menu copy enhances the communication process and enables better understanding.

Some menus can be built around a general descriptive copy featuring the history of the establishment or around the local area in which the establishment is situated. Alternatively, descriptive copy can be based on a speciality dish which has significant cultural importance to the area or the establishment. In so doing, the description may wish to feature the person responsible for creating and preparing the dish – especially if the chef is reasonably well known and has appeared on national or local television or radio. The chef may also have had their recipes featured in the local press. This too may be included in the menu to create further interest.

Menu copy should be set in a style of print that is easy to read and well spaced. Mixing typefaces is often done to achieve emphasis; if overdone, the overall concept is likely to look a mess and therefore unattractive to the eye and difficult to understand. Emphasis may also be achieved by using boxes on the menu. Also, menu paper and the colour of the print can carefully be contrasted to make certain dishes stand out.

Further information on modern European menu construction can be found in Gillespie (2001).

## HEALTH AND SAFETY

The dual responsibility of employers and employees at work is to ensure that the premises and equipment are safe and that they are kept safe so as to prevent accidents. Employers need to assess any hazards or risks and implement procedures to deal with any accidents. All employees should receive training in accident prevention. Safety signs must be used to inform and instruct people using the premises in order both to prevent accidents and of what they must do should an accident occur. All potential hazards should be reported.

## Safety regulations

Six new health and safety at work regulations came into force in 1993:

1 The management of Health and Safety at Work Regulations 1992:
   (a) risk assessment
   (b) control of hazardous substances
   (c) training.

2 The workplace (Health, Safety and Welfare Regulations 1992):
   (a) floors to be of suitable construction
   (b) floors free from hazardous articles or substances
   (c) steps taken to avoid slips, trips or falls.

3 Manual Handling Operations Regulations 1992:
   (a) reducing incorrect handling of loads
   (b) preventing hazardous handling.

4 Fire precautions:
   (a) means of firefighting
   (b) evacuation procedures
   (c) raising the alarm.

5 Provision and use of work equipment:
   (a) ensure correct usage
   (b) properly maintained
   (c) training given.

6 Health and safety (display screen equipment):
   (a) ensure that members of staff using visual display units have a suitable workplace, and
   (b) they take regular breaks.

## Developing safety policies

Managers are required to develop workable policies, which address real workplace issues that are of practical use and are tailored to the operation and processes. When five or more persons are employed, the foodservice operator has a legal responsibility under the Health and Safety at Work Act 1974 to write down a statement of the operation's general policy organisation and arrangements for health and safety. Safety policies should identify all hazards found within the business and attempt to deal with them, reducing the risk of injury '*in so far as is reasonably practicable*'. There is, therefore, an inseparable link between policy and risk assessment, the first stage of development of a comprehensive safety policy. A summary of an approach to the development of a safety culture for a foodservice operation is given in Figure 3.1.

## Developing a positive health, safety and hygiene culture

It is an important function of management to develop a culture of safety. Good management involves stimulating staff interest and motivating employees to set goals to achieve the highest standards of hygiene and safety within the organisation.

A positive safety culture establishes safety systems; achieving the culture requires time and effort from management. Management must be caring, committed and well organised,

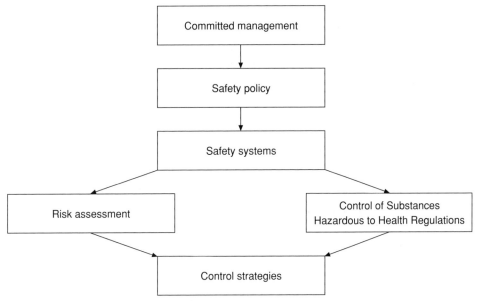

**Figure 3.1**   Developing a safety culture

identifying named individuals who are competent to guide company policy and know-ledgeable staff who are able to contribute to the business through safety committees.

## Control of Substances Hazardous to Health (COSHH) Regulations 1989

Substances dangerous to health are labelled very toxic, toxic harmful, irritant or corrosive. Whilst only a small number of such chemicals are used in foodservice operations for cleaning, it is necessary to be aware of the regulations introduced in 1989. Those persons using such substances must be made aware of their correct use and proper dilution, and to wear protective goggles, gloves and face masks. It is essential that members of staff are trained to take precautions and not to take risks.

The COSHH Regulations require the employer to do the following:

■ Assess the risk to health arising from work and what precautions are needed.

■ Introduce measures designed to prevent or control the risk.

■ Ensure that control measures are used and that equipment is properly maintained and procedures observed.

■ Where necessary, monitor the exposure of the workers and carry out an appropriate form of surveillance of their health.

■ Inform, instruct and train employees about the risks and the precautions to be taken.

Assessment is an essential requirement for all employers. As in tackling any problem, it is important to know what the problem is, and the extent of it, before deciding what, if anything, needs to be done about it. By going through the assessment procedure step by step, the health of those who could be affected by the work activities is protected, and money and effort are correctly spent and not wasted. The assessment must be a systematic review of the substances present, their effect, and how they are used and handled. For example, are there any harmful fumes given off?

## Risk assessment

Prevention of accidents and preventing food poisoning in foodservice establishments are essential, therefore it is necessary to assess any possible hazard or risk and decide what action is to be taken. The outcome of the risk assessment is that potential hazards or risks can be classified under four levels:

- Minimal risk – safe conditions with safety measures in place.
- Some risk – acceptable risk; however, attention must be given to ensure safety measures operate.
- Significant risk – where safety measures are not fully in operation, also includes foods most likely to cause food poisoning. Requires immediate attention.
- Dangerous risk – requires the cessation of the process and/or discontinuing of the use of the equipment in the system and the complete checking and clearance before continuation.

To operate an assessment of risks the following process should be considered:

1 Assess the risks.

2 Determine preventative measures.

3 Decide who carries out safety inspections.

4 Determine the frequency of inspections.

5 Detail the methodology of reporting back and to whom.

6 Detail how to ensure inspections are effective.

7 See that on-the-job training in safety is related to the job.

The purpose of the exercise of assessing the possibility of risks and hazards is to prevent accidents. Firstly, it is necessary to monitor the situation and to have regular and random checks to observe that the standards set are being complied with. It is essential that an investigation is made if any incidents or accidents occur. The investigation must aim to track down any defects in the system and proceed to remedy these at once.

Some of the potential hazards in food production areas are as follows:

- *Falls*  The highest numbers of accidents occurring in foodservice premises are due to people falling, slipping or tripping on kitchen floors. A major reason for the high incidence of this kind of accident is that water and grease are likely to be spilt, and in combination they are treacherous. Staff must be trained to clean floors immediately after spillages.

  Another cause of people falling is the placing of articles on the floor in corridors, passageways or between stores and tables. Persons carrying trays and containers have their vision obstructed and items on the floor may not be visible. As the fall may occur on to a hot stove and the item being carried may be hot, these falls may have serious consequences. Nothing should be left on the kitchen floor. Kitchen staff must be trained to think and work safely.

- *Manual handling*  The incorrect handling of heavy and awkward loads causes accidents. This is especially important when lifting goods and equipment on to and off of trolleys, tables, and within service areas.

- *Fire regulations*  All food production staff must have knowledge of the fire drill. They should be trained in how to extinguish small fires, and clearly understand which extinguisher is used for which fire.

- *Provision and use of work equipment*  All equipment must be suitable for the job for which it is to be used. All equipment must be regularly maintained and serviced. All equipment must comply with safety legislation, such as Electricity at Work Regulations 1989, Gas Safety and Use Regulations 1994, Prescribed Dangerous Machines Order 1964, and other health and safety regulations.

- *Personal protective clothing*  All kitchen staff must wear protective clothing and protective safety footwear.

- *Kitchen equipment*  All equipment must be maintained so that it is both safe and in working order. Manufacturers' instructions should be adhered to. All new equipment, especially gas and electrical equipment, must also comply with the legislation.

- *Health and safety committees*  Each organisation is required to have a health and safety committee to regularly review safety at work.

- *Individual health*  The health of an individual can also affect that individual's safety and the safety of others. For this reason, many companies have an occupational health policy which aims to promote good health practices at work. This involves regular medical checks and advice on maintaining a healthy lifestyle. In many cases such a policy has helped to reduce staff absenteeism through illness.

## Food hygiene policies

Food hygiene policies set down a commitment by the organisation to encourage food hygiene practices within its working environment. These must be seen as laying down clear guidelines and objectives for management, chefs and other personnel. Some of these policies have been modelled closely on health and safety lines giving a detailed set of broad objectives with guidance in relation to particular processes. Emphasis must be on clear, accurate guidance to ensure that members of the kitchen staff comply and that the policy is accepted by all who work for the organisation. Some establishments ask staff to sign a form to indicate that they understand the policy and that they mean to comply with its objectives to maintain high standards of hygiene. Failure to comply once signed may lead to disciplinary action. The success of the policy must be judged on the commitment of the workforce, therefore before formulating any document it is advisable to consult with staff. It is important that any policy is simple to understand and is practical to operate.

## Hygiene committees

Food hygiene involves everyone in the production system, from goods inwards to final product. In order to focus attention on the subject and to maintain a continued interest throughout the workforce it is advisable to set up a hygiene committee. Such a committee comprises those who have immediate responsibility for maintaining hygiene standards, quality control, production, service, training, and so on. Staff representatives from various areas should be involved. Members should be changed from time to time to avoid complacency and to maintain interest.

## The Food Safety (Temperature Control) Regulations 1995

These regulations came into force in September 1995 and replace earlier and quite complex regulations. There are now only two important temperatures: 8°C and 63°C (82°C in Scotland).

Foods which may be subject to microbiological multiplication must be held either at no more than 8°C or above 63°C. There are a few exceptions, which include foods in display. These foods can be displayed for up to four hours. Low-risk and preserved foods can be stored at ambient temperature. It is possible to reuse food that has been displayed at ambient temperatures provided it has not exceeded four hours at that temperature, and is then subsequently served directly from a refrigerator. Manufacturers can vary upward the 8°C ceiling if there is a scientific basis to do so. Food which is served hot should be held at over 63°C. Under Scottish regulations, reheated food must attain a temperature of 82°C provided this does not adversely affect the quality of the food.

## Hazard analysis and critical control point (HACCP)

Developed in the USA in the mid-1970s, HACCP is widely used by food manufacturers and processors and is now being applied in the foodservice industry. HACCP is a procedure that examines each stage in the production process, which may appear vulnerable in terms of introducing a hazard into the food. Particular attention is then given to this stage in the process. HACCP critically examines each stage of food production through to the final product and the consumer.

Once a potential hazard in the processes has been identified, whether it is within the preparation, processing, storage or service, then attention must be given to either eliminating or minimising the hazard. One of the advantages of HACCP is that a multi-disciplinary team is involved because it covers the wide range of activities associated with the food product. Staff must be trained in HACCP and, for the process to be successful, they too must have commitment.

On introducing the HACCP process into food production the following elements have to be implemented:

■ A detailed flowchart needs to be drawn up showing the path of the food throughout the manufacturing or kitchen process.

■ All production details need to be identified so that any special characteristics are noted that could become a cause for concern.

■ Each stage in the production must be carefully examined to see if there is the possibility that a hazard could occur. The risks are then recorded as high, medium or low. Monitoring controls are then implemented.

Taking food samples and bacterial swabs also helps to complement the HACCP programme.

HACCP can be adapted by all sectors of the foodservice industry – the process is not confined to large operators. A simplified version of HACCP has also been introduced called Assured Safe Catering.

Examples of critical control points (CCPs) are:

■ Inspection (including temperature checks) of goods on delivery and before use.

■ Separate storage and handling of ingredients and the finished product.

■ Correct temperature ranges for refrigerated and frozen goods.

■ Cleaning procedures for equipment and utensils.

■ Cross-contamination with other menu items in process.

■ Personal hygiene and health standards.

■ Proficiency in use and cleaning of equipment.

### How to establish HACCP

1 Select a specific menu item or group of menu items.

2 Draft a flow diagram showing how it is/they are made (see Figure 3.2).

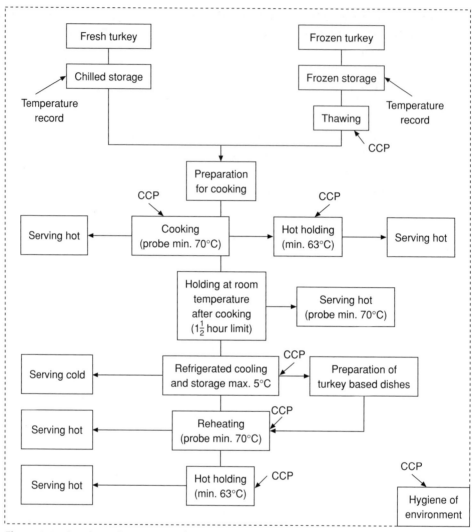

**Figure 3.2**   Specimen flow diagram (*source*: HCIMA Technical Brief 1991)

3 Select the most relevant person who should:
   (a) amend the flow diagram if necessary;
   (b) examine each stage and identify where significant hazards could occur under both normal and occasional conditions;
   (c) list all probable causes of each hazard;
   (d) identify each CCP at which these causes can be controlled.
4 Specify the control procedures at each CCP and change working practices as necessary.

A specimen flow diagram is shown in Figure 3.2. (This diagram is indicative only and is not applicable to turkey in all situations.)

### How to maintain HACCP

- Monitor the information (for example, temperature record charts) and take effective action when appropriate.
- If any feature of ingredients, processes or environment changes, alter the HACCP system as necessary.
- Carry out periodic checks to ensure the accuracy of any instruments.
- Periodic laboratory testing of the microbiological condition of raw materials, equipment, environment and product should be made wherever possible.
- Ensure adequate personnel monitoring, training and retraining.

### Use of HACCP in foodservice operations

The most important aspects to be considered are:

- Handling and storage procedures from delivery to service of the menu items.
- Holding items and temperatures.
- Cooling times.
- Personnel training.

## Assured Safe Catering

As HACCP is a system designed principally for manufacturing it is seen by many foodservice operators as being too complex. Therefore, a simpler system was developed which takes a slightly different approach in that it takes a generic view of all operations in a kitchen, for example, temperature monitoring. Assured Safe Catering (ASC) is based on the HACCP approach but tends to look at the many steps or individual subprocesses involved in getting all the supplies from the supplier to the customer. At each point where a risk is identified, a control measure needs to be designed, implemented and monitored. These may include:

**Subprocesses**

- Specification
- Buying
- Receiving
- Storage
- Preparation

- Cooking
- Holding – hot or cold
- Reheating
- Serving
- Waste disposal
- Cleaning.

### Risks

- Contamination
- Temperature
- Cross-contamination.

### Measures include:

- Supplier checks
- Checks for condition
- Temperature checks
- Colour-coding knives and boards.

### *The Assured Safe Catering system*

The process of setting up the ASC system includes the following stages:

1 Planning the system.

2 Organising the system.

3 Setting up an organisational flowchart:
  (a) listing the hazards
  (b) identifying the controls
  (c) determining the critical controls
  (d) monitoring and recording
  (e) implementing procedures
  (f) checking procedures.

4 Checking the system to ensure effectiveness.

5 Reviewing to take account of changes; introducing improvements.

## Food hygiene audits

Food hygiene audits are carried out by management to scrutinise the food production operation. The audit is intended to record deficiencies and areas for improvement and to monitor performance at certain points. These may be linked to any quality assurance (including ISO 9002) criteria.

The audit usually requires a suitably qualified person to carry out a detailed inspection of the premises, plant and practices. The report is presented to management and includes observations and makes recommendations.

Many foodservice establishments change their techniques and procedures of operation without being aware of hazards that are introduced. It is all too easy for people who are familiar with the kitchen or plant to fail to see what, to outsiders, are obvious problem areas emerging. Buildings may also be suffering from wear and tear and lack of repair. Equipment may also need overhauling. Often, a hygiene audit is the only way of looking critically at the environment and thus picking up the problem areas or practices.

The frequency of these audits may vary, depending on the type of premises. High-volume production will justify more frequent audits. Establishments processing high-risk fresh commodities will also require more frequent audits. All inspections require properly recorded documentation, which provides the basis for reports to go to the people who are able to take action. Otherwise their value is diminished. Reports should prioritise, to assist management in their decision-making, especially when financial implications have to be assessed and considered. It is always advisable to inform the local environmental health officer of the audits and the prioritised reports. The process of food hygiene management is shown in Figure 3.3.

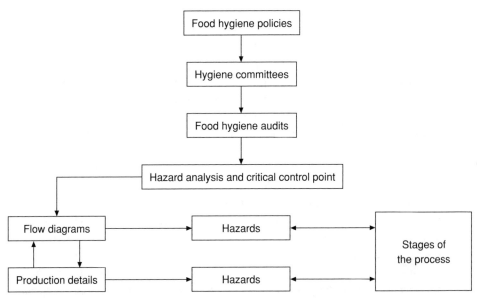

**Figure 3.3** The process of food hygiene management for food production

## Registration of premises

Under the Food Premises (Registration) Regulations 1991 as amended by the Food Premises (Registration) Amendment Regulations 1993, all existing food premises in England, Wales and Scotland have to register with their local authority. Anyone starting a new food business must register 28 days before trading. It is an offence not to register.

## FOOD PRODUCTION SYSTEMS

A production system has to be organised to produce the right quantity of food at the correct standard, for the required number of people, on time, using the resources of staff, equipment and materials effectively and efficiently.

As costs of space, equipment, fuel, maintenance and labour continue to rise, more thought and time have to be given to the planning of a production system and to kitchen design. Research is often lacking in this area of the foodservice industry, although research from equipment manufacturers concentrating on new technology is increasing. New technology enables us to plan production systems more effectively.

The requirements of the production system have to be clearly matched to the type of food that is to be prepared, cooked and served, to the required market at the correct price. All allocation of space and the purchase of the different types of equipment have to be justified, and the organisation of the kitchen personnel has to be planned at the same time.

Many food production operations are based on the process approach, as opposed to the *partie* system (product approach). The process approach concentrates on the specific techniques and processes of food production. The system places importance on the identification of these common techniques and processes across the full range of required dishes. In developing the production system, groupings are not then based on the types of dish or food, which is the basis of the *partie* system, but on the clustering of similar production techniques and processes which apply a range of common skills and encourage flexible open-endedness.

Food production is an operating system and can be managed through the application of the systems approach. A whole range of different cuisines are able to fit more neatly into this approach because the key elements focus on the process, the way the food is prepared, processed (cooked) stored and served. Using this approach, food production systems may be identified using the input/process/output model of systems and the elements may be set out as in Figure 3.4.

This identification of the seven stages of food production shows the types of *foods in*, the *processes* and the *foods out* or presentation stages. Using this approach a generic model of food production can be developed, and this is shown in Figure 3.5.

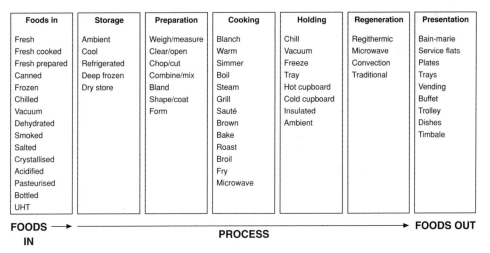

| Foods in | Storage | Preparation | Cooking | Holding | Regeneration | Presentation |
|---|---|---|---|---|---|---|
| Fresh | Ambient | Weigh/measure | Blanch | Chill | Regithermic | Bain-marie |
| Fresh cooked | Cool | Clear/open | Warm | Vacuum | Microwave | Service flats |
| Fresh prepared | Refrigerated | Chop/cut | Simmer | Freeze | Convection | Plates |
| Canned | Deep frozen | Combine/mix | Boil | Tray | Traditional | Trays |
| Frozen | Dry store | Bland | Steam | Hot cupboard | | Vending |
| Chilled | | Shape/coat | Grill | Cold cupboard | | Buffet |
| Vacuum | | Form | Sauté | Insulated | | Trolley |
| Dehydrated | | | Brown | Ambient | | Dishes |
| Smoked | | | Bake | | | Timbale |
| Salted | | | Roast | | | |
| Crystallised | | | Broil | | | |
| Acidified | | | Fry | | | |
| Pasteurised | | | Microwave | | | |
| Bottled | | | | | | |
| UHT | | | | | | |

FOODS IN → ——————————————— PROCESS ——————————————— → FOODS OUT

**Figure 3.4**   Elements of food production

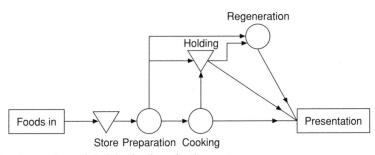

**Figure 3.5**   A generic model of the food production system

Developing this approach further, nine standard production systems can be identified, and these are shown in Table 3.2 on page 80.

## CENTRALISED PRODUCTION SYSTEMS

Centralised production has recently been considered by a large number of employers in the foodservice industry. Considerations have been based on:

■ Labour cost – using staff more effectively and efficiently.

■ Food costs – greater control over wastage and portion sizes linked to standardised recipes and standardised purchasing specifications.

■ Equipment – more use of technology reducing commitment in individual units.

**Table 3.2   Methods of food production**

| No. | Method | Description |
| --- | --- | --- |
| 1 | Conventional | Term used to describe production utilising mainly fresh foods and traditional cooking methods |
| 2 | Convenience | Method of production utilising mainly convenience foods |
| 3 | Call order | Method where food is cooked to order either from customer (as in cafeterias) or from waiter. Production area often open to customer area |
| 4 | Continuous flow | Method involving production line approach where different parts of the production process may be separated (e.g. fast food) |
| 5 | Centralised | Production not directly linked to service. Foods are 'held' and distributed to separate service areas |
| 6 | Cook–chill | Food production storage and regeneration method utilising principle of low temperature control to preserve qualities of processed foods |
| 7 | Cook–freeze | Production, storage and regeneration method utilising principle of freezing to control and preserve qualities of processed foods. Requires special processes to assist freezing |
| 8 | Sous-vide | Method of production, storage and regeneration utilising principle of sealed vacuum to control and preserve the quality of processed foods |
| 9 | Assembly kitchen | A system based on accepting and incorporating the latest technological development in manufacturing and conservation of food products |

## Cook–chill system

Cook–chill is a foodservice system based on normal preparation and cooking of food followed by rapid chilling, storage in controlled low-temperature conditions above freezing point, 0–3°C (32–37°F), and subsequently reheating immediately before consumption. The chilled food is regenerated in finishing kitchens which require low capital investment and minimum staff.

## The purpose of chilling food

The purpose of chilling food is to prolong its storage life. Under normal temperatures, food deteriorates rapidly through the action of microorganisms and enzymic and chemical reactions. Reduction in the storage temperature inhibits the multiplication of bacteria and other microorganisms and slows down the chemical and enzymic reactions. At normal refrigeration temperature, reactions are still taking place but at a much slower rate, and at frozen food storage temperatures (−20°C (−4°F) approx.) nearly all reactions cease. A temperature of 0–3°C does not give a storage life comparable to frozen food but it does produce a good product.

It is generally accepted that, even when high standards of fast-chilling practice are used and consistent refrigerated storage is maintained, product quality may be acceptable for only a few days (including day of production and consumption). The storage temperature of 0–3°C is of extreme importance to ensure both full protection of the food from microbiological growth and the maintenance of maximum nutritional values in the food. It is generally accepted that a temperature of 10°C (50°F) should be regarded as the critical safety limit for the storage of refrigerated food. Above that temperature, growth of microorganisms may render the food dangerous to health.

## The cook–chill process

1 The food should be cooked sufficiently to ensure destruction of any pathogenic microorganisms.

2 The chilling process must begin as soon as possible after completion of the cooking and portioning processes, within 30 minutes of leaving the cooking process. The food should be chilled to 3°C (37°F) within a period of 60–90 minutes. Most pathogenic organisms will not grow below 7°C (45°F), whilst a temperature below 3°C (37°F) is required to reduce growth of spoilage organisms and to achieve the required storage life. However, slow growth of spoilage organisms does take place at these temperatures and for this reason storage life cannot be greater than 5 days.

3 The food should be stored at a temperature between 0 and 3°C (32–37°F).

4 The chilled food should be distributed under such controlled conditions that any rise in temperature of the food during distribution is kept to a minimum.

5 For both safety and palatability, the reheating (regeneration) of the food should follow immediately upon the removal of the food from chilled conditions and should raise the temperature to a level of at least 70°C (158°F).

6 The food should be consumed as soon as possible and not more than 2 hours after reheating. Food not intended for reheating should be consumed as soon as convenient and within 2 hours of removal from storage. It is essential that unconsumed reheated food is discarded.

7 A temperature of 10°C (50°F) should be regarded as the critical safety limit for chilled food. Should the temperature of the chilled food rise above this level during storage or distribution then the food concerned should be discarded.

Cook–chill is generally planned within a purpose-designed, comprehensive, new central production unit to give small-, medium- or large-scale production along predefined flow-lines, incorporating traditional foodservice/chilling/post-chilling packaging and storage for delivery to finishing kitchens.

Within an existing kitchen, where equipment is retained with possible minor additions and modifications, chilling/post-chilling packaging and additional storage for cooked chilled food are added.

### Finishing kitchens

Finishing kitchens can consist of purpose-built regeneration equipment plus refrigerated storage. Additional equipment, such as a deep fat fryer for chips, boiling table for sauces and custards, and pressure steamer for vegetables and so on can be added if required to give greater flexibility.

Where chilled food is produced to supply a service on the same premises, it is recommended that the meals should be supplied, stored and regenerated by exactly the same method as used for operations where the production unit and finishing kitchens are separated by some distance. Failure to adhere to just one procedure could result in disorganised production and reduce productivity. Once a decision is taken to sever production from service this method should be followed throughout the system.

### Distribution of cook–chill

Distribution of the chilled food is an important part of the cook–chill operation. Fluctuations in storage temperature can affect the palatability and texture of food and lead to microbiological dangers requiring the food to be discarded.

The distribution method chosen must ensure that the required temperature below 3°C (37°F) is maintained throughout the period of transport. Should the temperature of the food exceed 5°C (41°F) during distribution, the food ought to be consumed within 12 hours; if the temperature exceeds 10°C (50°F) it should be discarded (Department of Health Cook Chill guidelines). Because of this, refrigeration during distribution is to be encouraged in many circumstances.

In some cases, the cook–chill production unit can also act as a centralised kitchen and distribution point. Food is regenerated in an area adjacent to the cook–chill production area and heat retention or insulated boxes are used for distribution. During transportation and service the food must not be allowed to fall below 62°C (145°F).

### Maintenance

All equipment used in the process must be checked and maintained regularly. The accuracy of thermometers should be checked every 2–3 months against a calibrated thermometer.

## Quality control

All staff working in a cook–chill production unit must be trained to the highest standard and must work under skilled supervision. Adequate control of bacterial contamination and multiplication, which are hazards in any kitchen, can be achieved by a survey of the initial installation by a qualified analyst and batch checks thereafter. In a very large production kitchen, producing between 10 000 and 15 000 meals per day, a full-time microbiologist would normally be employed.

## Management of quality assurance

Because of the potential risks to health, strict quality assurance is of paramount importance. This involves the HACCP (hazard analysis critical control point) approach (see page 75). This involves identifying critical points in the system, establishing monitoring procedures and training staff.

## Regeneration food service system for hospitals

In hospitals, the system utilises specially designed porcelain or stainless steel dishes with stainless steel covers. Centrally produced meals are chilled in a purpose-built chilling unit. The chilled meal packs are distributed for ward-level regeneration to service temperature in a purpose-designed trolley/oven unit. This thermal heating system is based on quartz radiant heaters, proportionally spaced to ensure even and simultaneous heat distribution on both the porcelain dish and the stainless steel cover. Alternatively, regeneration may be carried out in convection ovens with steam injection; a humidifier oven will prevent the food's drying out and counteract any loss of moisture that may have occurred during the chilling process.

## Employee self-service

The employee self-service system utilises bulk stainless steel dishes into which cooked food is portioned prior to chilling and storage. At service time the food is batch regenerated behind the service counter for self-help or self-service. One central kitchen can supply chilled meals to numerous satellite services where cooking operations are virtually eliminated.

## Banqueting

The banqueting system utilises ceramic banquet dishes, divided into ten to twelve portions, into which the food is normally placed after chilling. Banquet meals are stored in cold rooms prior to regeneration which can take place in portable thermal units; this is particularly suitable for hotels where banquets and seminars occur in different venues or on different floors.

## Production

- Skilled staff are employed in the production operation.
- It is largely unskilled staff, under strict supervision, who carry out packaging, chilling, storage and regeneration.

Maximum efficiency should follow if the production area is set up in a new location, but, depending on circumstances, a simple layout can be established in an existing kitchen for possible use in room service, banqueting, small-scale staff catering (night-shifts) and as a pilot scheme for a potentially larger operation.

## Cook–freeze system

Blast freezers have increasingly been introduced with success into foodservice operations. The ability to freeze cooked dishes and prepared foods, as distinct from the storage of chilled foods in a refrigerator or already frozen commodities in a deep-freezer, allows a foodservice operator to make more productive use of kitchen staff. It also enables economies to be introduced into the staffing of dining rooms and restaurants.

### The cook–freeze process

Cook–freeze uses a production system similar to that used in cook–chill. The recipes used have to be modified, enabling products to be freezer-stable and modified starches are used in sauces so that on reheating and regeneration the sauce does not separate. Blast freezers are used in place of blast chillers. The freezing must be carried out very rapidly to retain freshness and to accelerate temperature loss through the latent heat barrier, thus preventing the formation of large ice crystals and rupturing of the cells.

Blast freezing takes place when low-temperature air is passed over food at high speed, reducing food in batches to a temperature of at least $-20°C$ ($-4°F$) within 90 minutes, Blast freezers can hold between 20 and 400 kg (40–800 lb) per batch, the larger models being designed for trolley operation.

1 *Preparation of food*  The production menu for a month is drawn up and the total quantities of different foods required calculated. Supplies are then ordered, with special attention given to their being:
   (a) of high quality;
   (b) delivered so that they can immediately be prepared and cooked without any possibility of deterioration during an enforced period of storage before being processed.

   The dishes included in the menu must be cooked to the highest standards with rigid attention to quality control and to hygiene. It will be remembered that deep-freeze temperatures prevent the multiplication of microorganisms but do not destroy them. If, therefore, a dish were contaminated before being frozen, consumers would be put at risk months later when the food was prepared for consumption.

   The exact adjustment of recipes to produce the best results when the food is subsequently thawed and reheated is still in the process of being worked out by chefs, using numerous variations of the basic system. The single change needed in recipes involving sauces is the selection of an appropriate type of starch capable of resisting the effects of freezing. Normal starches will produce a curdled effect when subsequently thawed and reheated.

In order to achieve rapid freezing with a quick reduction of temperature to $-18°C$ ($0°F$) or below, the cooked food must be carefully portioned (close attention being paid to the attainment of uniform portion size). Each portion is placed into a disposable aluminium foil container, may be placed conveniently into aluminium trays holding from six to ten portions each, sealed and carefully labelled with its description and date of preparation.

2 *Freezing*   The food thus divided into portions and arranged in trays is immediately frozen. An effective procedure is to place the trays on racks in a blast-freezing tunnel and expose them to a vigorous flow of cold air until the cooked items are frozen solid and the temperature reduced to at least $-5°C$ ($23°F$). The quality of the final product is to a significant degree dependent on the rapidity with which the temperature of hot cooked food at, say, $80°C$ ($176°F$) is reduced to below freezing. The capacity of the blast freezer should be designed to achieve this reduction in temperature within a period of $1-1\frac{1}{4}$ hours.

3 *Storage of frozen items*   Once the food items are frozen they must at once be put into a deep-freeze store maintained at $-18°C$ ($0°F$). For a foodservice operation involving several dining rooms and cafeterias, some of which may be situated at some distance from the kitchen and frozen store, a four weeks' supply of cooked dishes held at low temperature allows full use to be made of the facilities.

4 *Transport of frozen items to the point of service*   If satisfactory quality is to be maintained, it is important to keep food frozen in the cooked state, frozen until immediately prior to its being served. It should therefore be transported in insulated containers to peripheral kitchens, if such are to be used, where it will be reheated.

If frozen dishes are to be used in outside catering, provision should be available for transporting them in refrigerated transport and if necessary, a subsidiary deep-freeze store should be provided for them on arrival.

5 *Reheating of frozen cooked portions*   In any foodservice system in which a blast-freezing tunnel has been installed to freeze pre-cooked food, previously portioned and packed in metal foil or other individual containers, it is obviously rational to install equipment that is designed for the purpose of reheating the items ready to be served. The blast-freezing system is effective because it is, in design, a specially powerful form of forced convection heat exchanger arranged to extract heat. It follows that an equally appropriate system for replacing heat is the use of a force convection oven, especially for the reception of trays of frozen portions. Where such an oven is equipped with an efficient thermostat and adequate control of the air circulation system, standardised setting times for the controls can be laid down for the regeneration of the various types of dish that need to be reheated.

6 *Quality control*   Adequate control of bacterial contamination and growth, which are hazards in any kitchen, can be achieved by a survey of the initial installation by a qualified analyst and regular checks taken on every batch of food cooked. Very large kitchens employ a full-time food technologist/bacteriologist. In smaller operations the occasional services of a microbiologist from the public health authority should be used.

## Overall benefits of cook–chill and cook–freeze

### For the operation

- Good portion control and reduced waste.
- No overproduction.
- Central purchasing – bulk-buying discounts.
- Full utilisation of equipment.
- Full utilisation of staff time.
- Overall savings in staff.
- Savings on equipment, space and fuel.
- Fewer staff with better conditions – no unsocial hours, no weekend work, no overtime.
- Simplified delivery to units – less frequent.
- Solve problem of moving hot food. (EC regulations forbid the movement of hot foods unless the temperature is maintained over 65°C (149°F). Maintaining 65°C is regarded as very difficult to achieve and high temperatures inevitably will be harmful to foods.)

### For the customer

- Increased variety and selection.
- Improved quality, with standards maintained.
- More nutritious foods.
- Services can be maintained at all times, regardless of staff absences.

The advantages of cook–freeze over cook–chill are:

- Seasonal purchasing provides considerable savings.
- Delivery to units will be far less frequent.
- Long-term planning of production and menus becomes possible.
- Less dependent on price fluctuations.
- More suitable for vending machines incorporating microwave.

And the advantages of cook–chill over cook–freeze are:

- Regeneration systems are simpler: infrared and steam convection ovens are mostly used and only approximately 12 minutes is required to reheat all foods perfectly.
- Thawing time is eliminated.
- Smaller-capacity storage is required: 3–4 days' supply as opposed to up to 120 days.
- Chiller storage is cheaper to install and run than freezer storage.
- Blast chillers are cheaper to install and run than blast freezers.

■ Cooking techniques are unaltered (additives and revised recipes are needed for freezing).

■ All foods can be chilled so the range of dishes is wider (some foods cannot be frozen). Cooked eggs, steaks and sauces such as hollandaise can be chilled (after some recipe modification where necessary).

■ No system is too small to adapt to cook–chill.

## Sous-vide

Sous-vide is a form of cook–chill: a combination of vacuum sealing in plastic pouches, cooking by steam and then rapidly cooking and chilling. The objective is to rationalise kitchen procedures without having a detrimental effect on the quality of individual dishes. Vacuum pressures are as important as the cooking temperatures with regard to weight loss and heat absorption. The highest temperature used in sous-vide cooking is 100°C (212°F) and 1000 millibars is the minimum amount of vacuum pressure used.

As there is no oxidation or discoloration it is ideal for conserving fruits, such as apples and pears, for example pears in red wine, fruits in syrup. When preparing meats in sauces the meat is pre-blanched and then added to the completed sauce.

Sous-vide is a combination of vacuum sealing, tightly controlled *en papillote* cooking and rapid chilling. Potential users are brasseries, wine bars, airlines, private hospitals and function foodservice operators seeking to provide top quality with portion convenience.

### The sous-vide process

1 Individual portions of prepared food are first placed in special plastic pouches. The food might be fish, poultry, meats or vegetables, to which seasoning, a garnish, sauce, stock, wine, flavourings, vegetables, herbs and/or spices can be added.

2 The pouches of food are then placed in a vacuum-packing machine which evacuates all the air and tightly seals the pouch.

3 The pouches are next cooked by steam. This is usually in a special oven equipped with a steam control programme, which controls the injection of steam in the oven, to give steam cooking at an oven temperature below 100°C (212°F). Each food item has its own ideal cooking time and temperature.

4 When cooked, the pouches are rapidly cooled to 3°C (37°F), usually in an iced water chiller, or an air blast chiller for larger operations.

5 The pouches are then labelled and stored in a holding refrigerator at an optimum temperature of 3°C (37°F).

6 When required for service the pouches are regenerated in boiling water or a steam combination oven until the required temperature is reached, cut open and the food presented.

The advantages of the sous-vide process are:

■ Long shelf-life, up to 21 days if refrigerated.

■ Ability to produce meals in advance means better deployment of staff and skills.

■ Vacuum-packed foods can be mixed in cold store without the risk of cross-contamination.

■ Reduces labour costs at point of service.

■ Beneficial cooking effects on certain foods, especially moulded items and pâtés. Reduced weight loss on meat joints.

■ Full flavour and texture are retained as food cooks in its own juices.

■ Economises on ingredients (less butter, marinade).

■ Makes pre-cooking a possibility for à la carte menus.

■ Inexpensive regeneration.

■ Allows a small operation to set up bulk production.

■ Facilitates portion control and uniformity of standards.

■ Has a tenderising effect on tougher cuts of meat and matures game without dehydration.

Its disadvantages are:

■ Extra cost of vacuum pouches and vacuum-packing machine.

■ Unsuitable for some meats (for example, fillet steak) and vegetables which absorb colour.

■ All portions in a batch must be identically sized to ensure even results.

■ Most dishes require twice the conventional cooking time.

■ Unsuitable for large joints as chilling time exceeds 90 minutes.

■ Complete meals (for example, meat and two vegetables) not feasible – the meat component needs to be cooked and stored in separate bags.

■ Extremely tight management and hygiene controls are imperative.

■ Potentially adverse customer reaction (boil-in-the-bag syndrome).


## VOLUME IN FOOD PRODUCTION

The food production process may be seen in the elements for food production as shown in Figure 3.4 (page 79). This figure identifies seven stages in the general food production process. These are:

1 foods in

2 storage

3 preparation

**4** cooking

**5** holding

**6** regeneration

**7** presentation.

Each of these stages has an effect on the potential volume of the operation. Also differing operations will route foods in different ways. The generic model is identified in Figure 3.5 (page 79). Thus, for instance, a fast food process will flow from 'foods in' to 'store' to 'preparation' or 'cooking', then to 'holding' and then to 'presentation'. A cook–chill process will flow from 'foods in' to 'store' to 'preparation' to 'holding' or 'cooking' then to 'holding', and then to 'regeneration' and then to 'presentation'.

It is, however, difficult to determine the key process in any food production system that limits the potential volume, as each of the stages has a separate effect on the capacity of food able to be processed at any time, as follows (Cousins 1994):

■ *Foods in*  The availability of food and the frequency of delivery clearly have an impact on the maximum food capacity of the operation. Greater and more frequent delivery opportunities increase the potential capacity. In addition, the variety of foods being bought in terms of either food type or supplier source will also affect food capacity.

■ *Storage*  The storage space and type of storage available determine the type of food that can be bought and the quantities that can be available at a given time. Capacity can be increased by altering the nature of foods being bought, for instance from fresh to convenience, or by increasing the delivery frequency.

■ *Preparation*  The extent to which food has to be prepared also affects capacity. High preparation requirements increase the space and the layout required. This stage can be greatly affected by increasing the use of ready prepared foods and by the use of equipment for bulk preparation activities.

■ *Cooking*  The availability of cooking space and the time that cooking takes can limit capacity. Again this can be affected by variations in the needs for cooking and the type of cooking required. In addition, the type of equipment used for the cooking processes can be altered to increase the volume of cooking that can be done at a given time.

■ *Holding*  Food capacity is limited by the type and availability of holding space. Variations in the need for holding in a given operation can vary the potential food capacity.

■ *Regeneration*  This stage follows from holding and has similar characteristics. However, the regeneration potential can be less than the full holding potential depending on the nature of demand required at a given time.

■ *Presentation*  The food capacity at this stage is usually determined by the speed of the service process. This assumes that a critical path analysis approach has been used to ensure that the full range of foods required at a given time is available at the same time.

Overall, the need to meet the demands of the presentation stage is determined by the expected volume of business at a given time. Each of the previous stages, through the application of careful critical path analysis approaches, should be able to be planned and operated to meet the presentation demand.

## PURCHASING AND CONTROL

Once a menu is planned, a number of activities must occur to bring it into reality. One of the first and most important stages is to purchase and receive the materials needed to produce the menu items. Skilful purchasing with good receiving can do much to maximise the results of a good menu. Six important steps must occur if purchasing and receiving functions are to be successful:

1 Know the market.

2 Determine purchasing needs.

3 Establish and use specifications.

4 Design the purchase procedures.

5 Receiving.

6 Evaluating the purchasing task.

Since markets vary considerably, to do a good job of purchasing a buyer must know the characteristics of each market.

A market is a place in which ownership of commodity changes from one person to another. This could occur using the telephone, on a street corner, in a retail or wholesale establishment or at an auction.

It is important that the purchaser for a foodservice operation has knowledge of the items to be purchased. For example:

- where they are grown
- seasons of production
- approximate costs
- conditions of supply and demand
- laws and regulations governing the market and the products
- marketing agents and their services
- processing
- storage requirements
- commodity and product, class and grade.

## Classification of markets and methods of purchasing

### The primary market

Raw materials may be purchased at the source of supply, the grower, producer or manufacturer or from central markets such as Smithfield or Nine Elms (Covent Garden) in London. Some establishments or large organisations will have a buyer who will buy directly from the primary markets. Also, a number of small establishments may adopt this method for some of their needs, i.e. the chef patron may buy fish, meat and vegetables directly from the market.

### The secondary market

Goods are bought wholesale from a distributor or agent; the foodservice establishment will pay wholesale prices and possibly obtain discounts.

### The tertiary market

The retail or cash and carry warehouse is a method suitable for smaller companies. A current pass obtained from the warehouse is required in order to gain access. This method also requires the user to have their own transport. Some cash and carry organisations require a VAT number before they will issue an authorised card. It is important to remember that there are the added costs of running the vehicle and the person's time in going to the warehouse.

Cash and carry can often be an impersonal way of buying as there are often no people to discuss quality and prices with.

## The buyer

The buyer is the person who makes decisions regarding quality, amounts, price, what will satisfy the customers, and profit of commodities. The wisdom of the buyer's decisions will be reflected in the success or failure of the operation. The buyer must not only be knowledgeable about the products, but also have the skills required to deal with salespeople, suppliers and other market agents. The buyer must be prepared for hard and often aggressive negotiations.

Buying demands integrity, maturity, bargaining skills and an even disposition. Often, buyers are subjected to bribes and other inducements by unscrupulous suppliers. Many suppliers will use pressure in order to get the buyer to purchase from specific sources. It is important to remember to treat the company's money as if it were your own. Use firm, friendly tactics, and socialise only if it means that it will improve your buying position or benefit the company in some way. A buyer must always retain the right to be a free agent.

Buying associations have ethical codes to which members subscribe. They require a high standard of ethical relationship between buyer and seller.

A buyer must have knowledge of the internal organisation of the company, especially the operational needs, and be able to obtain the product needs at a competitive price. The buyer must also be acquainted with the procedures of production and how the items are going to be used in the production operations, in order that the right item is purchased. For example, the item required need not always be of prime quality. Examples here would be tomatoes for soups and sauces: to be cost-effective these items do not need to be grade A or class 1. Another example is certain types of nut which do not have to be whole prime quality nuts for certain pastry goods or salads: to reduce costs it is better to purchase broken nuts.

A buyer must also know the storage requirements for each item and the space available, and the ability of the operation to finance special purchases in order to make good use of market conditions. For example, if there is a glut of fresh salmon at low cost, has the organisation the facility to make use of the extra salmon purchases? Is there sufficient freezer space? Can the chef make use of salmon by creating a demand on the menu? The buyer must also have a knowledge of yield testing procedures and know how to work closely with the chef and food production team to establish a specification so the right item is obtained.

## Buying methods

Buying methods will depend on the type of market and the kind of operation. Purchasing procedures are either formal or informal, and both have advantages and disadvantages. Informal methods are suitable for casual buying, where the amount involved is not large and speed and simplicity are desirable. Formal contracts are best for large orders of commodities purchased over a long period of time. Prices do not vary much during a year, once the basic price has been established. Using informal methods, prices and supply tend to fluctuate.

### Informal buying

Informal buying usually involves oral negotiations, talking directly to salespeople, face to face or using the telephone. Informal methods vary according to market conditions and include the following:

- *The quotation and order sheet method*  This uses a list of particular commodities always wanted in quantity and quality. Columns are provided to record prices from different suppliers. Prices are compared and orders given.

- *The blank cheque method*  This is when there is an extreme shortage of a commodity or some other market condition exists where the buyer must get the commodity at any cost. This usually operates only in extreme circumstances.

- *The cost-plus method*  This is used when prices are not known or the market is unstable. Many suppliers like this arrangement because they do not have to add a safety factor to take care of risk if commodities fluctuate considerably in price. They are free to buy at the most favourable price and then add on what they require to cover costs and give a profit. The amount over and above the cost paid for the item charged to the buyer is usually a standard percentage. Thus a supplier may buy fruit and vegetables and charge the buyer the price paid plus 10 per cent.

### Formal buying

This is known as competitive buying, giving suppliers written specifications and quantity needs. Negotiations are normally written. Methods are detailed as follows.

■ *The competitive bid method*  The sellers are invited to submit bids through written communications. The suppliers then send prices and other information on the commodities to the buyer. Bids are opened at a specified time to determine awards. Only those sellers able to meet the established purchase conditions of the buyer will be considered in awarding bids. The invitation to bid usually contains certain conditions. These will include:
  – terms of payment
  – discounts
  – method of delivery
  – invoice requirements.

■ *The negotiated method*  This is used when suppliers are hesitant to bid because of time restrictions, fluctuating market conditions, or a high perishability of the product. Negotiations may occur using the telephone and later confirmed in writing. Several suppliers are usually contacted to compare prices. This method is useful in that it allows competitive bidding whilst giving flexibility.

■ *The futures and contract method*  This is used by large organisations that have sufficient capital and staff to contract for future delivery of commodities at an established bid price. The advantage is that it ensures an adequate supply at an established price and avoids shortages and price fluctuations that affect prices. Sometimes this system is used to establish a buying agreement for only a week or month for commodities such as meat, fresh fruits and vegetables, but arrangements can also extend to a short season. Items more stable in price, such as canned goods, potato powder, tea and coffee, and frozen goods, are often placed on contract for long periods, possibly up to one year.

The quantity under contract may vary and the amount purchased will depend on the amount used over a period. Contract and industrial foodservice operators are able to forecast fairly accurately how much of each commodity they are likely to consume. A price is agreed along with quality and the quantity may also be set. For example, the price of baked beans may be dependent on the number of cases a buyer is guaranteeing to take over a period. Frequencies of delivery of the baked beans will also be determined. The maximum stock of baked beans held at any one time is determined by the buyer according to what was needed over a period of time. This is directly related to the operational need, how many food outlets have baked beans on the menu and the sales forecast of baked beans over a given period. When the stock diminishes to the reorder level, the buyer will contact the supplier for a new delivery. In some cases the supplier's salesperson may visit the company regularly to bring the inventory of the operations up to an established point. Whichever the case, such an arrangement is often called par stock supplying.

This ensures that a safety stock level on the quantity of the items to be used between the time of reorder and the time of delivery is maintained. A reserve stock (or safety stock) is essential in case the delivery is late.

## Selecting suppliers

Selecting suppliers is important in the purchasing process. Firstly, consider how a supplier will be able to meet the needs of your operation. Consider:

- price
- delivery
- quality/standards.

Information on suppliers can be obtained from other purchasers. Visits to suppliers' establishments are to be encouraged. When interviewing prospective suppliers, you need to question how reliable a supplier will be under competition and how stable under varying market conditions.

Suppliers are also selected on experience. A buyer soon gets to know the reliable suppliers. New suppliers are often tried out; some are retained. Considerations leading to a decision to continue to do business with a supplier include:

- If the supplier anticipates the needs of the organisation. The supplier notes market conditions and informs the company buyer.
- Suppliers regularly give product and market information.
- Does the supplier break quantities down as and when required, or does the buyer have to take a minimum quantity, which may be double the requirement needed?
- The supplier should always maintain adequate stocks.
- Evaluate credit terms and discounts available.
- Assess delivery conditions.
- A supplier may be able to offer a wide range of goods and services. Savings can often be made by consolidating products and services.

Many suppliers offer fresh fruit and vegetables, and part-prepared fresh vegetables such as peeled and turned potatoes, peeled and sliced carrots, prepared fresh beans. They will also offer a full range of frozen vegetables and speciality goods.

## Three types of need

Within a foodservice operation three types of purchasing and stock need can be identified. These are:

■ *Perishables*   These cover fresh fruit and vegetables, dairy products, meat and fish. Prices and suppliers may vary. Informal means of buying are frequently used. Perishables should be purchased to meet menu needs for a short period only.

■ *Staples*   These include supplies of canned, bottled, dehydrated and frozen products. Formal or informal purchasing can be used. Because items are staple and can be easily stored, bid buying is frequently used to take advantage of quantity price purchasing.

■ *Daily-use needs*   Daily-use or contract items are delivered frequently on par stock basis. Stocks are kept up to the desired level and supply is automatic. Supplies may be delivered daily, several times a week, weekly or less often. Most items are perishable, therefore supplies must not be excessive, only sufficient to get through to the next delivery.

## Determining quantity and quality

Determining quantity and quality of items to be purchased is important. This is based on the operational needs. The buyer must be informed by the chef or other members of the production team of the products that are needed. The chef and their team must establish the quality and they should be encouraged to inspect the goods on arrival. The buyer with this information then checks the market and looks for the best quality and best price. Delivery arrangements and other factors will be handled by the buyer. In smaller establishments the chef may also be the buyer.

When considering the quantity needed, certain factors should be known:

■ The number of people to be served in a given period.

■ The sales history.

■ Portion sizes, determined from yield testing a standard portion control list drawn up by the chef and management teams.

Buyers need to know production, often to be able to decide how many portions a given size may yield. They must also understand the various yields. Cooking shrinkage may vary, causing problems in portion control and yield.

The chef must inform the buyer of quantities. The buyer must also be aware of different packaging sizes, such as jars, bottles, cans and the yield from each package. There must be an indication of grades, styles, appearance, composition, varieties and quality factors such as:

■ colour

■ texture

■ size

■ absence of defects

■ bruising

■ irregular shape

■ maturity.

The chef and management team should establish quality standards when the menu is planned. Menus and recipes are developed using standardised recipes which directly relate to the buying procedure and standard purchasing specifications.

## The standard recipe

Standard recipes are a written formula for producing a food item of a specified quality and quantity for use in a particular establishment. It should show the precise quantities and qualities of the ingredients together with the sequence of preparation and service. It enables the establishment to have a greater control over cost and quantity.

### Objectives

One objective of the use of the standard recipe is to predetermine the following:

- the quantities and qualities of ingredients to be used stating the purchase specification
- the yield obtained from a recipe
- the food cost per person
- the nutritional value of a particular dish.

Another is to facilitate:

- menu planning
- purchasing and internal requisitioning
- food preparation and production
- portion control.

In addition, the standard recipe will assist new staff in preparation and production of standard products – which can be facilitated by photographs or drawings illustrating the finished product.

## Standard purchasing specification

Purchasing specifications have two functions:

- They communicate to a supplier what the specifier wishes to have supplied in terms of goods and services.
- They provide criteria against which the goods and services supplied can be compared.

The main advantages of specification buying are:

- Drawing up the specifications requires careful thought and a review of the buyer's needs. This frequently results in a simplification of the variety of products purchased and often reveals the possibility of using less expensive commodities. Both factors result in economies.

■ Buying according to specifications frequently induces more suppliers to bid on an order, because all suppliers know exactly what is wanted and that their chances are as good as those of other suppliers because they are bidding on identical items. This increased competition for the business often results in lower prices.

■ Specifications ensure the identical nature of items purchased from one or two sources. When the purchaser has more than one supplier of an item, this identity is essential and specification buying is a virtual necessity.

■ Purchasing to specifications gives the person receiving the order an exact standard against which to measure the incoming materials and results in accurate inspection and a uniform quality of commodities.

■ If specification buying is combined with quality control on the part of the supplier, it may be possible for the buyer to save money by doing a less complete inspection.

■ Specification buying is a necessary step towards industry-wide standardisation and standardisation programmes hold the promise of substantial savings.

The principal disadvantages of buying by specifications are:

■ It is not economical to prepare specifications for small-lot purchases. This rules out the possibility of specification buying for many items.

■ Specification buying adds to the purchaser's responsibilities. They must be able to state precisely what they want and the supplier's obligations extend only to complying with those terms. If the product does not live up to expectations, the liability rests with the buyer.

■ In specification buying, the cost of inspection is greater than in purchasing by brand name where the buyer is guaranteed a standard through experience. Items purchased to specification must be examined, whereas branded items need little more than a casual check and count.

■ There is always the danger of becoming overdefined in preparing specifications and, as a consequence, paying more than necessary for items.

■ There is also a danger of assuming that after specifications are established, the characteristics of the item have been permanently set. Unless specifications are periodically reviewed, there is a chance that the buyer will lose out on product improvements.

The content of a specification varies according to whether it is written for a user, designer, manufacturer or seller. A simple item may require only a brief description, whereas in the case of a complex assembly, the specification will be a comprehensive document, perhaps running to several pages. The content that may be required in a specification is listed in the *Guide to the Preparation of Specifications* issued by the British Standards Institution (PD 6112) in May 1967. These are categorised under the following headings:

■ characteristics

■ performance

■ control of quality

■ packaging and protection.

Most books available suggest that when writing specifications it is convenient to write them in a standard form. An example of information is as follows.

■ *Definition of the item* Care must be taken so that a common catering term used by the buyer means exactly the same thing to the supplier. For example, 'whole sirloin' means with bone, and 'strip loin' without the bone; 'washed and sliced potatoes' means after they have been peeled and of a thickness of no more than the specification.

■ *Grade or brand name* For example, apples – grade extra class, or Granny Smiths; Lea and Perrins Worcestershire Sauce; where available it should state the desired variety and next acceptable substitute.

■ *Weight, size or count* For example, pounds, kilos; A2s or A10s; lemons 120s, pineapples 12s. Counts vary from country to country; therefore desired country of origin should be quoted against the count and the substitute country with the alternative count noted.

■ *Unit against which prices should be quoted* For example, per pound, per case, per box, per sack, each.

■ *Special notes for the commodity* For example, for meat the notes could contain details of the preparation of a particular cut of meat, or details of special packaging and delivery requirements. With regard to the Food Safety Act 1990/1995, chilled delivery vehicles are a legal requirement.

### The contents which may be required in a specification

These are taken from the *Guide to the Preparation of Specifications* issued by the British Standards Institution (PD 6112) in May 1967.

1 Title of specification.

2 List of contents.

3 Foreword including why the specification has been written and on whose authority.

4 Scope of the specification. (If the specification is limited to certain aspects only, for example workmanship and dimensions, these should be stated. Attention should be drawn to excluded factors.)

5 The purpose of the equipment or material.

6 Definition of terminology, symbols, abbreviations and measuring systems.

**7** Relevant authorities to be consulted.

**8** Reference to related documents such as statutory regulations, national and international standards.

**9** Conditions in which the item or material is to be installed, used, manufactured or stored.

**10** Characteristics. These may be shown by:
  **(a)** design, samples, drawings, models, preliminary tests or investigations;
  **(b)** properties, for example strength, dimensions, weight, safety, with tolerances where applicable;
  **(c)** interchangeably (functional dimensional);
  **(d)** material and their properties (including permissible variability, approved or excluded materials);
  **(e)** requirements for a manufacturing process, for example heat treatment. (This should be specified only when critical to design considerations);
  **(f)** appearance, texture, finish, including colour, protection, and so on;
  **(g)** identification marks, operating symbols on controls, weight of items, safety indications, and so on;
  **(h)** method of marking.

**11** Performance:
  **(a)** performance under specified conditions;
  **(b)** test methods and equipment for assessing performance; where, how and by whom carried out; reference to correlation with behaviour in operation;
  **(c)** criteria for passing tests, including accuracy and interpretations of results;
  **(d)** acceptance standards;
  **(e)** certification and/or reporting, i.e. reports, test schedules or certificates required.

**12** Life.

**13** Reliability, i.e. under stipulated conditions and tests and control procedures for assessing reliability.

**14** Control of quality checking for compliance with specification:
  **(a)** method of checking compliance;
  **(b)** production tests on raw materials, components, subassemblies and assemblies;
  **(c)** assurance of compliance, for example by supplier's certificates or independent certification schemes;
  **(d)** inspection facilities required by the user/designer or offered to the manufacturer/supplier;
  **(e)** instructions regarding reject materials or items;
  **(f)** instructions with regard to modifications of process;
  **(g)** applicability of quality control to subcontracts, and so on;
  **(h)** acceptable conditions.

15 Packaging protection:
   (a) specification of packaging, including any special conditions in transit;
   (b) condition in which the item is to be supplied, for example protected, lubricant free;
   (c) period of storage;
   (d) marking of packaging.

16 Information from the supplier to the user, for example instructions and advice on installation, operation and maintenance.

17 After-sales service.

## Centralised purchasing within a company operating a number of units

There are advantages for large organisations in establishing a specialist department through which all purchasing is channelled. These include the following:

- Economies of scale enabling the use of bargaining power and resources to the best effect. This is done thus:
  - a consolidation of quantities can take place resulting in quantity discounts;
  - suppliers dealing with a central purchasing department have the incentive of comparing for the whole or substantial proportion of the requirements;
  - cheaper prices may result since the fixed overheads of the supplier can be spread over longer production runs (however, as food is a perishable commodity this may not have a major impact);
  - specialist purchasing staff can be employed for each of the major categories of purchase;
  - cheaper prices may be achieved by going directly to the grower and not via the marketplace – for example buying the whole crop of one farm at a negotiated rate;
  - lower administrative costs apply – for example it is cheaper to process one order for £10 000 than ten each of £1000;
  - the use of computerisation can be used to facilitate the collection, summary and analysis of data, which in turn can improve purchasing efficiency;
- Coordination of the activity:
  - uniform policies can be adopted;
  - uniform purchasing procedures can be followed;
  - standardisation is achieved by the use of company specifications;
  - back-up services, especially stock control, can be coordinated;
  - staff training and development can be undertaken on a smaller scale with better results;
  - research into sources, qualities and supplier performance can be achieved;
  - it is more convenient for the supplier to approach a central purchasing department.

- Control of the activity:
  - the performance of the purchasing department can be monitored by fixing objectives and comparing actual results with predetermined standards;
  - stock rotation is achieved and loss of wastage due to out-of-date stock can be minimised;
  - uniform pricing is achieved and assists in standard costings nationwide.

A centralised role in a company such as foodservice retail (family foodservice restaurants) can work very well, as each of the restaurants has a set menu and therefore is limited to the commodities it requires, perhaps 200 at most. In a unit where there is a contract foodservice operator the requirement varies from unit to unit. A directors' dining room will require fillet steak and smoked salmon; a school kitchen would never order such commodities. Therefore a centralised purchasing department would have to order many thousands of different commodities because of the diversity of the business.

Purchasing may be completely decentralised, with each unit undertaking its own purchasing, although unit buyers are given some guidelines upon which to purchase. It is at this level that food specifications are most needed to give the non-specialist food purchasers some technical guidelines upon which to buy.

A combination of centralisation and decentralisation may apply. It could be said that the function of the purchasing administration is already done centrally under the purchasing director, but no physical purchasing is done at this level. It is necessary to have central administration to ensure the achievement of company purchasing standards.

However, it is possible for non-perishable goods and commodities with an extended shelf-life to be bought centrally and delivered to the unit on a weekly basis. This would improve the effectiveness of this area. But the perishable items, i.e. bakery goods, dairy produce, fresh meat and fish, fresh fruit and vegetables, would be purchased straight into the unit. Alternatively, there could be a system whereby the unit informs a central office, operated by purchasing specialists, of its requirements, which then places the order and organises delivery to the unit.

## Purchasing specifications

No matter what purchasing system is adopted, there is always a need for purchasing specifications to assist in the task. Even specialists with technical training need to know the standard that the company expects its suppliers to reach. A standard indicated in a specification lends itself to the ultimate standard which a company wants to achieve. Good specifications aimed at the right standard will ensure:

- quality products
- quality service
- acceptable prices.

Commodities which can be specified include:

- Grown (primary):
  - butcher's meat
  - fresh fish
  - fresh fruit and vegetables
  - milk and eggs.
- Manufactured (secondary):
  - bakery goods
  - dairy products.
- Processed (tertiary):
  - frozen foods including meat, fish and fruit and vegetables
  - dried goods
  - canned goods.

It can be seen that any food product can have a specification attached to it. However, the primary specifications focus on raw materials and ensuring the quality of these commodities. Without quality at this level, a secondary or tertiary specification is useless. For example, the specification for a frozen apple pie would use a primary specification for the apple, a secondary specification for the pastry and a tertiary specification for the process, i.e. freezing. But no matter how good the secondary or tertiary specifications are, if the apples used in the beginning are not of a very high quality, the whole product is not of a good quality. Therefore, primary specifications are most important as they lay down the basic foundations upon which manufacturing and processing specifications can be built. The most useful specifications at unit level are likely to be for basic raw materials, as it is the chefs who implement the manufacture or process of the commodity. Control can be gained in this area by developing a series of standardised recipes so that the customer can be guaranteed a constant product at all times. It can therefore be seen that further development of primary specifications is necessary to continue the development of quality.

### Problems in preparing purchasing specifications in the UK

Preparing specifications in the UK and many other countries is rather difficult owing to a lack of government grading of many foods. However, the position of fruit and vegetable suppliers has improved in recent years with the grading of fruits and vegetables produced in the UK. This is also the case with the recommended classification of carcass meat by the Meat and Livestock Commission.

An important factor in finding suppliers interested in selling commodities to a specification prepared by a foodservice operator is that of the purchasing power of the foodservice operator. A large foodservice operator is able to influence the supply trade quite easily. The small foodservice operator has a problem of purchasing only what suppliers have readily available to sell, as the small operator has only a low purchasing power. It is rare to find suppliers that will prepare commodities to the specifications of small operators, and those that do exist are likely to charge premium prices for this service. Sometimes the difficulty can be overcome by finding suppliers who are already producing an item for a larger concern to a similar specification and who therefore can accept a compromise that will go towards the needs of the small foodservice operator's specification.

The Agriculture and Horticulture Act 1964, which gave the Minister for Agriculture, Fisheries and Food power to prescribe grades for fruit and vegetables, to enforce labelling and size of packaging units, and powers of inspection at the wholesale level, is seen as a very good aid to the foodservice operator when preparing purchasing specifications. Since February 1973, there has been a gradual introduction of the EC quality grading for fresh fruit and vegetables on the UK market. Each product is graded at one of four levels: extra class, class 1, class 2 or class 3.

## OPERATIONAL CONTROL

Food is expensive, and efficient stock control levels are essential to help the profitability of the business. The main difficulties of controlling food stocks are as follows:

- Food prices fluctuate because of inflation and falls in the demand and supply through poor harvests, bad weather conditions and so on.
- Transport costs, which rise owing to wage demands and cost of petrol.
- Fuel costs rise, which affects food companies' and producers' costs.
- Removal of food subsidies to bring the UK into line with the EU.
- Changes in the amount demanded by the customer; increased advertising increases demand. Changes in taste and fashion influence demand from one product to another.
- Media focus on certain products, which are labelled healthy or unhealthy, will affect demand, for example butter is high in saturated fats, sunflower margarine is high in polyunsaturates.

Each establishment should devise a control system to suit its own needs. Factors that adversely affect the establishment of an efficient control system are:

- Regular changes in the menu.
- Menus with a large number of dishes.
- Dishes with a large number of ingredients.
- Problems with assessing customer demand.
- Difficulties in not adhering to or operating standardised recipes.
- Raw materials purchased incorrectly.

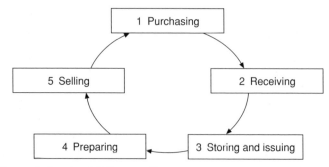

**Figure 3.6** The control cycle of daily operation

Factors assisting in the establishment of an efficient control system are:

■ Constant menu, for example McDonald's, Harvester.

■ Standardised recipes and purchasing specifications.

■ Menu with a limited number of dishes.

With some of all these factors present in a foodservice operation, stock control is often easier and costing more accurate.

In order to carry out a control system, food stocks must be secure, refrigerators and deep-freezers should be kept locked. Portion control must be accurate. A bookkeeping system must be developed to monitor the daily operation. The control cycle of daily operation is shown in Figure 3.6.

## Purchasing

The purchasing transaction can be shown diagrammatically as in Figure 3.7. It is important to determine yields from the range of commodities in use, which will determine the unit costs. Yield testing indicates the number of items or portions that can be obtained and helps to provide the information required for producing purchasing specifications. Yield testing should not be confused with product testing, which is concerned with the physical properties of the food texture, flavour and quality. In reality, tests are often carried out which combine both of these requirements.

Unless communication lines are set up to inform buyers of production needs and to inform receiving clerks, accounting personnel and others of orders and expected arrival times, poor buying and control occur. Management will establish many requirements that must be met in control: the routing of paperwork, payment policies, receiving procedures, checks to ascertain quality.

Requisition and inventory control must be implemented. Control begins with the calculation of the amount and the writing of the specification. Orders are usually placed

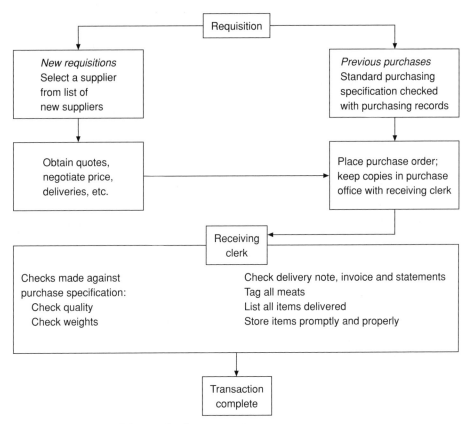

**Figure 3.7** Summary of the purchasing transaction

through a purchase order. This states the item or items required, amount, size, weight and other pertinent information.

All purchase orders have numbers so that they can be quickly identified. Purchase orders should be signed only by an authorised person. One copy is normally held by the individual issuing it, one may go to the accounting department, and another to the receiving rooms. Copies are sent to the supplier. In some cases, it may be a requirement to have the purchase order signed and returned by some individual in the supplier's company so it is known that the order will be honoured.

Regular purchase orders are for one single order to be delivered at a specified date. 'Open delivery' purchase orders establish the purchase of items over a period of time. Items needed daily or weekly are often purchased by open delivery orders.

A purchase record may be maintained. This record may indicate what was ordered and from whom, as well as any other information that may need to be maintained. A purchase price record usually is maintained on cards to keep information on the price paid for a particular item.

## Receiving

Receiving practices vary with different organisations. The general principles of control are as follows:

1 Check delivery note to see if the products delivered agree with it.

2 Inspect products/raw materials to determine if they are in agreement with the purchase order and specification.

3 Tag all meats with date of receipt, weight and other information needed to identify the delivery properly.

4 List all items received on the daily receiving report.

5 Accept the products/raw materials by signing the delivery note and returning the copy to the delivery driver.

6 Store or deliver goods to the correct place.

In large organisations, receiving is a specialised job. This job may be combined with the storeroom job. Authority and responsibility must be given to the individual receiving. This must include jurisdiction over those who help receive and store.

- *Invoice receiving*  If the invoice accompanies the delivery with the delivery note, check the invoice against the delivery and check with the purchase order or the quotation and the order sheet, or other documents. Note any discrepancies. Check quality and quantity against documentation.

- *Blind check receiving*  A blind receiving method may be used. For this the clerk is given a blank invoice or purchase order listing the incoming products or raw materials. The quantities, quality, weights and prices are omitted. The receiving clerk must add these in when the products/raw materials are delivered. This enforces a formal checking system and entails more than merely glancing to see if the goods agree with the figures on the invoice. The receiving clerk must weigh items to record their correct weight. A count is required in addition to a quality check. Another invoice with quantities, weights, quality and prices is sent to the finance office. This is checked against the invoice of the receiving clerk and the figures verified. Blind receiving is an accurate method of checking merchandise and verifying deliveries. It does take more time and costs more since it requires the clerk to prepare a complete record of all incoming products or raw materials.

- *Partial blind receiving*  This is a combination of invoice receiving and blind receiving. The receiving clerk has itemised purchase orders, delivery notes and invoices with the quantities omitted. When the goods, products and raw materials are checked, the quantity of each item is listed in the space provided. This is not as accurate as the previous method, but is faster and less costly. It is essential in both methods that the supplier's invoice does not accompany the goods, products or raw materials. If it does, the information on quantity must be omitted or made invisible by a blank area where such information would appear.

Good principles of receiving are important for control. These are:

■ Being ready and prepared for the delivery.

■ Checking the incoming goods thoroughly against the purchase order and the purchase specification. Open cases if they appear to be damaged or tampered with. Date all canned goods before storing.

■ Weigh items separately. When receiving bulk items, remove excess paper, ice, and so on.

■ Weigh meats and tag them. The practice prevents disputes with the supplier about over- and under-weights. Tagging also reduces the chance of spoilage or excess weight loss. It also simplifies calculation of food costs, since a good record of meat withdrawals can be obtained from the tags taken from meat as it comes from the inventory.

Meat tags should be used on all large cuts of incoming meats for the following reasons:

■ To show the supplier, should there be a question of quality and quantity.

■ To prevent reweighing on issuing (provided the entire unit is used).

■ To provide a check on the accuracy of the receiving clerk.

■ To help stock rotation.

■ To speed inventory-taking.

■ To facilitate ordering (lower half is sent to purchasing agent when item is used).

■ To check for quality. Checking for quality is often neglected by the receiving clerk. It is important to see that the grade and quality of the raw materials or goods agree with those shown on the delivery note and invoice, i.e. purchase order.

■ To store items promptly and properly.

An example meat tag is shown in Figure 3.8.

Recording incoming deliveries is as important as checking quality and quantity. The form or style of doing this may vary.

## Storing and issuing

Raw materials should be stored correctly under the right conditions and temperature. A method of pricing the materials must be decided and one of the following should be adopted for charging the food to the various departments. The cost of items does not remain fixed over a period of time: over a period of one year a stores item may well have several prices. The establishment must decide which of the following prices to use:

■ actual purchase price

■ simple average weight

■ weighted average price

| No: | _____ |
|---|---|
| Date: | 20-08-2000 |
| Supplier: | Meadowbank Meats |
| Origin: | Scottish Aberdeen Angus |
| Cut: | Strip loin |
| Weight: | 7 kg |
| Unit price: | £14.50 per kg |
| Checked by: | Mr Williams Head Storekeeper |
| No: | _____ |
| Date: | 20-08-2000 |
| Supplier: | _____ |
| Origin: | _____ |
| Cut: | _____ |
| Weight: | _____ |
| Unit price: | _____ |
| Checked by: | _____ |

**Figure 3.8**   Meat tag – the lower half is sent to the purchasing agent when the item is used

■ inflated price (price goes up after purchase)
■ standard price (fixed price).

As an example, weighted average price might be used for dried fruit, as follows:

    10 lb × 40p =   400p
    20 lb × 50p = 1000p
    Total           1400p

So 1400 divided by 30 lb = 46.6p per lb, weighted average price.

## Food preparation and production

Food preparation is an important stage of the control cycle. The cost of the food consumed depends on two factors:

■ the number of meals produced
■ the cost per meal.

In order to control food costs the operation must be able to:

■ control the number to be catered for, and

■ control the food cost per meal in advance of production and service by using system of pre-costing, using standardised recipes, indicating portion control.

## Sales and volume forecasting

Forecasting requires predicting the volume of sales for a future period. In order to be of practical value the forecast must both:

■ predict the total number of covers (customers), and

■ predict the choice of menu items.

Therefore, it is important to:

■ Keep a record of the numbers of each dish sold from a menu.

■ Work out the average spent per customer.

■ Calculate the proportion, expressed as a percentage, of each dish sold in relation to total sales.

Forecasting is in two stages:

■ *Initial forecasting* This is done once a week in respect of each day of the following week. It is based on sales histories, information related to advance bookings and current trends. When this has been completed, the predicted sales are converted into the food/ingredients requirements. Purchase orders are then prepared and sent to suppliers.

■ *The final forecast* This normally takes place the day before the actual preparation and service of the food. This forecast must take into account the latest developments such as the weather and any food that needs to be used up. If necessary, suppliers' orders should be adjusted.

Sales forecasting is not a perfect method of prediction, but it does help with production planning. Sales forecasting, however, is important when used in conjunction with cyclical menu planning.

## Storekeeping

Keeping a properly run and efficient storeroom is essential in order to maintain the unified process of control throughout the operation. A clean, orderly food store, run efficiently, is essential in any foodservice establishment for the following reasons:

- Stocks of food can be kept at a suitable level, so eliminating the risk of running out of any raw material.
- All food entering and leaving the stores can be properly checked; this helps to prevent wastage.
- A check can be kept on the percentage profit of each department of the establishment.

## Control and profitability

A summary of the factors that will help the profitability of the foodservice operation is as follows:

- Ensuring correct cooking of food to minimise portion loss.
- Efficient preparation of raw materials.
- Correct portion control.
- Minimising wastage, sufficient use of raw materials, utilising left-over food.
- Reducing theft.
- Accurate ordering procedures.
- Adequate checking procedures.
- Reference marks to standardised recipes and yield factors.
- Sufficient research into suppliers.
- Accurate forecasting.
- Proper menu-planning.

**SUMMARY**

The chapter has aimed to identify the principles, practices and applications of food production in the foodservice industry. Inherent in the process is the hygienic management concept necessary to deliver a clean, safe and healthy product all the time. It has focused on the knowledge required by a manager to operate and manage a food production system effectively. This knowledge is gained through an understanding of the basic principles of menu-planning and food production systems, which are also linked to the purchasing and storage processes. As with every manufacturing system, standardisation is essential to maintain the consistency of the products within the financial constraints, and therefore the chapter has also attempted to demonstrate the principles and importance of operational control.

## REFERENCES

Cousins, J. (1994) 'Managing capacity' in *The Management of Food-service Operations*, Jones, P. and Merricks, P. (eds), London: Cassell, pp.174–87.

Gillespie, C. (2001) *European Gastronomy into the 21st Century*, Oxford: Butterworth Heinemann.

## FURTHER READING

Kinton, R. Ceserani, V. and Foskett, D. (1999) *The Theory of Catering*, 9th edition, London: Hodder and Stoughton.

# BEVERAGE PROVISION

This chapter considers beverage provision within foodservice operations.

**OBJECTIVES**

This chapter is intended to support you in:

- working within the licensing framework for the sale of alcoholic beverages

- developing wine, drink and other beverage lists

- developing specific skills in managing the purchasing, storage and control of wine stocks

- pricing of wine and drink lists

- developing sales and increasing profits

- operating purchasing, storage and control systems for wine and drinks.

## THE LICENSING FRAMEWORK

In order to sell intoxicating liquor in the UK, licences are required. These licences govern the type of liquor that can be sold, the extent of the market that can be served and the times of opening (or permitted hours). There are also regulations on restrictions for 'off sale', supply to young persons and 'on measures'. Restrictions are made by the government and penalties for infringement are applied, not only to the licensee or their staff, but also to the customer. In all cases of doubt as to legal issues and concerns, a licensing solicitor should be consulted.

English and Scottish legislation are very different. The manner in which the licences are granted also differs significantly. Scottish liquor licensing is regulated by the Licensing (Scotland) Act 1976, as amended, which regulates both the sale and supply of alcoholic liquor. Scottish legislation is noted separately in this chapter.

Alcoholic beverages are sold in two main types of licensed establishment. These are known as free houses and tied houses:

- *Free house*  This is a licensed establishment which has no attachment to one particular supply source.
- *Tied house*  This is a licensed establishment which is tenanted or managed and is linked (tied) to a particular source of supply:
  - *tenanted*  The tenant leases the property from the brewer and is tied to that brewer for the purchase of beer and possibly other drinks.
  - *managed*  A manager is paid a salary to run the premises which are owned by a particular brewery.

Traditionally it is the premises which are licensed, and the person who holds the licence is known as the licensee. The National Licensee's Certificate, a requirement for new licensees in the UK, is establishing a common standard covering the law and comprises training in such areas as the law, moral responsibilities, drugs, violence and its alleviation. The development is supported by the British Institute of Innkeeping and by a number of brewery and pub chains who have incorporated the certificate into their training programmes. Having the certificate can be useful when applying for licences as this is increasingly being taken into account when applications for new licences are being considered.

## Types of licence

The various types of licence available in the UK are described below.

(*Note*: The definitions for the licences quoted here apply to England and Wales. The licensing pattern in Scotland is similar although there are differences in the definitions and in the permitted hours (see page 118). Licensing definitions in Northern Ireland are similar to those in England and Wales.)

### Full on-licence

A full on-licence allows the licensee to sell all types of intoxicating liquor for consumption on and off the premises. However, there are a few examples of on-licences where the type of alcohol is limited, for example beer only or beer and wine only.

### Restricted on-licence

There are three types of restricted on-licence:

- *Restaurant licence* This applies to the sale of alcoholic liquor to persons taking main meals only. A restaurant licence is granted for premises which are 'structurally adapted and bona fide used' for the purpose of providing meals for individuals frequenting the premises. No alcoholic liquor may be sold for consumption off the premises.
- *Residential licence* This applies to the sale of alcoholic liquor to persons residing on the premises or to their private friends who are being genuinely entertained by the guests at the guests' expense.
- *Combined licence* This is a combined restaurant and residential licence.

### Club licence

Club licences fall into two categories:

- *Licensed club* Normally this is a licence to run a club which is operated by individuals or a limited company as a commercial enterprise. The sale of alcoholic liquor is to members only.
- *Members' club* A licence to run a club, normally by a committee of members, as a non-profit-making organisation. The members own the stock of liquor and sale is to members only.

### Off-licence

An off-licence is a licence authorising the sale of intoxicating liquor for consumption off the premises only. Off-licences are granted in respect of premises which authorise sale or supply of alcohol off the premises only.

### Occasional licence

An occasional licence is granted to holders of on-licences and restaurant or combined licences enabling them to sell alcoholic liquor at another place for a specific time, for example a licensee may be able to set up a bar for a local village hall function.

### Occasional permission

Occasional permission is similar to an occasional licence but may be applied for by non-licence holders, for example a charity may apply for occasional permission in order to sell drink at a fund-raising event.

### Music and dancing licences

These licences are not liquor licences but are required for public music and dancing. The licences are granted by local councils and the law varies from place to place. Licences are not required where radio, television and recorded music are used or when there are no more than two live performers, although if dancing takes place, a licence is required. The music and dancing licences referred to here are under English law; for Scottish law see note below.

### Permitted hours

Permitted hours are as follows in England and Wales:

| | |
|---|---|
| Weekdays | 1100 to 2300 |
| (including Good Friday) | (off-licences 0800 to 2230 or 2300) |
| Sundays | 1200 to 2230 |
| | (off-licences may open from 1000 on Sundays) |
| Christmas Day | 1200 to 1500 and 1900 to 2230 |
| | (the hours for off-licences are the same) |

Local magistrates may also allow weekday opening from 1000.

Within these permitted hours the licensee can choose when and for how long to close the premises. Regular extensions and occasional extensions obviously allow trading outside these hours.

## Exemptions to permitted hours

The following exemptions apply to permitted hours:

- The first 20 minutes after the end of permitted hours is for consumption only.
- The first 30 minutes after the end of permitted hours for those taking table meals is again for consumption only.
- Residents and their guests may be (but do not have to be) served at any time as long as only the resident makes the purchase.

## Extensions to permitted hours

- *Special Order of Exemption*   This is available for specific occasions such as a wedding, dinner dance or carnival.
- *General Order of Exemption*   This applies to an area where a particular trade or calling is going on, for example market day or food markets, which are operating early in the morning.
- *Supper Hour Certificate*   This allows for an additional hour at the end of permitted hours for licensed restaurants.

■ *Extended Hours Certificate* This is an extension for establishments which already hold a Supper Hour Certificate and provide some form of entertainment. The extension is until 1 a.m.

■ *Special Hours Certificate* This allows for extensions of permitted hours to premises which are licensed, hold a music and dancing licence and provide substantial refreshment. The extension can be until 3 a.m. in the West End of London and until 2 a.m. elsewhere.

## Young persons

It is an offence for persons under 18 to be served in a licensed bar. It is also an offence to allow persons under 18 to consume alcoholic beverages in a bar. Similarly, it is an offence for the person under 18 to attempt to purchase or to purchase or consume alcoholic beverages in a bar. The position regarding young persons is summarised in Table 4.1.

Since January 1995, the holder of an on-licence has been able to apply to the local Licensing Committee for a Children's Certificate. The certificate allows children to enter a bar, accompanied by adults, up to 9 p.m. There is also 30 minutes drinking up time. A later time may be applied for different parts of the year such as the summer months.

The certificate applies to publicans and other licensees with ordinary bars from which children under 14 are currently prohibited during permitted hours. The main requirements are that there must be 'an environment in which it is suitable for persons under fourteen to be present' and that meals and soft drinks must be available at the times when children are allowed.

Young persons under 18 may not be employed in a bar unless they are over 17 and registered as a Modern Apprentice. However, persons under 18 may be employed in a restaurant (which is not a bar) where, for instance, the restaurant is a place set aside for the consumption of table meals and where the drink is ancillary to the meal. Persons under 18 years may also serve alcoholic drinks as long as the drink orders are obtained from a dispense bar for instance.

**Table 4.1  Young persons and licensed premises**

| Age | Purchase in a bar | Consume in a bar | Enter a bar | Purchase in a restaurant | Consume in a restaurant |
|-----|-----------|-----------|-------------|--------------|--------------|
| Under 14 | No | No | No[a] | No | Yes[b] |
| Under 16 | No | No | Yes | No | Yes[b] |
| Under 18 | No | No | Yes | Yes[c] | Yes |

[a] See note on Children's Certificates in text
[b] As long as the alcoholic beverage is bought by a person over 18
[c] Beer, cider and perry only
*Note:* Tobacco should not be sold to persons under 16.

## Rights of entry

The police and customs and excise officers have right of entry to licensed premises. This is because the sale and consumption of intoxicating drinks is carried on within the framework of the law. The police can enter premises at any time if they suspect an offence against the licensing law is being, or is about to be, committed. They can also enter during permitted hours and 30 minutes afterwards for the purpose of preventing or detecting offences against licensing laws even with no grounds for suspecting such offences are taking place or are about to take place. Customs and excise officers have right of entry and can remove goods liable to forfeiture, such as goods that have fraudulently evaded duty.

## Weights and measures

The Weights and Measures Act 1985 and the Intoxicating Liquor Order 1988 make the following requirements:

- *Beer and cider* Unless sold in a sealed container, beer and cider may only be sold in measures of $1/3$ or $1/2$ pint or multiples of $1/2$ pint. This does not apply to mixtures of two or more liquids, for example a shandy.
- *Spirits* Whisky, gin, vodka and rum, where sold by the measure, must be sold in measures of 25 ml, 35 ml or multiples thereof. A notice must be clearly displayed in the establishment indicating the measure that is being used. Only one of these measures (i.e. 25 ml or 35 ml) can be used. This restriction does not apply to mixtures of three or more liquids, for example for cocktails.
- *Wines* Wines sold open in carafes must be sold in measures of 25, 50 or 75 cl or 1 litre. For wine by the glass, measures are 125 ml, 175 ml or multiples thereof. Both measures may be used in the same establishment. The licensee must display a statement which documents the measures in use. This could be included in the wine list.

## Other matters

There have been changes in the grounds on which licensing justices decide on applications, which include consideration of the suitability of the licensee, the premises and the likelihood of public nuisance or threat to public safety. This might also include taking into account the number of licences already granted for a particular area.

In 1999, the Justices Clerk's Society together with the Magistrates' Association published a good practice guide (GPG). This is a very helpful guide, and many committees have adopted it in whole or in part. Additionally, the Home Office has published a White Paper proposing reform of the licensing system for the UK, which includes proposals for an integrated licensing scheme for premises, the introduction of 'personal licences', and more flexible permitted hours.

## Alcoholic strength

There is no longer a requirement for indicating the alcoholic strength of wine and other drinks on wine and drink lists. The alcoholic content of drinks by volume, is now virtually always shown on labels. The scale used is the Organisation Internationale Métrologie Légal (OIML) scale, which is directly equal to the percentage by volume of pure alcohol in a drink at 20°C. 'Low Alcohol' drinks may contain up to 1.2 per cent of alcohol, 'de-alcoholised' must have not more than 0.5 per cent, and 'alcohol-free' not more than 0.05 per cent alcohol by volume.

## Other legal requirements

In addition to the licensing requirements for the sale of alcoholic beverage, note must be taken of the law regarding:

- sale of goods and trades descriptions
- discrimination
- the provision of services
- price list requirements
- health and safety
- customers' property and debt
- weights and measures
- service, cover and other minimum charges.

## Licensing in Scotland

Licensing in Scotland is similar to that in England. In terms of sole licences, those available in Scotland are: restaurant license; refreshment licence; public house licence; restricted hotel licence; hotel licence. The music and dance licensing in England has an equivalent in Scotland termed 'public entertainment licences'. However, if in any doubt, a licensing solicitor can always provide advice.

Permitted hours in Scotland are:

Weekdays   11 a.m. to 11 p.m.
Sundays    12.30 p.m. to 2.30 p.m. and 6.30 p.m. to 11 p.m.

Regular extensions and occasional extensions obviously allow trading outside these hours. For off-sale premises, no off-sale is allowed in respect of refreshment, entertainment, restricted hotel, restaurant or registered club licences. Also, for off-sale premises and parts of public house or hotel licences, which have been set aside for the sale or supply of alcohol off the premises, may trade with the maximum hours of 8 a.m. to

10 p.m. Off-sale premises may open on a Sunday; however, alcohol may not be sold until 12.30 p.m.

It is worth noting that the Act does not contain a requirement on premises to be open for the sale or supply of alcohol during the permitted hours and a licensee is therefore entitled but not obliged to do so. Individual licensing boards may also make bylaws requiring premises to be closed on New Year's Day and, in terms of Section 38 of the Act for up to a further four days of each year.

In Scotland, a drinking up time is allowed for those consuming alcohol as ancillary to a meal of 30 minutes and those simply consuming alcohol of 15 minutes. No alcohol may be sold or supplied during that time.

## COMPILING WINE AND DRINKS LISTS

Wine and drinks lists are primarily a selling aid. The lists identify for the customer what is on offer, the price of the item and details such as the measure in which the item is to be sold. Wine and drinks lists come in a variety of styles, usually reflecting the type of establishment. In compiling wine and drinks lists a number of factors need to be considered:

- The overall presentation and style, including the colour scheme, should be in keeping with the style of operation.
- The size, shape and durability of the list, in order to make it easy to handle and use for both guests and staff.
- Flexibility in design and construction so as to be able to make changes as vintages change and for the inclusion of special promotions.
- The length of time that the list will be in operation.
- The overall design and legibility of the lists, including features such as illustrations, or a contents page if the list is extensive.
- Ensuring that the information included assists the customer as well as meeting legal requirements.
- How to make decisions on the actual content of the list.
- The availability of supply, storage capacity and the capital investment required.
- The inclusion of bin numbers which will simplify inventory and reordering for wine lists and assist both internal personnel and guests.

The wine and drinks lists are part of the expression or character of the operation. Presentational style can mark one operation out as special even though there may be very similar content to other operations in the vicinity. Poor presentation can adversely affect customers' judgement of the business and the food and beverage product.

## Types of wine and drinks lists

Wines and drinks included in a list would be:

■ Non-alcoholic drinks including natural spring and mineral waters, aerated waters, squashes, juices and syrups.

■ Cocktails, including non-alcoholic cocktails.

■ Bitters as aperitifs and for mixed drinks and cocktails.

■ Wines, including still wine, sparkling wines, alcohol-free, de-alcoholised and low-alcohol wines, fortified wines and aromatised wines.

■ Spirits and liqueurs.

■ Beers, including draught and packaged beers and reduced alcohol beers, cider and perry.

The order of wines and drinks on the list tends to follow the order of consumption or to be grouped under types of wine or drink:

■ cocktails

■ apéritifs

■ cups

■ spirits

■ wines

■ liqueurs

■ beers, minerals and squashes.

Wines are often listed by area, with the white wines of one region first followed by the red wines of that region. A more modern trend is to list all the white wines available area-by-area followed by the red wines arranged in a similar way. This type of layout is often more useful to the customer. However, sparkling wines, and therefore the champagnes, are often listed before all other wines available.

### Bar and cocktail lists

These may range from a basic standard list offering the common, everyday aperitifs, a selection of spirits with mixers, beers and soft drinks together with a limited range of cocktails, to a very comprehensive list offering a wide choice in all areas.

When setting up a cocktail bar or preparing a bar and cocktail list, it is necessary to consider the availability of the specialised equipment, preparation requirements and stocks which are necessary for presentation, including specialised glassware and garnishes. Additionally, in order to profit from yield management techniques, it is imperative that the majority of beverages have standard recipes and measures.

## Apéritif lists

Apéritif lists can be combined with the restaurant wine list, although they are more frequently presented separately along with digestif and liqueur lists. For apéritif lists it is common to include lighter, drier styles in wines and fortified drinks, although drinks with some acidity are useful to enhance appetite. The contents might include:

- champagne – non-vintage, vintage, premier cuvées, champagne rosé
- Kir Royale
- other sparkling wines, sparkling rosé
- dry sherry – fino, manzanilla through to dry oloroso
- dry white wine – for example, Muscadet and New Zealand Sauvignon Blanc
- lighter Mösel, Austrian and Swiss wine styles
- Pineau des Charentes
- Sercial Madeira, Rainwater, Verdelho
- ratafia
- vermouths
- bitters
- white port
- dry Marsala
- tawny port (served chilled).

## Restaurant wine lists

Customers can tell a lot about a restaurant from the content and presentation of its wine list. The list must inform, although too much information is just as bad as having none. Careful consideration also needs to be given to the extensiveness of the wine as it can cost a vast amount of money to maintain.

Examples of types of wine list are:

- A full and very comprehensive list of wines from all countries, but emphasis on the classic areas such as Bordeaux/Burgundy plus a fine wine/prestige selection.
- A middle of the road, traditional selection, for example some French, German, Italian together with some 'new world' wines.
- A small selection for well-known or branded wines.
- A prestige list predominantly with wines of one specific country.

In constructing a restaurant wine list it is worth considering the following points:

- The extent to which the list will allow suitable pairing with the menu(s) on offer.
- The range to be covered, such as covering the 'old' and 'new worlds' and include sparkling wines, champagne, red and white wines, rosé and fortifieds.

- Balance in terms not only of country of origin but also of styles, prices, grapes, countries, tradition and fashion.
- The inclusion of a small selection of well-known or branded wines, where required.
- Stating who the producer or merchant is and what the vintage is, if appropriate.
- The availability of some wines by the glass, half bottle, bottle and magnum.
- The inclusion of half bottles which, although in the main are likely to be taken up by individuals eating on their own, will also be of interest to individuals wishing differing wines with each course or to parties of guests with differing preferences.
- The opportunity for effective marketing of a reserve or special list of rare wines.
- Ensuring that prices per item are clear and unambiguous.
- The extent to which the list excites the customer and communicates commendable value.

### After-meal drinks lists (digestifs)

After-meal drinks are frequently presented as a separate digestif or liqueur list. Digestif lists should comprise soothing, mellowing, heavier, sweeter, richer styles but also list settling beverages. The contents can include:

- Good sweet wines such as sweet German, Austrian, Loire and Jurançon wines which can refresh the palate.
- Sweet fortified wines like port, sherry, Madeira, Marsala, Malaga, rich and liqueur muscats which are all good digestifs.
- Vintage and LBV (late bottled vintage) port.
- A specialist range of Cognac, Armagnac and brandies and/or a specialist range of malt and 'older malt' whiskies.
- A range of liqueurs.
- Settling digestifs including Chartreuse, richer bitters, Strega and good cognac.
- A range of speciality liqueur/spirit coffees might also be included.

### Banqueting wine lists

For banqueting wine lists, the following apply:

- The length of the list is generally according to size and style of operation.
- There should be a range of prices from house wines to some fine wines to suit all customer preferences.
- In some instances the banqueting wine will draw wines from the restaurant wine list – this reduces the need for double-stocking.
- There is usually a selection of popular wine names or styles on offer.

An operation is in essence endeavouring to achieve ease of availability, strong gross profit margin and high recognition. Some considerations in drawing up banqueting wine lists are:

- Ensuring that the list will allow suitable pairing with the menu(s) on offer, especially if there is a range of suggested standard menus.
- Because banqueting lists are often sent out months in advance of an event, care needs to be taken to ensure ongoing supplies.
- A disclaimer might be useful which advises that an alternative may be necessary, or substitutions may be made if the client does not request that wines be set aside for their event.
- Ensuring that sales mix data are able to distinguish between banqueting lists sales and from restaurant sales, as wines may appear to be performing more strongly simply through an order placed from a banquet.

### Room service drinks list

These lists tend towards less formality. However:

- They usually offer a limited range of wines and other drinks although it can be helpful if the customers can purchase from the main lists if required.
- There may be a mini-bar/refreshment centre or choice from a standard bar list.
- In some instances, a fixed stock in sealed decanters is provided for VIP and other guests.

### Other beverage lists

Cocktails, spirits, liqueurs, beers, cider and perry all make up the beverage directory on offer in many establishments. More recently the attention being given to other beverages has increased, with even the most simple operations offering a range of teas and coffees and other proprietary drinks as a matter of course. Additionally, even the best destination hotels, restaurants and resorts are offering freshly prepared juices, some of which mimic the look and gravity of wines both red and white.

Increased travel and growing numbers of European tourists have impacted on tea and coffee service in no small way. The impetus is towards ever-higher standards of fresh preparation and an accelerating demand for continental styles.

Coffee being offered includes filter, cafetière, espresso and cappuccino as standard. Additional offerings can include:

- ristretto – intense form of espresso, often served with a glass of water in Europe
- café crème – regular coffee prepared from fresh beans ground fresh for each cup, resulting in a thick cream coloured, moussy head
- espresso macchiato – espresso spotted with a dollop of milk foam

■ latte macchiato – steamed milk spotted with a drop of espresso

■ espresso con panna – espresso with a dollop of whipped cream on top

■ caffè latte – shot of espresso plus hot steamed milk, with or without foam as desired

■ caffè mocha – chocolate compound followed by a shot of espresso; the cup or glass is then filled with freshly steamed milk topped with whipped cream and cocoa powder.

Single-estate coffees are also entering the market with exceptional taste profiles.
Teas can include:

■ Assam – full, rich and malty, served at breakfast usually with milk

■ Darjeeling – delicate and light, usually served in the afternoon or evening with lemon or a touch of milk

■ Earl Grey – blended Darjeeling and China teas scented with oil of Bergamot; served with lemon or a touch of milk

■ Jasmine – fragrant and light green tea dried with jasmine blossom

■ Kenya – refreshing and light tea served with milk

■ Lapsang Souchong – smoky, tarry, highly aromatic tea, delicate on the palate with a rewarding acquired taste; can be served with lemon

■ Sri Lanka – golden tea from a Ceylon blend served with lemon or milk.

Offering a range of beverages other that wines and drinks can provide for superior opportunities for increasing revenue. It is also possible, however, to offer additional revenue generators with these beverages such as biscuits, scones, open or closed sandwiches, savouries and so on.

Innovative approaches to the service of the beverages generally can also allow for increased gross profit margins. The service of these beverages can be enhanced through using, for instance, glass teapots with warmers to display herbal infusions or exotic varieties, house or rare blends and even special first flush teas. Individual teas and coffees can also be served in differing vessels to attract attention and invigorate sales. Equally, liqueur coffees have equal potential to be displayed in manners others than simply the traditional fashion.

## PRICING OF WINES AND DRINKS

Restaurant wine and drink pricing tends to be based on three basic methods of pricing:

■ *Cost-plus pricing* Here, the selling price of a drink is determined by the addition of a specific percentage of the cost price to the cost of the drink in order to achieve a predetermined percentage gross profit (gross profit = sales less the cost of sales). In practice, percentages are varied to achieve standard pricing for similar groups of products, for example all spirits or all minerals.

- *Rate of return* Here, the total costs of the business are determined for a given business level and from this the percentage of the cost price required to be added to the cost price is determined in order to ensure that the business will be viable.

- *Market orientated* Here, selling prices are determined by considering both what the customer is likely to pay as well as what others in similar operations locally are charging. It is also worth considering that there is a certain naivety on the part of some consumers who expect restaurant prices to reflect those of the retail market.

In practice, a combination of these methods is used. For drinks other than wine, it is usual to find that similar products will have the same prices. This avoids each item having a different price and it makes it easier for staff to remember prices. In addition, the percentage of the cost price that is added will vary in order to achieve a balance of selling prices between various items. This is to ensure that the selling prices are in line with what the customer is likely to expect. Thus, lower-cost items such as minerals tend to have a higher percentage of the cost price added to them, whereas higher-cost items such as spirits have a lower percentage of the cost price added.

For wines, the simple cost-plus approach (aiming for a gross profit of 66 per cent for instance) tends to be used as well as various formula approaches. One such formula approach is double the cost-plus. This takes the cost price of the wine, doubles it and then adds a fixed amount. The difficulty with both the cost-plus and formula approaches is that the more expensive wines tend therefore to have a disproportionately higher selling price on the wine list and this does not encourage the sales of these higher-priced items.

An alternative to the cost-plus and formula approaches is to recognise that the gross profit cash contribution derives from the total number of sales of an item multiplied by the cash profit that the item provides. Thus, the most profitable item is the one that gives the highest total cash contribution. In this approach, the pricing of wines achieves a potential profit irrespective of the cost price of the wine. Prices in this method are determined by adding a fixed amount to the cost price. In some cases a banding system is used where the fixed amount is increased slightly the higher the cost price of the wine. With this approach, the higher-priced wines look more attractive to the customer and this encourages sales.

## PURCHASING

The objective of good purchasing is to achieve the right amount of stock, at the right quality, at the right level and at the right price. In contrast to food, beverages generally have longer shelf-lives with the exception of cask and keg beers. However, all items do have a limited life, although in the case of good wines this could be several decades.

Although longer shelf-lives will mean that greater stocks can be held, the cost of storage both in fuel and space costs has to be taken into account. In addition, the holding of high-value stock ties up capital that could be used for other purposes.

For tied house premises, where the establishment is linked to a particular brewer, the sources for purchasing beverages are determined by the brewer. It is common for brewers to own or have links or associations with specific suppliers of spirits, minerals and other drinks. In these cases, the opportunities for selective purchasing are limited.

For free house premises, the establishment can determine who they wish to buy from. Some considerations are as follows:

- *Using one main supplier*  This has the advantage of buying from one supplier rather than many, which reduces administrative costs. Deliveries will be regular and will cover all items. There are also additional benefits from the support that can be had from suppliers in producing wine and drinks lists and menu covers and from discounts that are available depending on amounts purchased. On the other hand, the range of beverages may be limiting in some way, thus reducing the potential range of beverages on offer in a particular establishment. In addition, using one main supplier can make the establishment overly dependent on that source.

- *Using a variety of suppliers*  This has the advantage for the establishment of being able to achieve a particular range of beverages and reduces dependency on any one source. It also means that advantage can be taken of special promotions or discounts at different times and from differing sources. Potential disadvantages are that this approach increases the number of separate deliveries, increases paperwork and can lead to inconsistencies in the range of beverages on offer.

Generally, establishments use a combination of the two approaches: using one main supplier but with additional purchases coming from other sources. Depending on the policy of the establishment, the buying of wines needs some further consideration. Buying for laying down and service at some future time can build up a good stock of fine wines which can, when sold, produce good profits. However, the downside is the storage and initial capital costs together with the risks that could be associated with this approach.

## The costs of purchasing

There are three areas of cost associated with purchasing. These are:

1 The costs of acquisition:
   (a) preliminary costs, for example:
   - preparation and specifications
   - supplier selection
   - negotiation
   (b) placement costs, for example:
   - order preparation
   - stationery
   - postage
   - telephone

(c) post-placement costs, for example:
- progressing
- receipt of goods
- inspection of goods
- payment of invoices
- other clerical controls.

2 The holding costs:
   (a) financial costs, for example interest on capital tied up in inventory cost of insurance
   (b) losses through deterioration, pilferage
   (c) storage costs, for example:
   - space
   - handling and inspection
   - stores lighting
   - heating/refrigeration
   - clerical costs, for example stores records and documentation.

3 The cost of stockouts:
   (a) cost of alternatives, for example:
   - buying at enhanced prices
   - using more expensive substitutes.

## Determining stock levels

Stock levels may be determined by using past sales data. A formula which can be useful is:

$$M = W (T + L) + S$$

where:

$M$ is the maximum stock,
$W$ the average usage rate,
$T$ the review period,
$L$ the lead time and
$S$ the safety stock (buffer or minimum).

An example using this formula could be:

$W = 24$ bottles per week
$T = 4$ weeks
$L = 1$ week
$S = 1$ week's usage, i.e. 24 bottles

Therefore:

$M = 24 (4 + 1) + 24$
$\quad = 144$ bottles

Minimum stock (buffer or safety stock) may also be calculated as follows:

$$L \times W = 1 \times 24$$
$$= 24 \text{ bottles}$$

ROL (reorder level) may also be calculated as follows:

$$(W \times L) + S = (24 \times 1) + 24$$
$$= 48 \text{ bottles}$$

Using this type of approach can enable operations to determine the appropriate stock holding to meet the needs of the establishment whilst at the same time minimising the amount of capital tied up in the stock being held. Good stock control can be used to apply *just in time* (JIT) approaches to stockholding, rather than stock levels being determined through *just in case* approaches.

## FURTHER CONSIDERATION ON WINE PROVISION

Wine is to a great extent part of everyday life, and guests, whether dining or imbibing for business or pleasure, can be assumed to be more informed than at any other point in time. It is also a field where the professional becomes the eternal novice as each change of vineyard ownership or vinifier, operating technique or change in technology, every vintage and each climatic change, has its effect on the final product. Also, wine in many vine-growing regions of the world is viewed quite simply as a primary agricultural commodity, and techniques in vinification have changed enormously in the past two decades in response to consumer demand for quicker-maturing wines. Professionals therefore do need to keep abreast of the subject.

The expertise required of contemporary sommeliers' therefore has to comprise exemplary advanced communication skills paired with deep knowledge which can be translated into a manner which allows the guest to freely understand and select with confidence. Wine adds flair to a meal, and in many social settings it is becoming the drink of preference.

## Types of wine cellar

There are basically two types of commercial wine cellar: the 'restaurant cellar' and 'long-term investment cellar', in some cases the two are combined. Restaurant cellars usually stock three categories of wine:

- Inexpensive well-made wines for everyday casual consumption possibly forming the mainstay of the list.
- Moderately priced, well-crafted wines from known producers such as Petits Châteaux and lesser known varieties possibly forming the mainstay of the list.

■ Special-occasion expensive wines from known producers such as premium older vintage, rarer vintages, crus bourgeois and classed growths.

The centre of activity within the wine cellar will alter with the seasons. In winter months investment in hearty reds matching heavier dishes produced during this period will increase. In warmer months it may be necessary to invest in more light wines, rosé and sparkling wines. These will be refreshing both indoors and outside.

The long-term investment cellar ensures supply as well as value. It is often found in fine dining restaurants and hotels, and houses specific styles of wines (for laying down) whose value will potentially increase over time. Great wines if stored correctly will have the potential to achieve more harmony over time, and, as other individuals consume these vintages prematurely the remaining stocks will increase their value. These wines will include most claret, red and white Burgundies, red Rhône wines, reds from Piedmont such as Barolo, good Rioja, some of the exceptional Alsace and German whites and also vintage champagne, most fortified wines, vintage port and Madeira.

Proper storage is necessary in order to protect the investment, although young wines in particular are much more resilient and robust than many believe, and surprising amounts of short-lived ill treatment can be withstood. Nevertheless, the importance of good storage cannot be emphasised too much. Being reputed for having a well-kept and well-stocked cellar and selling fine, well-crafted wines can increase reputation, making it good commercial sense.

However, it is also important for management to know the impact on working capital. Capital invested in fine wines and spirits can seriously affect the cash flow of a business, so it is important for management to know what beverages to purchase and where and what optimum stock levels to keep. For example, The Breakers, a Mobil Five Diamond, AAA Five Star Resort in Palm Beach, Florida, has at any one time 15 000 bottles (1250 cases) in inventory. Between banqueting and its various restaurants, the resort will purchase in excess of 100 000 bottles (8333.33 cases) of wine per year. To give an idea of scale: total value of beverage purchases per year is around, $1.9 million; total food approximately $7 million. For all that the numbers are large, there is obviously efficient management in that The Breakers holds only two months' stock.

## Purchasing wines

How wine will be purchased and from where will depend on the scale of the operation, the level of interest, purchasing freedom, specialisation, location and how much time can be devoted to sourcing wine. The range of options open to the foodservice operation is listed in Table 4.2.

Many businesses will be interested purely in the price of specific wines. However, the purchasing decisions will be better shaped if serious consideration is given to value for money and obtaining the return that an operation feels is justified for a particular outlay.

**Table 4.2** Sources for wine purchasing

| Source | Description |
|---|---|
| Fine wine merchant/distributor | Most frequently used by establishments seeking best-quality wines from well-known, well-established producers |
| (Branded) wine merchant/distributor | Most frequently used by small, medium and many large businesses |
| Wine division of a brewery | For example Carlsberg, Tetley, Scottish and Newcastle. Purchasers may be locked into purchasing from only one brewery |
| Direct from producer | Usually dependent on buyer's proximity to producers and volume requirements |
| *En primeur* | Where ageing cellar space permits, this can prove profitable. (See Brokers below) |
| Wine retailers | Much less likely in larger establishments, but can be very effective; for example Oddbins |
| Wine clubs | Rarely used by larger businesses |
| Internet | Some good finds can be had |
| Wine fair | Rarely used by the largest businesses; good for the small and medium-sized business |
| Auction rooms | Good for small and medium-sized businesses |
| Brokers | Good for small, medium- and large-sized businesses; the bulk of *en primeur* purchasing is now being managed through brokers |
| Tastings | Held by wine merchants, can invigorate sales as hoteliers and restaurateurs have ample opportunity to sample a broad range of wines |

Most suppliers do not surmise that operations select simply on price and operate with the understanding that there has to be a price–value balance.

## Using merchants

Good merchants can steer buyers towards not only added-value options but also the composition of award winning wine lists. This should be their objective when talking to a quality establishment. Writing wine lists should be the merchant's main area of expertise, but the merchant should also be both food and marketplace aware. They should be able to propose the right level of wine list and the right quality of wine, which will be in keeping with the level of the establishment within the marketplace.

Larger hotels and restaurants tend to use more than one supplier and, especially if they are part of a group, there may be one nominated supplier for the basic stock. The best merchants supply bespoke services for wine list printing and consultancy services in wine, and these services are part of the merchant's main added value. They should be specialists in constructing wine lists, even to the extent of putting together a wine list with the wines from perhaps two other suppliers. A caveat, however, is that you must be knowledgeable enough to detect bluffers and weaknesses or gaps in the merchants' knowledge and portfolio.

Reputable wine merchants can also provide information on food and wine combining, but it should be remembered that:

- They are not absolute experts as this is such a subjective area.

- Anyone who is offering you wine, particularly fine wines, should be able to tell you enough of how that wine fits in and have enough of an opinion to help out with food and wine combining.

- In recent years there has been a revolution in our appreciation of wine and food in restaurants. Especially fine wine and fine food. Attendant to this, new-style wine consultants and wine buyers have emerged in response, more able to give good advice on food and wine combining for fusion and international cuisines.

When a merchant is reviewing a list or suggesting a list to a client, they must be able to suggest wines for current drinking, and be able to state clearly that twelve months from that period they will review the wines listed in terms of a development statement on the list. However, it may perhaps be more appropriate to change some of the wines completely at this stage.

Many individuals agonise over the profitability of wine on their lists, and many more get it completely wrong. The merchant can offer advice in this area if requested:

- The merchant can do many of the calculations, suggesting a total open margin, a total margin across the list and individual margins for each of the wines.

- The merchant should also give advice if the operation is perhaps a little greedy in pricing some of the finer wines, which could establish the operation's credibility, but are out of people's reach.

Wine merchants should also be able to undertake on-site promotions, and contribute to merchandising, training, tasting events, and be speakers at gastronomic events. However, it is worth booking these possibilities in advance, as merchants are generally busy.

## STORAGE AND CELLAR MANAGEMENT

Factors and practices, which determine good cellar management, are:

### Key factors

■ Good ventilation.

■ High levels of cleanliness.

■ Even temperatures of 13–15°C (55–59°F).

■ Strong draughts and wide fluctuation of temperature should be avoided.

### Good practices

■ On delivery all casks should be placed immediately upon their stillions.

■ Casks remaining on the floor should have the bung uppermost to withstand the pressure better.

■ Correct humidity.

■ Spiling should take place to reduce any excess pressure in the cask.

■ Tappings should be carried out 24 hours before a cask is required.

■ Pipes and engines should be cleaned at regular intervals.

■ Beer left in pipes after closing time should be drawn off.

■ Returned beer should be filtered back into the cask from which it came.

■ Care should be taken that the cellar is not overstocked.

■ All spiles removed during service should be replaced after closing time.

■ All cellar equipment should be kept scrupulously clean.

■ Any ullage should be returned to the brewery as soon as possible.

■ All beer lines should be cleaned weekly with diluted pipe-cleaning fluid and the cellar floor washed down weekly with a weak solution of chloride of lime (mild bleach).

## Wine cellarage

■ A subterranean northerly aspect is ideal where possible.

■ Excessive temperature variation should be avoided – a constant cool temperature of 7–12.5°C (45–55°F) should be maintained which will assist the wines to develop gradually.

■ Wine should be stored away from excessive heat, hot water pipes, heating plant or hot unit.

■ Excessive dampness should be avoided and a relative humidity of between 55 and 70 per cent maintained. Humidity assists in keeping the cork from drying out, but the very important labels require protecting in the cellar (this can be achieved by spraying with ordinary hair spray which provides years of protection).

- Draughts and unwanted odours should be avoided, so the cellar should be clean and well ventilated.

- Fluorescent light (it does not give off heat) can be used in a cellar area. Otherwise 20–40 watt maximum lighting should be used throughout. Wine can lose its colour followed by its flavour if exposed to too much light. Some wines are partially protected from light, by their coloured glass bottles. Bright light, however, especially sunlight or ultraviolet light, should be avoided, especially with champagne and Chardonnay.

- Table wines should be stored on their sides in bins so that the wine remains in contact with the cork. This keeps the cork expanded and prevents air from entering the wine – a disaster which quickly turns wine to vinegar;

White wines, sweet wines and champagne are more fragile than reds. White, sparkling and rosé wines should be kept in the coolest part of the cellar and in bins nearest the ground (because warm air rises). Red wines are best stored in the upper bins. Some red Burgundies, which are not filtered – in efforts to preserve their full flavour characteristics – are more likely to suffer from adverse cellarage. Syrah and Cabernet Sauvignon wines are more resilient than Pinot Noirs.

Special refrigerators or cooling cabinets can keep sparkling, white and rosé wines at serving temperature. These may be stationed in the dispense bar – a bar located between the cellar and the restaurant – to facilitate prompt service.

Many restaurants around the world place their dispense bar in a prominent position as a dramatic design statement – as in the Mandarin Oriental in London – or in the restaurants themselves – as is the case in the Mandarin Oriental in Munich, The Atlantic Hotel in Hamburg and the Sheraton Grand Hotel in Edinburgh. In terms of innovative cellarage, Anton Mosimann, in his exclusive London dining club, a former Presbyterian Church, utilises the organ loft area for his cellar. In this way his members can look up from where they are dining to the glass cellar where you can walk through the chilled white wine cellar and into the red wine cellar and choose your wines in person.

If fine wines cannot be cellared effectively in-house, location of the cellarage at a wine merchant's premises should be considered. There are also self-storage systems around the UK, based on the US practice of renting temperature-controlled vault storage.

## Storage of other drinks

Spirits, liqueurs, beers, squashes, juices and mineral waters are usually stored upright in their containers, as are fortified wines. If screw-caps are used, stand the bottles upright; if in cork, lay the bottles on their sides. Stopper caps and served caps are generally used for sherries and most ports, which are also stored upright once opened. Vintage and crusted ports are stored horizontally but require time upright to allow sediment to settle at the bottom of the bottle prior to decanting. Sherries rarely improve in bottle. Finos, manzanillas and tawny ports are best consumed as soon as possible after purchase.

## Stock control

The purchase of an establishment's alcoholic and non-alcoholic beverage stock is carried out by the individual responsible for the cellar. The order should be written in duplicate on an official order form. The top copy is then sent to the supplier and the duplicate remains in the order book for control purposes when the goods are delivered. In some instances there may be three copies of the order sheet. If so they are distributed as follows:

- top copy to the supplier
- duplicate copy to the control and accounts department
- third copy remains in the order book.

When the goods are delivered to an establishment, either a delivery note or an invoice should accompany them. Whichever document it may be, the information in the document should be exactly the same, with one exception: invoices show the price of all goods delivered whereas delivery notes do not. The goods delivered must first of all be counted and checked against the delivery note to ensure that all the goods listed have been delivered. The individual responsible for the cellar may carry out an extra check by comparing the delivery note with the copy of the order kept in the order book. This is to ensure that the items ordered have been sent and in the correct quantities and that extra items have not been sent which were not listed on the order sheet, thereby incurring extra cost without immediately realising it. At this stage all information concerning the goods delivered must be entered in the necessary books for control purposes.

### Goods received book

All deliveries should be recorded in full detail in the goods received book. Each delivery entry should show, basically, the following:

- name and address of the supplier
- delivery note/invoice number
- order number
- list of items delivered
- item price
- quantity
- unit
- total price
- date of delivery
- discounts if applicable.

The amount and deposit cost of all containers such as kegs, casks and the number of carbon dioxide cylinders delivered can also be recorded in this book or in a separate returnable containers book.

### Cellar stock ledger

The cellar stock ledger (see Figure 4.1) may be used as either an extension of, or in place of, the goods received book. It shows movement of all stock into the establishment and issues out to the bars or dispensing points. All movement of stock in and out of the cellar is normally shown at cost price.

| Name or drink | Bin No. | Opening stock | Received | Total | Closing stock | Consumption stock | Price per unit | £ |
|---|---|---|---|---|---|---|---|---|
|  |  |  |  |  |  |  |  |  |

**Figure 4.1**  Stock book

### Bin cards

Bin cards (see Figure 4.2) are used to show the physical stock of each item held in the cellar. The movement of all stock 'in and out' of the cellar is recorded on each appropriate bin card. The bin cards are also often used to show the maximum and minimum stock.

| Stock item | | Bin No. | |
|---|---|---|---|
| Date | Received | Balance | Issued |
|  |  |  |  |

**Figure 4.2**  Heading of a bin card

The minimum stock determines the reordering level, leaving sufficient stock in hand to carry over until the new delivery arrives. The maximum stock indicates how much to reorder and is determined by such considerations as storage and space available, turnover of a particular item and to some extent by the amount of cash available within the budget.

No item should be issued from the cellar unless it is being accounted for by the top copy of an official requisition form, correctly filled in, dated and signed by a designated person from each of the departments concerned. It can be helpful if all requisitions are handed in before a set time each day so that the issues can be prepared together. In certain instances, however, depending on the organisation of an establishment, it may be necessary to issue more than once per day. All requisition sheets are written in duplicate. The top copy of the requisition comes to the cellar for the items required to be issued, and the duplicate remains in the requisition book for bar personnel to check drink on receipt from the cellar.

### Requisitioning from the cellar

Each unit dispensing alcoholic beverages should use some form of requisition to draw items from the cellar. These requisitions may be controlled either by colour or serial number, and are normally in duplicate or triplicate. The copies are sent as follows:

- top copy to the cellar
- duplicate to the beverage control department
- triplicate would be used by each unit to check its goods received from the cellar.

Information listed on the requisition would be:

- name of dispensing unit
- date
- list of items required
- quantity and unit of each item required
- signature of authorised person to both order and receive the goods.

The purpose of the requisition is to control the movement of items from the cellar into the dispensing unit and to avoid too much stock being taken at one time, thus over-stocking the bar.

The level of stock held in the bar is known as par stock. The amount ordered on the requisition, each day, should bring the bar stock back up to par. The amount to reorder is determined simply by taking account of the following equation: opening stock plus additions (requisition) less closing stock equals consumption (the amount to reorder, each item to the nearest whole unit).

In the outlets, as all drink is checked before issue, a daily consumption sheet (see Figure 4.3) is completed each day after the service by copying down the sales shown on the top copy of the wine checks or from electronic point-of-sale (EPOS) control systems.

At the end of the week the consumptions are totalled, thereby showing the total sales for that period. These totals may then be transferred on to a bar stock book for costing purposes. Where drink consumed is not checked in any way then either a daily or weekly stock is taken so that the amount to be requisitioned from the cellar may be noted. This then brings the bar stock up to its required level, which is the par stock. The daily or

| Name or drink | Bin No. | Mon | Tues | Wed | Thurs | Fri | Sat | Sun | Total |
|---------------|---------|-----|------|-----|-------|-----|-----|-----|-------|
|               |         |     |      |     |       |     |     |     |       |
|               |         |     |      |     |       |     |     |     |       |
|               |         |     |      |     |       |     |     |     |       |
|               |         |     |      |     |       |     |     |     |       |
|               |         |     |      |     |       |     |     |     |       |

**Figure 4.3**   Daily consumption sheet

weekly consumption (sales) would then be costed and the cash total for sales arrived at would be related to the daily or weekly income.

### Ullage, allowance, off-sales book

Each sales point should have a suitable book for recording the amount of beer wasted in cleaning pipes, broken bottles, measures spilt, or anything that needs a credit. The number of bottles, whether beer or spirits, at off-sales prices and the difference in price must also be recorded, either in the same book or in a separate one, the off-sales book. This difference will be allowed against the gross profit.

### Transfer book

The transfer book is used in multi-bar units to record movement of stock between bars.

## Analysing sales

In order to make decisions about the beverage provision over time, an analysis and evaluation of a number of factors needs to be made. These factors include:

- gross profit margin
- beverage sales per customer
- average number of bottles sold per customer
- sales mix data, such as the ratio of white wine to red wine consumption
- assessing the average price per bottle sold per period
- making stock considerations and changes to the lists based on popularity and profitability of items
- logging requests for wines not on the list
- understand the competition.

Chapter 7 considers the whole range of issues involved with the appraisal of performance and making strategic decisions

## Determining cost of sales

The traditional approach to determining usage, or cost of sales, is to take the value of the opening stock, add to it the value of the purchases during the period and then deduct the value of the closing stock. This value is usually the cost prices. For outlets with differing gross profit mark-ups, the issue to the various outlets is also costed at selling price to ensure that the revenue is reconciled with that expected from the issues records. This is a very laborious process.

An alternative is as follows. The beverage stock of an establishment is located in two main areas, the cellar and the outlet or outlets. The outlet stock is usually set at a par level and returned to this level at a set time. This could be each day or each week. For control purposes, all that is important is the cost of actual sales. Therefore, only the cost of goods issued to the outlets needs to be calculated.

For the cellar, all that is important is the physical stock. Its actual value is required only for the end-of-year accounts. If this is true then the stock control of the cellar can be undertaken as follows. For each stock item, a bin card or entry in the stock book is drawn up as:

■ item – the name of the item

■ quantity – the stock unit, this could be a dozen, six or single

■ reorder level – the level of stock at which a new order is placed; this is predetermined for all items, as is the quantity of the stock to be ordered

■ opening stock – in unit terms

■ deliveries – in unit terms

■ issues to outlets – in unit terms

■ closing stock – in unit terms

■ current cost price.

From this record for each trading period, the cost price of issues can be determined. This is the consumption as issued from the cellar to the outlets. In addition, stock levels can be first determined from the book and then physically checked against what is actually in the cellar.

The advantage of this system is that it is only the cost of the issues that needs to be calculated. For each bar or outlet, a similar system exists. There is a par stock and each day or week this is returned to the par level. Over a period of time it will be found that the stock value of the outlet, at selling price, will be more-or-less constant. Thus the cost of goods issued to this outlet, at selling price, should equal revenue.

This approach does require the predetermining of the stock levels, the reorder levels and ensuring that issues to the outlets within the operation are in whole units only (single, dozen and so on).

## SUMMARY

This chapter has considered the complexity of the legal framework within which alcoholic beverages are sold and the factors that affect the compilation of wine and drinks lists. The various types of wine and drinks list have been examined as well as pricing considerations and it has been suggested that pricing systems need to move away from the traditional cost-plus methods, especially for wine. Approaches to purchasing have been identified and further consideration has been given specifically to wine provision. Finally the factors affecting the purchasing, storage and stock control for wine and other drinks have been examined.

## FURTHER READING

Durkan, A. and Cousins, J. (1995) *The Beverage Book*, London: Hodder and Stoughton.

Kelly, E. M. and Doyon, R. (1991) *Professional Bar Manager's Handbook*, New York: Van Nostrand Reinhold.

*Larousse Encyclopaedia of Wine* (1994) London: Larousse International.

Lipinski, R. A. and Lipinski, K. A. (1992) *The Complete Beverage Dictionary*, New York: Van Nostrand Reinhold.

Robinson, J. (1999) *The Oxford Companion to Wine*, Oxford: Oxford University Press.

Simon, J. (1999) *Wine with Food: The Ultimate Guide to Matching Wine with Food for Every Occasion*, London: Mitchell Beazley.

# CHAPTER FIVE

# OPERATIONAL AREAS, EQUIPMENT AND STAFFING

**AIM**

This chapter aims to outline the broad and some detailed considerations in the planning, design, equipping and staffing of foodservice operations.

**OBJECTIVES**

The chapter is intended to support you in:

■ developing a systematic approach to the planning, designing, equipping and staffing of foodservice operations

■ making operational choices which contribute to meeting both customer and operational needs.

## GENERAL CONSIDERATIONS

Many food and beverage managers are having to develop skills in design, amongst the wide range of other aspects of the role. The character of the food, beverages and service offered by any foodservice operation needs to be supported by an atmosphere and ambience which can make the experience of dining more memorable, and encourage repeat business and recommendation.

In addition to dealing with direct reports, reviewing financial performance, monitoring quality standards, overcoming obstacles and fine-tuning the operation, the food and beverage manager responsible for a large operation also has to consider innovation. Creating new operations, or renovating existing ones, means being involved in developing new concepts or rethinking old ones. This can include activities such as creating new design, developing new menus, beverage lists and rethinking approaches to production and service, which then includes looking for new plant, equipment such as china, glassware, flatware and cutlery, through to uniforms and so on.

## What is design?

In architecture and interior design, 'design' as a term describes the alchemy of all of the decisions determining how a particular object, space or building will appear. It is design that can distinguish one foodservice operation from another and also allow personal determinations of preference, one against another.

The designer takes into account function (practical purpose of the area under design) the image, style, operating efficiency and consumer comfort. The work also incorporates space-planning and drawing, interior and exterior elements, form and colour, finishes and durability, technology, lighting and audio-visual systems and the planning and regulation of what is visible and what is concealed. In a time when memorable experiences are an important commodity in the marketplace, design can immediately differentiate one operation from another.

## The food and beverage manager and design and trends

Trends in the international market have an impact on foodservice businesses, so it is necessary to stay in touch with forming trends. The dangers for foodservice businesses are that they can flounder because too much has been spent on interior design that could not be afforded or the business has suffered because the concept is not harmonised with effective staffing and menu and beverage list design. There is a tangible relationship between the nature of the market, the type of demand being met and the budget available.

In a competitive market, unless the operation is unique, it has to be more attractive than its rivals. Successful hotel restaurants, for instance, often have street entrances and separate identities. Some are franchised. If customers have to go through a lobby, the restaurant becomes isolated, hidden, and possibly remains unknown if the hotel is not entered. Customers need a reason to go to a particular operation in preference to another offering similar products. Modern restaurants, in particular, are more about entertainment than at any time previously.

Kitchens and restaurants are becoming closer. More open areas can be seen: chefs and the process of making food fascinate people. The distance from the kitchen to the table is also getting shorter, less complicated and more streamlined. Pan-Asian hoteliers, for instance, are building open kitchens – even the glass panel between the dining area and the kitchen has been removed, and this provides the possibility of a heightened sensory experience. Aroma, combined with visual and auditory senses can create an enlivened and richer experience.

As well as an increasing closeness in the production and service areas there is also nowadays a much closer relationship between bar and restaurant activity. Overall there is great emphasis on creating foodservice environments that are more easily cleaned and maintained.

## A systematic approach

The systematic approach to designing, planning, equipping and staffing of a foodservice operation includes giving consideration to a wide variety of factors. These can be grouped under five broad headings:

- market needs
- operational needs
- space allocation and requirements
- finance availability
- hygiene, health and safety.

### Market needs

The needs of the market, or rather the need of the establishment to provide products to meet the determined market needs, may be ascertained by working through the first three stages of the catering cycle (see page 2). These are:

- Consideration of the potential market and the needs of the consumer.
- The determination of policies and the business objectives, including the determination of the scope of the market needs that the operation is intended to serve.
- The interpretation of demand, which identifies the type, range and scale of the food and beverage services to be provided.

Giving consideration to and making decisions within the first three stages of the catering cycle (much of which has been discussed in Chapters 1–4), a framework will have been established within which systematic consideration can be given to the planning and design of the facilities for the food and beverage operation and determining the plant, equipment and staffing required.

### Operational needs

Included in the consideration of the planning and design of facilities and the staffing of the operation, is the determination of the various operational methods that will be used. These include:

- receiving and storage methods
- production systems and methods
- service system and methods
- dining arrangements
- clearing methods
- control methods
- dishwashing methods.

The consideration of these operational aspects also needs to take into account the customer usage of food and beverage service areas. This will include issues such as access to the premises and facilities such as toilets. It should also include the needs of the disabled and of children.

### Space allocation and requirements

Taking into account the various considerations outlined above, Figure 5.1 gives a rough guide to the space allocation required for different types of foodservice operation.

| **Meals** | Square metres per meal served/hour | | |
|---|---|---|---|
| | *Up to 200* | *200–500* | *500+* |
| Cafeteria | 0.45–0.70 | 0.35–0.45 | 0.25–0.35 |
| Hotels | 0.35–1.60 | 0.35–0.70 | 0.35–0.45 |
| Restaurants | 0.35–0.90 | 0.35–0.45 | 0.30–0.35 |

**Fast food outlets**

The average overall size of most fast food outlets is currently around 1000–1500 $m^2$.

**Restaurant and hotel dining areas**

(NB Space allocation includes sideboards, aisles, etc.)

| *Style* | *Space per cover* $(m^2)$ |
|---|---|
| Traditional restaurant | 1 |
| Banqueting | 0.9 |
| High-class restaurants | 2 |

(NB For safety reasons all aisles should be 1 metre wide)

| *Production areas* | *Space per cover* $(m^2)$ |
|---|---|
| Up to 100 covers | 0.5 |
| 100–1000 | 0.3–0.4 |
| 1000 or more | 0.25 |

**Figure 5.1**  Space allocation (courtesy of Croner's Catering)

### Finance availability

The main financial objectives of the operations will have been considered under stage 2 of the catering cycle (determination of policy). Under this stage the finance available will also have been determined. Consideration will also have to be given to:

■ The cost of the space to be used.

■ The purchasing policies, for example buying equipment, leasing equipment, lease/rental, new or used.

■ The expected life of the operation in terms of the product life cycle and therefore the expected life of the equipment.

### Hygiene, health and safety

The design of catering facilities must at all stages reflect the need for safe and hygienic practices. Legislation concerning food preparation areas is not comprehensive and includes:

■ The Food Hygiene Act 1970

■ The Office, Shops and Railway Premises Act 1963

■ The Health and Safety at Work Act 1974

■ The Public Health Act 1936

■ The Food Safety Acts 1990/1991/1995.

The early involvement of the local environmental health officer (EHO) will reduce the risk of costly later amendments bearing in mind the legal powers of the EHO to close catering premises considered unfit for food production. The limited legislation covering food preparation areas means that very much is left to local interpretation, and consultation with the EHO is strongly advised. Similarly, the local fire officer should be consulted prior to any significant alterations or changes of use.

## FOOD PRODUCTION AREAS

Factors which influence kitchen planning and design are:

■ the size and extent of the menu and the market that it serves

■ services – gas, electricity and water

■ labour, level of skills

■ amount of capital expenditure, costs

■ use of prepared convenience foods

- types of equipment available
- hygiene and the Food Safety Acts 1990/1991/1995
- design and decor
- multi-usage requirements.

## Design of the kitchen

The size and space of the kitchen should enable staff to work safely, efficiently, speedily and in comfort. The aim when planning a kitchen is for food to be prepared and served without waste of either time or effort. Therefore, layout design must consider working methods which improve productivity and utilise equipment to reduce labour. The main considerations are:

- To design an efficient work flow.
- To provide adequate workspace.
- To create appropriate sections.
- To ensure access to ancillary areas.
- To determine number, type and size of equipment.
- To consider ease of supervision.

Kitchens must be designed so that they can be easily managed. The managers must have easy access to the areas under their control and have good visibility in the areas which have to be supervised.

## Work flow

Food preparation rooms should be planned to allow a work flow whereby food is processed through the premises, from the point of delivery to the point of sale or service, with the minimum of obstruction. The various processes should be separated as far as possible and food intended for sale should not cross paths with waste food or refuse. Staff time is valuable, and a design which reduces wasteful journeys is both efficient and cost-effective. The overall sequence of receiving, storing, preparing, holding, serving and clearing needs to be achieved by:

- minimum movement
- minimal backtracking
- maximum use of space
- maximum use of equipment with minimum expenditure of time and effort.

## Workspace

Approximately 4.2 m² (45 ft²) is required per person; too little space can cause staff to work in close proximity to stoves, steamers, cutting blades, mixers and so on, which creates the potential for accidents. Aisle space of approximately 1.37 m (4½ ft) is desirable as aisles must be adequate to enable staff to move safely. The working area must also be suitably lit and ventilated with extractor fans to remove heat, fumes and smells.

## Working sections

The size and style of the menu and the ability of the staff will determine the number of sections and layout that are necessary. A straight-line layout would be suitable for a snack bar whilst an island layout would be more suitable for an hotel restaurant.

## Access to ancillary areas

A goods receiving area needs to be designed for bringing in supplies easily, with nearby storage facilities suitably sited for distribution of foods to preparation and production areas.

Hygiene considerations must be planned so that kitchen equipment is cleaned and all used equipment from the dining area is cleared, cleaned and stored. Stillroom facilities may also be required.

## Preparation surfaces

The choice of surfaces on which food is to be prepared is vitally important. Failure to ensure a suitable material may provide a breeding ground for bacteria. Stainless steel tables are the best, as they do not rust and their welded seams eliminate unwanted cracks and open joints. Sealed tubular legs are preferable to angular ones because again they eliminate corners in which dirt collects, although tubular legs have often been found to harbour pests. Preparation surfaces should be:

- jointless
- durable
- impervious
- of the correct height
- firm-based.

Surfaces must withstand repeated cleaning at the required temperature without premature deterioration through pitting and corrosion. General considerations are:

- Water absorbency – softwoods draw fluids into them, and with the fluids bacteria can also be drawn in.

- Resistance to stains, cleaning chemicals, heat and food acids.
- Toxicity – cutting boards must not give off toxic substances.
- Durability – cutting boards have to withstand wear and tear, split or warp.

## Colour coding

To avoid cross-contamination, it is important that the same equipment is not used for handling raw and high-risk products without being disinfected. To prevent the inadvertent use of equipment for raw and high-risk foods, it is recommended that different colours and shapes be used to identify products or raw materials; for example:

- red – raw meat
- blue – raw fish
- brown – cooked meats
- green – vegetables
- white – general purpose
- yellow – sandwiches.

## Fixing and siting of equipment

Where practicable, equipment should be mobile to facilitate its removal for cleaning, ideally castor-mounted with brakes on all the wheels.

Pipework and equipment directly above open food should not expose the food to any risk of contamination from dirty condensation, rust or flaking paint.

Gas and electrical supply pipes should be flexible and capable of being disconnected. In the case of gas supply the coupling to the mains must incorporate a self-sealing valve and a shut-off cock immediately upstream of the fitting. The flexible tube must conform to the UK gas specifications and the appliances must be secured to a fixed point by a strong detached wire or chain, shorter in length than the tube to avoid accidental stretching.

Machinery must be mounted on covered raised platforms of concrete to facilitate cleaning. The bases and lower parts of machines, including motors and gears, may be difficult to clean and consequently collect dust and spillages which make ideal breeding sites for pests. In such circumstances the bases should be completely sealed. Skirting or cover plates tend to trap dust.

## Stationary equipment

For planning purposes, stationary equipment must be 500 mm (20 in) from the walls and there must be 250 mm (10 in) clearance between the floor and underside of the equipment. This allows for the cleaning of wall and floor surfaces. Alternatively, the machines should be fixed firmly to the floor without a gap. However, the design must avoid narrow areas or angles in contact with the floor.

Electrical equipment, such as motors and switches, do pose problems for cleaning. Such equipment must always be earthed and capable of removal without tools prior to cleaning the main equipment. Ideally motors should be sited outside food rooms, to reduce cleaning problems. Trailing wires and cables must be avoided.

When pipework is installed, consideration must be given to future cleaning. There must be sufficient space left between the pipes and the floor or the wall to allow access for easy cleaning. Pipes may also be built into the walls. When pipes are lagged, an impervious cleansable finish is required.

Guards on machinery which are required under health and safety legislation should be capable of being thoroughly cleaned and, where necessary, removed quickly and easily without the use of special tools.

Newly built premises should comply fully with the requirements of the appropriate hygiene and safety legislation. Plans should be discussed with the enforcement officers as it is much easier and cheaper to provide satisfactory finishes and facilities.

The use of satisfactory building materials and a well-planned layout is essential to achieve high standards of hygiene. The size of the premises must be adequate to allow efficient operation and the site must be large enough to accommodate possible future expansion, if this is a management objective.

## Building fabric

Considerations for design are as follows.

### Ceilings

The choice of materials for ceilings presents problems because kitchen ceilings are exposed to extreme temperature, fumes and steam and are not readily accessible for cleaning. All surfaces including ceilings must be capable of being thoroughly cleaned and have smooth continuous surfaces. Ceilings may be suspended or solid, as detailed below.

### Suspended

- Suspended ceilings cover horizontal pipework and services are concealed.
- Access should be built for inspection of pest control and to allow for maintenance.
- Structural walkways are often necessary and should always be provided in large premises.
- Suspended ceilings can be of various materials but they are normally made of metal lattice, incorporating cleansable panels, aluminium backed and faced fibreboard.
- Flush-fitting ventilation grilles should also be provided.

**Solid**

■ Solid ceilings give less scope for hygienic finish.

■ They should be well insulated to avoid condensation and mould growth.

Ceilings should be:

■ smooth

■ fire-resistant

■ light in colour

■ covering wall joints

■ easy to clean.

The ceiling height must provide a satisfactory working condition and allow for the installation of equipment. A ceiling height of 3.0–3.6 m (10–12 ft) will not only ensure that the ceiling is accessible for cleaning but also mean that extremes of temperatures are unlikely to arise.

## *Walls*

Walls must as a general rule be:

■ smooth

■ impervious

■ non-flaking

■ light of colour

■ capable of being thoroughly cleaned and if necessary disinfected

■ solid (as those with cavities may harbour pests)

■ free of crevices and ledges which cause cleaning problems.

False panelling should not be used.
    Wall surfaces should be:

■ resin-bonded fibre glass

■ ceramic-faced blocks

■ glazed tiles (with water-resistant grouting)

■ stainless steel

■ plastic sheeting

■ polypropylene.

Depending on the operation, surfaces adjacent to walls surface may need to be resistant to:

- spillages
- chemicals
- grease
- heat
- impact.

Stainless steel splashbacks for sinks and working surfaces are advisable. Use wall and floor stops to prevent damage to wall surfaces. Wall corners are usually made of non-corrosive metals or PVC. Stainless steel is also used. Crash rails may be placed along walls where there is a high volume of traffic to avoid trolleys' damaging wall surfaces.

Pipework and ducting should be bracketed at least 150 mm (6 in) from walls to facilitate cleaning. All lagging on pipes must be smooth and impervious. Pipes passing through external walls must be effectively sealed to prevent the ingress of pests.

### Doors, windows, stairs and platforms

Doors, windows, stairs and platforms must be designed to prevent the accumulation of dirt and to facilitate easy cleaning. These areas can allow the entry of insects, dirt, dust and contamination.

- Windows should be in north-facing walls to reduce glare and solar heat gains.
- Solar film on windows will assist in counteracting heat.
- Cleansable fly screens must be fitted to opening windows.
- Windows must be constructed in an uncomplicated design to facilitate cleaning.
- Internal window sills should be sloped to prevent their use as shelves.
- The design of frames and windows and doors should avoid acute angles.
- Right-angled joints between frames and walls should be beaded and filled to form smooth continuous surfaces.
- All woodwork should be well seasoned, properly knotted, stopped, primed and given three coats of polyurethane paint.

Doors must be:

- smooth
- made of non-absorbent surfaces
- capable of being thoroughly cleaned
- tight-fitting
- self-closing
- fitted with finger plates if necessary.

External doors should:

■ be proofed against entry of insects

■ have metal kick-plates to prevent gnawing of rodents.

Doorways must be large enough to allow for the movement of mobile equipment and possible replacement of fixed equipment.

Swing doors which open both ways should be fitted with sight panels. Stairs, ladders and platforms must be capable of being thoroughly cleaned and should not expose food to risk of contamination.

## Flooring

The basic rule is that floors should be smooth, impervious and capable of being readily cleaned. When selecting a floor covering, the following criteria should be considered:

■ The volume and nature of traffic.

■ Whether the area is wet or dry.

■ How the area will be cleaned.

■ What chemical resistance is necessary.

■ Whether production will need to be curtailed to effect repairs to the floor.

■ The type of subfloor.

The manager/owner of the establishment must assess the cost-effectiveness of a finish. The following must be considered:

■ initial cost

■ durability

■ performance

■ safety.

Floors should be:

■ durable

■ non-absorbent

■ anti-slip

■ without crevices

■ capable of being effectively cleaned

■ resistant to acids, grease and salts

■ sloping to allow liquids to drain to trapped gulleys (a slope of 1 in 60 is the minimum recommendation).

The angle between walls and floors should be level.

Floor coverings might be:

- epoxy resin
- granolithic
- welded anti-slip vinyl sheet
- anti-slip ceramic or quarry tiles.

A *screed system* – for example, magnesium oxychloride formulation – is incombustible and will not support bacterial growth or allow surface contamination by grease.

Resins are available as coatings – a thin-layer screed put on to a heavy-duty screed. A thin-layer screed is 4–10 mm thick. A heavy-duty screed is used as an underlay – and as a finished floor surface. These range in depth from 10 to 35 mm.

Resins which are typically used for flooring are:

- epoxies
- acrylics
- polyurethanes.

Epoxy resins have the widest application as they have excellent binding properties and good general resistance to floor damage, acids, alkalines and so on. They can also be solvent-free, meaning that there is a minimal risk of tainting nearby materials.

## Water supplies and drainage

### Cold water
Cold water supplies used for washing in addition to food should be mains supplied and should not be fed via an intermediate tank, unless chlorinated.

The soteriological (life-supporting) and chemical quality of the water must be checked at frequent intervals to ensure that the water will not contaminate the product. Water companies are legally required to check the mains water continuously.

### Hot water
Hot water should be supplied to every sink with a discharge temperature of 60°C. In hard water areas, hot water supplies should be softened, otherwise scale build-up will cause cleaning and operational problems and add significantly to detergent usage.

### Water pipes
Water pipes should preferably be made of plastic, with screw or push-fit connections to enable easy dismantling to ease blockages.

### Grease traps

Grease traps should be fitted outside of food areas so as to avoid possible contamination of food and food surfaces during cleaning. All inspection chambers should also be placed outside of food rooms.

### Manholes

Manholes should be double-sealed, bedded in silicon grease and screwed down with brass screws.

### Potato peelers and dishwashers

If connected directly to the drainage system, potato peelers and dishwashers should be trapped to avoid waste pipes acting as vents for sewers.

### Drainage

Drainage in any catering establishment must be efficient, with smooth clear drainage which is continuously cleaned and in good order and repair. The drainage system must be adequate to remove peak loads quickly without flooding. Sufficient drains should be installed to facilitate effective cleaning of rooms by pressure-jet cleaners or by other means of cleaning.

It is advisable to use shallow, glazed, half-round floor channels for uncovered drainage provided they do not pose a risk to health and safety. If covers have to be used they should be made of non-corrosive material and be continuous, strong and easily removed for cleaning.

Drains must have sufficient access points to allow rodding in the event of blockages. The care of drains includes:

- Drains should be cleaned and degreased regularly.
- Construction should inhibit the harbourage and movement of vermin.
- Defective drains may result in effluent foul odours and rodents entering into food rooms.
- All external rainwater fall pipes should be fitted with balloon guards to deter rodents.
- Circumference guards should be fitted around vertical drainpipes fastening them to walls, to prevent the rodents climbing up them.

## Ventilation

Ventilation is a process which provides an effective supply of clean fresh air generally from the outside. It is basically dependent upon the movement or circulation of air at a sufficient rate, to ensure that moist, stale air is removed at regular intervals.

Adequate ventilation is essential in any food establishment in order to create a comfortable working environment. In doing so, ventilation must prevent:

- excessive heat
- condensation
- dust
- steam
- odours
- contaminated air.

Good ventilation will assist in:

- reducing grease
- reducing staining of ceilings.

A kitchen will require approximately 20–30 changes per hour, depending on the production needs of the kitchen. Many busy kitchens with high-volume production require 30 changes per hour. Those with specialist equipment such as tandoori ovens, require 60 changes per hour.

It is possible to find 120 changes per hour in small, low-ceiling basement kitchens. Ventilation can be achieved either naturally or artificially. Natural ventilation is supplied through windows and doors. Open windows cause problems as they allow the entry of dust and insects and in some cases birds. Because of this, windows should be covered by perforated gauze, although this does present additional cleaning problems. Although a kitchen may have sufficient windows, the windows may not be positioned to give the most effective circulation when open. Constant opening and closing by food handlers causes hazards as hands become contaminated. Nearly all kitchens, therefore, require mechanical ventilation, especially those in a basement or enclosed within a building.

Expert advice is needed in deciding which type of ventilation is best suited to the premises. Initial costs for ventilation are normally high; this cost depreciates over 15–20 years.

The simplest system is an electric extractor fan fitted into an external wall or window and operated by either a cord or switch. The positioning of the fan is of prime importance: it should be placed so that it picks up the majority of fumes from the kitchen. Externally it should not discharge at the face level of passers-by or where it might carry to other rooms.

Apart from creating a circulation and renewal of the total air within a kitchen, particular attention must be given to the sources of heat, fumes or steam. Equipment such as stoves, boilers, steamers, fryers and bratt pans release large volumes of heat and fumes into the atmosphere. Special provision must be built in to control these effluvia. The simplest way is to have a hood above the equipment to collect the fumes via a duct, which leads to the outside. The ducting should have a fan that creates an air current away from the source and a filter arrangement to arrest the majority of heavy materials, such as grease particles. The fan is normally situated well away from the source of heat to prevent damage to the motor. The filter is nearer the source, in order to absorb as much grease and dirt as possible to prevent any build-up in the ducting. Permission for ducting outside the building must be granted by the local planning office and the EHO.

Cooking smells can be a nuisance in some establishments but actively encouraged in others. If the smells have to be removed, the best way is to install an activated carbon filter. These still need to have residual deposits of grease and dust, to be removed. Some odours can be dealt with by installing an oxidiser. The effectiveness of oxidisers depends on the type and extent of the odour.

Modern buildings are often equipped with air conditioning, which provides a balanced system of purified air in each part of the building, and a separated ducted extraction of stale air.

As ventilation is a specialist subject always consult a ventilation engineer.

## Hygiene of ventilation and water systems

Clean air and safe water are vital for a pleasant working environment and hygienic food production. Risk of infection can be due to failure to carry out routine maintenance and cleaning of ductwork, pipes and cooling towers. This leads to what is commonly known as the sick building syndrome. Symptoms are:

- dry throat
- sore eyes
- dry nose
- drowsiness
- humidifier fever (caused by poor ventilation and humidity)
- raised temperature
- respiratory problems
- headaches.

## Lighting

Premises should take full advantage of natural lighting through large, well-placed windows. In addition, efficient artificial lighting is always required in food production areas for the following reasons:

- To enable staff to work in an agreeable working environment.
- To facilitate cleaning.
- To prevent accidents.
- To prevent eye strain.
- To discourage insects and rodents as these normally shun well-lit areas.

Adequate lighting is also essential in passageways, storerooms, stairs and in areas outside the building where staff need to go, such as refuse areas and delivery bays. Wall and ceiling finishes should be chosen to enhance available light by using light-reflecting colours.

The number and capacity of lights required in any establishment will depend on the size of the area to be illuminated. From a working point of view, a number of independent lights, positioned over those areas where staff work, are preferable to fewer, larger-wattage lights, which need positioning fairly high to spread the light and which may well lose intensity and cause shadows in the process.

Fluorescent lights give a more efficient light than tungsten filament bulbs. Both tubes and shades can be selected to give the most agreeable light, without glare, to those working on the premises. Tubes also have a longer life and are cheaper to run than tungsten filament bulbs.

All light fittings should be of simple design and preferably flush with the ceiling or wall to assist in cleaning. Press-button or recessed switches should be avoided as they encourage the build-up of food deposits.

Electrical fittings situated near sinks, cooking ranges and refrigerators should be sealed to keep out moisture and should be made of rubber, plastic or rustproof metal. Wiring should be laid in conduit and, where possible, chased into the wall to avoid unnecessary dust traps.

In large kitchens it may be preferable to have individual or groups of lights, operated by separate switches. This gives greater flexibility and reduction in electricity usage, and also eliminates the need to have a large cluster of switches which may become difficult to clean.

## Refuse storage and disposal

Refuse containers must be situated outside the building, preferably in a covered but not totally enclosed area.

Refuse can be divided into two types:

- Dry waste – paper, cardboard boxes.
- Wet waste – food and kitchen debris.

The best type of container for wet waste is either metal or plastic bins with a tight-fitting lid which keeps out flies and insects.

### The storage and disposal of waste

- Refuse must not be allowed to accumulate in food rooms and should not be left overnight.
- Waste may be stored in strong polythene bags and removed at the end of the working day. The stands for the bags must be maintained in a clean condition.

■ Staff must be trained to:
  – clean as they go
  – replace lids
  – wash their hands after receptacles are used
  – not overfill sinks
  – to tie full sacks to prevent problems from insects
  – prevent refuse collectors from entering food rooms or dining areas
  – keep waste food separate from paper and cardboard.

■ Where possible, food waste should be stored under refrigeration.

■ Food waste should be removed from food premises daily.

■ The number and type of receptacles used will depend on:
  – the type and quantity of waste
  – the frequency of collections
  – the access available for the refuse vehicle.

■ Dustbins should be stored clear of the ground on tubular steel racks to facilitate cleaning and removal of spillages.

■ All receptacles should be capable of being cleaned and have tight-fitting lids to prevent insects, birds and rodents gaining access.

■ The refuse area must be well drained, and have an impervious surface that is capable of being cleaned.

■ Standpipes, hoses and high-pressure sprays should be provided for cleaning purposes.

■ The receptacles and refuse area must be thoroughly cleaned after emptying.

■ Refuse areas must not be so far from the food rooms that they discourage their use, nor should they be so close that they encourage flies to enter the food rooms.

### Refuse compaction

■ A well-run compaction system improves hygiene.

■ Cleaning of refuse areas is also easier and spillages are reduced.

■ The capital cost of refuse compactors must be compared against collection charges, cleaning and pest control.

### Sanitary disposal

■ The law requires that suitable hygiene provision is made for the disposal of sanitary dressing where an establishment employs ten women or more.

■ Customer welfare must be considered when selecting a method of disposal.

■ A regular contract service is available which uses specially designed containers placed in WC cubicles to afford privacy. These are regularly collected and replaced by fresh, sterilised containers. The contractor is responsible for the safe disposal of the contents away from the customer's premises.

■ Contractors should be asked to undertake a survey to establish the optimum number of sanitary towel dispensers, rate of replenishment and the number and siting of disposal units.

## Cleaning and disinfecting facilities

Within the kitchen design there must be the following:

■ Adequate facilities for cleaning and disinfection of utensils and equipment must be provided.

■ Utensils and equipment should be constructed of corrosion-resistant materials such as stainless steel which is capable of being thoroughly cleaned.

■ Sinks must have adequate supplies of hot and cold water.

■ Taps should be wall-mounted with no direct connections to sinks, for easy cleaning.

■ Wastepipes should be of plastic push-fit ware.

■ The sink should be free-standing so that it can be removed easily after unscrewing the trap joint and easing free the wastepipe.

■ Sterilising sinks and the rinse of dishwashing and tray-cleaning machines should operate at 82°C for sterilisation purposes.

## Accommodation for staff

Good clean accommodation for staff is essential if they are to be encouraged to work cleanly and hygienically. If clean conditions are provided and maintained for staff then those individuals will be encouraged to take ownership of the working practices necessary to provide an ideal hygienic working environment. This is a necessary step in total quality management.

The accommodation must be readily accessible to staff, and whilst in smaller premises where only one or two are employed, a single lavatory may suffice, in larger premises involving numbers of employees, it will be necessary to have separate accommodation for each sex, which should be situated on different floor levels.

Adequate accommodation must be provided for outdoor and other clothing and footwear not worn by the staff during working hours. These articles of clothing must not be stored in a food room and therefore, must be stored in separate lockers allocated to each member of staff.

It is advisable that a separate room be designated as a cloakroom so that clothes can be stored conveniently. Adequate washing facilities should be provided in the cloakroom, to encourage staff to wash their hands frequently and to reinforce personal hygiene.

### Washing facilities

The kitchen and food premises must have adequate facilities for hand washing and drying in all areas of the kitchen where food processing, preparation and handling are carried out:

- Wash hand basins must be located in such a way that they are easily accessible and encourage hand washing. They should never be obstructed.
- Wash hand basins must be kept clean and maintained in a good condition.
- A minimum of two wash hand basins should be fitted in premises where both raw and high-risk foods are handled.
- Washing facilities provided in food rooms should be additional to those in conjunction with sanitary conditions.
- All basins and troughs should be preferably made of stainless steel and connected to drains by properly trapped wastepipes.

### Sanitary conveniences

Sanitary accommodation must be clean, well lit and in efficient working order. The walls, floors and ceilings must be smooth, impervious surfaces capable of being easily cleaned.

All WCs and urinals must:

- Be separately ventilated to the exterior or, if artificially ventilated, then they should be provided at six changes per hour.
- Be entered from an intervening space, separately ventilated to the external air – they must not be entered direct from a food room or work room.
- Have foot- or knee-operated devices if possible, or light-sensitive devices.
- Have doors to intervening space; doors to sanitary accommodation should be self-closing.
- Have notices posted in the appropriate languages, according to the profile of the employees – always in English but often supplementary languages are requested – telling users to wash their hands.
- Have one wash hand basin for each WC or three urinals.

## FOOD PRODUCTION EQUIPMENT

The type, amount and size of equipment will depend on the type of menu being provided. Not only should the equipment be suitably situated but also the working height is very important to enable the equipment to be used without causing excess fatigue. Kitchen equipment manufacturers and gas and electricity suppliers can provide details of equipment relating to output and size.

The various preparation processes require different types of equipment and facilities depending on what food is involved. A vegetable preparation area means that water from the sinks and dirt from the vegetables are going to accumulate and therefore adequate facilities for drainage should be provided. Pastry preparation, on the other hand, entails mainly dry processes.

Whatever the processes, there are certain basic rules that can be applied which not only make for easier working conditions but also help to ensure that the food hygiene regulations are complied with.

Kitchens can be divided into sections, based on the production process:

- Dry areas – stores, storage.

- Wet areas – fish preparation, vegetable preparation, butchery, cold preparation.

- Hot wet areas – boiling, poaching, steaming.
    - Equipment – atmospheric steamers, pressure steamers, combination oven, bratt pans, steam-jacketed boilers.

- Hot dry areas – frying, roasting, grilling.
    - Equipment – cool zone fryers, pressure fryers, bratt pans, roasting ovens, charcoal grills, salamanders, induction cookers, halogen cookers, microwave, cook-and-hold ovens.

- Dirty areas – refuse, pot wash areas, plate wash.
    - Equipment – compactors, refuse storage units, pot wash machines, dishwashers, glass washers.

Consideration must be given to the management policy on buying raw materials. Choice will determine kitchen plans on handling raw materials. Prepared food will require different types of equipment and labour requirements compared with part-prepared food or raw-state ingredients.

### Prepared food examples

- sous-vide products
- cook–chill
- cook–freeze
- prepared sweets.

### Part-prepared

- peeled and cut vegetables
- convenience sauces and soups
- portioned fish/meat.

### Raw state

- unprepared vegetables
- meat which requires butchering
- fish requiring filleting and portioning.

## The choice of layout

A selection of equipment will be made after detailed consideration of:

- The functions that will be carried out within the cooking area of the kitchen.
- The amount of equipment, which will depend upon the complexity of the menus offered.
- The quantity of meals served.
- The policy of management in use of materials, from the traditional kitchen organisation using only fresh vegetables and totally unprepared items, to the use of prepared foods, chilled items, frozen foods, where the kitchen consists of a regeneration unit only.

Given, however, that a certain amount of equipment is required, the planner has the choice of a number of possible layouts, within the constraints of the building shape and size and the location of services. The most common are the island groupings, wall siting and the use of an L- or U-shaped layout and variations upon these basic themes.

## Equipment design

The Food Safety General Food Hygiene Regulations 1995 require the following to be incorporated into equipment design:

- That all articles, fittings and equipment with which food comes into contact be kept clean and be constructed of such materials and maintained in such condition and repair so as to minimise the risk of contamination, enabling it to be thoroughly cleaned and, where necessary, disinfected.
- That equipment be installed in a way which allows the surrounding area to be cleaned.

Construction materials must be: non-toxic, non-flaking, corrosion-resistant, durable, resistant to heat and resistant to acids. Food contact surfaces should be:

- easy to clean
- smooth and continuous surfaces without breaks, cracks, open seams, chips or pitting. It is extremely difficult to clean internal corners and crevices.

Unless designed for cleaning in situ, all food contact surfaces must be accessible for cleaning and inspection by easy methods of dismantling.

Equipment containing bearings and gears which require unsafe lubricants should be designed and constructed so that the lubricant used cannot leak or drip or be forced into the food or on to food contact surfaces. Only safe lubricants should be used on equipment designed to receive lubrication of bearings and gears in or within food contact surfaces.

Food contact surfaces need regular disinfection, therefore care must be taken in selecting materials used for these surfaces. Stainless steel is recommended (the best available is 18/8 stainless steel: 18 per cent chromium, 8 per cent nickel).

Small items of equipment, for example knife handles and brushes, should be made of cleanable materials. Care must be taken in dealing with equipment made of copper, zinc or cadmium. These metals are absorbed by acid food and may cause metallic food poisoning.

## Design and construction of equipment

Equipment must be so designed, constructed and finished that it can be easily cleaned and disinfected, safely, thoroughly and rapidly, without the need for skilled fitters or specialised tools.

Equipment such as gravity feed slicers, mixers, processors and so on, which do require dismantling for cleaning must be easy to take apart and reassemble. All edges must be smooth and rounded. Rough and sharp edges constitute a serious hazard to cleaners. If equipment is difficult to dismantle and may result in a danger to operatives, those responsible for cleaning will be reluctant to do so. This results in a lowering of hygiene standards and possible health risks.

The buyer of the equipment should also check that all joints and welds are smooth, and that nuts, bolts and screw heads are absent from food contact surfaces. All hinges should be capable of being taken apart for cleaning. No crevices in fitting panels, open joints and rough seams should be present in the equipment; if any of these are, they have a tendency to become filled with accumulations of food, grease and dirt which in turn will support bacterial growth and may then provide a food source for pest infestation.

### FOOD AND BEVERAGE SERVICE AREAS

Food and beverage service areas fall into two categories: those for customer and staff usage and those for staff usage only. Staff and customer usage areas include consumption areas such as dining areas and service areas such as in cafeterias, bars and the associated services. Staff areas include stillroom, wash-up, storage and cellar areas.

The general considerations for staff usage areas are:

- Appropriate siting and with logical layout of equipment.
- Ease of delivery access.
- Ease of service.
- Ensuring hygiene, health and safety requirements are met.
- Ease of cleaning.
- Sufficient storage space for service equipment and food items.
- Security.

The general considerations for areas used by both customers and staff include first the general considerations for staff-only areas as above and in addition take into account the meal experience factor of atmosphere (see page 53). This includes consideration of:

- decor and lighting
- heating and ventilation
- noise
- the size and shape of the areas.

## Decor and lighting

The general considerations on decor are:

- Appropriateness to the type and style of the operation.
- Sufficient flexibility especially where the space has multi-usage, for example function rooms.
- Functional reliability.
- Ease of maintenance including soft (on-going) and programmed refurbishment.
- Industrial rather than domestic quality.
- Ease of cleaning and general housekeeping needs.

Lighting, itself an architectural feature, is a pivotal ingredient in foodservice operational design. Just as important is the fact that colours have cognitive and emotional content and are thus just as crucial in the overall design process. Contemporary lighting and colour designs tend towards a versatile system of lighting by which a food and beverage service area may have bright lighting at lunchtime and a more diffused form of lighting in the evening. Lighting can create image, generate atmosphere and seamlessly communicate a marketing and merchandising message. In tandem, it can determine quality, price and speed of turnover. The principal rule in lighting provision is that it be neither too bright nor too dark. Brilliant lighting does not create comfortable or intimate surroundings. Dim lighting limits sensory evaluation and may inhibit safe working practices. It is an advantage to be able to change the colour of the lights for special functions, and technology enhances these possibilities.

There used to be two main kinds of interior illumination: incandescent and fluorescent. Incandescent lighting is warmer in colour but less efficient to operate than fluorescent bulbs of the same wattage. It can be easily directed to specific spots such as a particular table or painting, however its warmth appeal can cause a colour problem. It may make surroundings cheerful and inviting, but the yellowish hue of its bulbs, especially when dimmed, makes meats and lettuce appear muddy in colour. Warmer bulbs such as pink light make red meats look natural but salads unappetising. Localised incandescent lighting can be perfect when teamed with other lighting like wall lamps and hanging lamps placed strategically. Brilliant overhead lighting spoils the feeling of personal space. It may be appropriate for places where volume social interaction is desirable, but it has no place in intimate dining environs.

Fluorescent lighting is generally unsuited to dining areas, being unattractive to food and to customers. Its lower operating cost means, however, it is often considered, and in this case warm-tone tubes should be specified. It is therefore felt that a balance is needed for both warmth and good food appearance. Incandescent and halogen lighting is preferred.

The average food and beverage service area needs to select the correct mix of decor and functional lighting. It is only the fast food areas, for instance, that may successfully eliminate decor or mood lighting altogether. Brighter lights subconsciously inform customers to eat more quickly and leave. A summary of contemporary lighting and usage is given in Table 5.1.

The colour scheme should reflect the main qualities of the operation. A well-designed colour scheme can easily be spoilt by a badly planned lighting system and therefore the two aspects should be considered together at the design stage. Warm colours stimulate appetite and create a pleasant environment but should be applied with caution.

## Heating and ventilation

There are two dimensions to heating and lighting:

■ The maintenance of a reasonable temperature.

■ The ventilation of the areas.

The temperature of food and beverage service areas will change depending on the volume of customers and how long they stay in an area. For every ten people this is equivalent to turning on a 1 kilowatt fire. Temperature control will therefore need to take this into account, especially where customers are in dining areas for a long period such as in function operations. Temperature also has an actual and a perceived reality. Customers will have preferred locations depending on their perceptions of the heating; they may ask to sit by a window, for example, as this is considered a cooler part of the room, or not by

**Table 5.1   Examples of contemporary lighting usage**

| Lighting type | Usage |
|---|---|
| Portable luminaires | Table lights, candles, lamps etc. all pool light in the centre of a dining table, offering a degree of intimacy |
| Pendants | Suspended over tables offer an alternative to the portable luminaires. Useful where tables are unlikely to be moved |
| Up lighting | Can provide dramatic, theatrical, architectural effects at any height |
| Down lighting | Should be directional so that they can provide table intimacy, defining one from another |
| Highlighting | Ideal for picking out architectural and design features. Considered to be a highly sophisticated tool in lighting/accenting foliage, paintings, sculptures etc. |
| Wall lighting | Can accent, highlight or softly wash walls. It can also provide lighting for artworks and other features |
| Ambient lighting | The sum total of the lighting creating the effect required |
| Gobos projectors | Providing theatrical effects, which under the right conditions, add greatly to the overall interior design. Gobos projectors offer colour transition with infinite possibilities. The projected light can be directed at floor, wall or ceiling height |
| Fibre optics | Can provide highly decorative and dynamic lighting with the capacity to provide smooth colour transition |
| Cold cathode | Providing long life and low voltage, this multi-functional lighting has the ability for dimming. |

the door because of suspected draughts, or not near the buffet because of the heat or cold. In all these examples, the actual temperature may be the same as other areas of the room.

In areas where food and beverages are served there are inevitably smells which come from these areas. It is a truism that a single food smell is generally liked, for example fresh coffee or freshly baked bread, but that a combination of food smells is usually unpleasant. Some restaurant environments, however, utilise the smell of food and beverage effectively to promote customer comfort and promote sales as part of merchandising. In general, though, food smells are best avoided and the ventilation systems should be able to take account of this requirement. The other aspects to take account of here are the smells that result from smoking or, more specifically, the drifting of smoke.

## Ambient noise

Because of equipment movement and customer and staff conversation, food and beverage service areas can be noisy. The customer expectation is that generally the higher the service level and price, then the lower the noise level that will be tolerated. This is also affected by the time of day, for instance breakfast can be more acceptably noisy than dinner. Care needs to be taken in the design and selection of materials and equipment in order to contain noise at appropriate and acceptable levels. Sound-absorbing materials in walls, floors and ceilings can assist greatly. Acoustical materials for ceilings and walls are generally the largest target areas for noise control. The floor space is another major surface area which, when carpeted, actively controls noise. Window treatments and tabletop linen also absorb noise pollution.

Another issue is that of noise transmission from one area to another, as in an adjacent bar, lounge and kitchen. Sound transmission should really be considered and alleviated at the planning phase; afterwards it is a matter of control and the effective use of acoustical materials. Background music systems can also cause problems. It is an area of great controversy, with very clear views being expressed, as to why background music systems can aid or hinder operations. In general it depends on the particular style of the operation and the image that it is trying to project. If background systems are to be used then it is worth investing in high-quality equipment. Cheap and badly regulated equipment is distressful and fatiguing for customers. Not surprisingly, our appetite can quickly become suppressed or even turned off by negative influences. Noise, poor lighting, impressions of unsanitary conditions and feeble interior architecture and design all play such a part.

## The size and shape of the areas

Not only do the size and shape of the room affect the customers' enjoyment of the meal but also, in table service areas, the location of the tables becomes important.

Some issues to consider are:

■ The location of tables in a food service area especially taking into account the needs of the single diner and couples.

■ Facing positions (for example, not towards service areas, walls, doors, or too close to service stations).

■ Access for those with disabilities.

■ Ease of work flow.

■ Evenness of temperature and ventilation (including avoiding air-conditioning, heating and extraction hot spots).

■ Access to exits and toilets.

■ Avoiding being directly in the path of live or piped music systems.

## FOOD AND BEVERAGE SERVICE EQUIPMENT

The general points to be considered when purchasing equipment for a food and beverage service area are:

- flexibility of use
- type of service being offered
- type of customer and the nature of demand being met
- design
- colour
- durability
- ease of maintenance
- part replacement
- stackability
- costs and funds available
- availability in the future – replacements
- storage
- rate of breakage, for example for china
- shape
- psychological effect on customers
- delivery time.

## Furniture

Furniture must be chosen according to the needs of the establishment and the variation in human body dimensions. The type of operation being run determines the specific needs as far as the dining arrangements are concerned. A summary of possible dining arrangements is given in Table 5.2.

In determining the specification for furniture for a foodservice operation, the following factors might be taken into account:

- comfort
- cost
- design
- durability
- function
- movability

**Table 5.2   Dining arrangement**

| Type | Description of furniture |
|------|--------------------------|
| Loose random | Free-standing furniture positioned in no discernible pattern within a given area |
| Loose module | Free-standing furniture positioned within a given area to a predetermined pattern with or without the use of dividers to create smaller areas within a module |
| Booth | Fixed seating, usually high-backed, used to create secluded seating |
| High density | Furniture with minimum dimensions and usually fixed in nature positioned within a given area to create maximum seating capacity |
| Module | Seating incorporates table and chairs constructed as one and may be fixed |
| In situ | Customers served in areas not designed for service, e.g. aircraft and hospital beds |
| Bar and lounge areas | Customers served in areas not conventionally designed for eating |

- multi-functionality
- safety
- structure and materials
- storage capacity (if required).

Very often, by using different materials, designs and finishes and by careful arrangement, the atmosphere and appearance of the food and beverage service area can be changed to suit different occasions. Restaurant and bar furniture needs careful consideration. It needs to reinforce the aesthetics, style and ambience of the operation. The ergonomics have to be carefully considered. Furniture needs to be sturdy yet easily moved, versatile, durable, low-maintenance and with a superior finish. Where possible prior to purchase, performance evaluation should be carried out. This should definitely be requested where consultants are employed.

Wood is the most commonly used material in food and beverage service areas. It is found as the principal material in chairs and tables in a variety of foodservice operations. There are various types of wood and wood-grain finishes, each suitable to blend with a particular decor. Wood is strong and rigid and resists wear and stains.

Although wood predominates, more metals, mainly aluminium and aluminium-plated steel or brass, are gradually being introduced into food and beverage areas. Aluminium is lightweight and hardwearing, has a variety of finishes, is easily cleaned and the costs are reasonable. Furniture made of more than one material includes a wooden-topped table with a metal base, or a chair with a lightweight metal frame and a plastic finish for the seat and back.

Formica and plastic-coated tabletops may be found in many cafeterias or staff dining rooms. These are easily cleaned, hardwearing and eliminate the use of linen. The tabletop comes in a variety of colours and designs suitable for all situations. If desired, place mats may take the place of linen.

Plastic and fibreglass are used extensively to produce dining room chairs. These materials are easily moulded into a single-piece seat and back to fit the body contours; the chair legs are usually made of metal. The advantages are that these chairs are durable, easily cleaned, lightweight, may be stacked, are available in a large range of colours and designs, and are relatively inexpensive. They are frequently found in bars, lounges and staff dining rooms.

With seating requirements generally, there is a relationship between comfort and the time the customer will tend to spend in the seat. Thus less comfortable but adequately functional seating tends to be used in fast service operations; in higher-level service areas more comfortable seating is provided. It is also true that, because of differences in physiology, women tend to sit up straighter for longer than men. Therefore chairs with arms are more useful in operations meeting the needs of a male-dominated clientele.

Consideration also needs to be given to the needs of children, people with disabilities and the manoeuvrability and stacking capability of seating, especially for function operations.

## Trays

Trays are used throughout foodservice operations. Their use ranges from carrying equipment and food to service on a tray, as in hospital, airline and room service operations.

Additional considerations in the purchase of trays include:

- Lightness and strength – trays should be able to be carried when fully loaded and not become misshapen when weight is placed upon them.
- Stackability.
- Heat resistance.
- Ease of cleaning.
- Resistance to slippage.
- Resistant to damage from spilt items or damp.

## Tables

Tables generally come in four shapes: round, oval, square and rectangular. An establishment may have a mixture of shapes to give variety, or tables all of one shape according to the shape of the room and the style of service being offered. These tables will seat two or four people, and two tables may be pushed together to seat larger parties, luncheons, dinners and weddings. By using extensions, a variety of shapes may be obtained, allowing full use of the room and getting the maximum number of covers in the minimum space.

Examples of sizes are:

**Square**

- 76 cm (2 ft 6 in) square to seat two people.
- 1 m (3 ft approx.) square to seat four people.

**Round**

- 1 m (3 ft approx.) in diameter to seat four people.
- 1.5 m (5 ft approx.) in diameter to seat eight people.

**Rectangular**

- 137 × 76 cm (4 ft 6 in × 2 ft 6 in) to seat four people and to which extensions would be added for larger parties.

Tables come in many differing sizes, design finishes, colours and bases. There is also the opportunity for custom design and finishing.

## Chairs

Chairs come in an enormous range of designs, materials and colours to suit all situations and occasions. Because of the wide range of styles, the chairs vary in height and width, but as a guide, a chair seat is 46 cm (18 in.) from the ground, the height from the ground to the top of the back is 1 m (39 in.) and the depth from the front edge of the seat to the back of the chair is 46 cm (18 in.).

Additional purchasing considerations are the size, height, shape and the variety of seating required – banquette, armchairs, straight-backed, action-backed and padded chairs – giving the guest a choice, and also including high chairs for toddlers and kiddy boosters or cushions for children. Care also needs to be taken in matching chairs and seating generally with table heights, especially where chairs and tables in both metric and imperial measurements are being used.

## Sideboards

The style and design of a sideboard vary from establishment to establishment. They are dependent upon:

- the style of service and the menu offered
- the number of waiters working from one sideboard or workstation

- the number of tables to be served from one sideboard
- the amount of equipment that the sideboard is expected to hold.

The majority of commercially available sideboards are insufficient in strength, storage capability and worktop provision. It is now more usual for operations to design and build their own sideboards or workstations, often incorporating them as part of the design of the dining area.

## Linen

There are many qualities of linen in use, from the finest Irish linen and cotton to synthetic materials such as nylon and viscose. The type of linen used would depend on the class of establishment, type of clientele, cost involved, and the style of menu and service to be offered. The main items of linen normally to be found are as follows:

- *Tablecloths*  As table sizes have varied over the years, it is no longer feasible to be overprescriptive in tablecloth sizes. A general guide is to have cloths that will give a 30–45 cm (12–18 in.) drop. Although there are standard sizes (rounds, squares and oblongs), many manufacturers will now supply cloths for a multiplicity of use in differing materials, patterns, weights and colours.
- *Buffet cloths*  Used in long runs for buffet displays, these again vary considerably in size.
- *Trolley cloths and sideboard cloths*  These are often custom made from well-worn tablecloths, which are no longer suitable for use on tables, and folded to fit a sideboard or trolley.
- *Waiter's cloth or service cloth*  Used by service staff as protection against heat and to keep uniforms clean, these cloths are available in a variety of sizes and materials.
- *Tea- and glasscloths*  Used for drying purposes, these lint-free cloths are available in a variety of sizes and qualities.

Operations need to make arrangement to ensure the availability of linen to meet operation needs. Decisions need to be made on whether the operation should:

- have an in-house laundry and its own linen
- purchase its own linen and use an off-site commercial laundry, or
- have a linen rental contract with an external commercial laundry.

In essence it comes down to the requirements and size of the operation, its capacity in terms of available space to site a laundry and available capital for initial steep outlay. If the business is part of a group, another option may well be to utilise a centralised laundry service for the group.

The advantages of having an in-house laundry are:

- Less stock required through quicker return of linen.
- Ability to handle emergency requirements.
- Complete control of the treatments.
- Greater stock control and increased life of articles.
- Lower charges and in the long term more economic processing of linen.
- Prestige.

The disadvantages are:

- Difficulty of providing the necessary space for an in-house laundry facility.
- High initial capital outlay and increasing maintenance costs through time.
- Usage limited to stock availability.
- Dependency on technical expertise.

The advantages of having off-site commercial laundering are:

- No capital outlay if using hire company.
- Less-skilled personnel required.
- No worries over repair or replacement of linen.
- Less storage required on-site so available space can be utilised for other purposes.
- Costs can be evened out and controlled.

The disadvantages are:

- The total process takes longer and there can be delivery and collection delays.
- Higher stock required if buying own linen.
- Tendency to be less flexible in peak periods or if unexpected business occurs.
- Extra costs can be incurred for special treatment of linen.
- Losses of stock can occur.
- If hiring linen then any damages have to be paid for.

## China

When purchasing china, factors to consider are:

- Every item of earthenware should have a complete cover of glaze to ensure a reasonable length of life.
- China should have a rolled edge, which will give added reinforcement at the edge and reduce the possibility of chipping.

■ The pattern should be under rather than on top of the glaze. However, this demands additional glaze and firing. Patterns on top of the glaze will wear and discolour very quickly. Therefore, china with the pattern under the glaze is more expensive but its life will be longer.

Some manufacturers stamp the date, month and year on the base of the item. From this the life of the china, under normal usage, can be determined more accurately.

Earthenware which is produced for catering purposes is often given a trade name by the manufacturer to indicate its strength. Some examples are: steelite, vitreous, vitrock, vitrex, vitresso, ironstone and vitrified. Of these, vitrified ware is recognised to be the strongest. This does not mean, however, that every foodservice operator buys vitrified hotelware, as other factors apart from strength and economy are often taken into account.

### Sizes

There are more manufacturers of china in the marketplace than ever before. Foodservice operations can now choose not simply in terms of durability, but with bespoke design, size, colour, weight and shape as just part of an overall package. There is a wide range of traditional items available and their exact sizes vary according to the manufacturer and the design produced. As a general guide, traditional sizes are as follows:

| | |
|---|---|
| Sideplate | 15 cm (6 in.) diameter |
| Sweet plate | 18 cm (7 in.) diameter |
| Fish plate | 20 cm (8 in.) diameter |
| Soup plate | 20 cm (8 in.) diameter |
| Joint plate | 25 cm (10 in.) diameter |
| Cereal/sweet plate | 13 cm (5 in.) diameter |
| Breakfast cup and saucer | 23–28 cl (8–10 fl oz) |
| Teacup and saucer | 18.93 cl ($6\frac{2}{3}$ fl oz) |
| Coffee cup and saucer (*demi-tasse*) | 9.47 cl (3.4 fl oz) |
| Teapot | 28.4 cl ($\frac{1}{2}$pt), 56.8 cl (1 pt) 85.2 cl ($1\frac{1}{2}$pt), 113.6 cl (2 pt) |

Other items of china required may include:

■ Salad crescent

■ Hot water jugs

■ Milk jugs

■ Cream jugs

■ Coffee pots

■ Hot milk jugs

■ Consommé cup and saucer

■ Sugar basin

■ Butter dishes

■ Ashtrays

■ Egg cups

■ Soup bowl/cup

■ Platter (oval plate)

The use of china varies. Some considerations are:

■ The extent to which there is to be common usage of items thus reducing the level of stock, for example using one size of plate for fish and sweet courses or using one bowl for items such as soup, fruit and cereal.

■ The extent to which different service areas and different service times might have different china. For example, different banqueting china from coffee shop china or larger cups for breakfast.

■ The extent to which the various china items should match. It has become quite common to have differing designs of china according to different types of dish and also to mix complementary patterns.

## Tableware

The term tableware covers:

■ *Flatware*  All forms of spoon and fork.
■ *Cutlery*  Knives and other cutting implements.
■ *Hollow-ware*  Any item made from silver, apart from flatware and cutlery, for example teapots, milk jugs, sugar basins, oval flats.

The majority of food service areas use either plated silverware or stainless steel.

For silver, the manufacturer will often quote 20-, 25- or 30-year plate. This denotes the length of life a manufacturer may claim for the plate subject to fair or normal usage. The length of life of silver also depends upon the weight of silver deposited. There are three standard grades of silverplate: full standard plate, triple plate and quadruple plate.

British Standard BS 5577 was introduced in 1978. In silver plated tableware, two grades are specified:

■ standard – for general use
■ restaurant – thicker grade for restaurant use and marked with an R.

The minimum thickness of silver plating quoted should give a life of at least 20 years, depending on usage.

Plain cutlery and flatware are more popular than patterned for the simple reasons that they are cheaper and easier to keep clean.

Stainless steel flatware and cutlery are available in a variety of grades. The higher-priced designs usually have incorporated in them alloys of chromium (which makes the metal stainless) and nickel (which gives a fine grain and lustre). Good British flatware and cutlery are made of 18/8 stainless steel. This is 18 per cent chromium and 8 per cent nickel. A higher grade is 18/10.

Stainless steel is finished by different degrees of polishing;

- high polish finish
- dull polish finish
- a light-grey matt, non-reflective finish.

General considerations for choosing a selection of tableware items can include the extent to which items will have more than one purpose, for example using jugs for hot water, hot milk or cold milk, or using standard ranges of cutlery such as sweet/soup spoons, and general-purpose knives and forks rather than having, say, separate fish knives and forks.

## Glassware

Glass contributes to the appearance of the table and the overall attraction of the room. There are many standard patterns available to the caterer (see Table 5.3). Most manufacturers now supply hotel glassware in standard sizes for convenience of ordering, availability and quick delivery.

Except in certain speciality restaurants or high-class establishments, where either coloured glassware or cut glassware may be used, hotel glassware is usually plain.

A good wine glass should be plain and clear so the colour and brilliance of a wine can be clearly seen; it should have a stem for holding the wine glass so that the heat of one's hand does not affect the wine on tasting; there should be a slight incurving lip to help hold the aroma and it should be large enough to hold the particular wine being tasted.

**Table 5.3   Glassware and sizes**

| Glass | Size |
|---|---|
| Wine goblets | 14.20, 18.93, 22.72 cl (5, $6^2/_3$, 8 fl oz) |
| German/Alsace | 18, 23 cl (6, 8 fl oz) |
| Flute | 18, 23 cl (6, 8 fl oz) |
| Saucer champagne | 18, 23 cl (6, 8 fl oz) |
| Cocktail glasses | 4, 7 cl (2, 3 fl oz) |
| Sherry, port | 4.735 cl |
| Highball | 23, 28 cl (9, 10 fl oz) |
| Worthington | 28, 34 cl (10, 12 fl oz) |
| Lager glass | 28, 34 cl (10, 12 fl oz) |
| Brandy balloon | 23, 28 cl, (9, 10 fl oz) |
| Liqueur glass | 2.367 cl |
| Tumbler | 28.40 cl ($^1/_2$ pint) |
| Beer | 25, 50 cl ($^1/_2$, 1 pint) |

## DISPOSABLES

The choice of which disposable to use may be determined by:

■ Necessity because of situations such as outdoor catering, automatic vending or fast food.

■ Cost considerations such as cost of laundry or savings on wash-up.

## Types of disposable

The main varieties of disposable available are used, broadly speaking, in the following areas:

■ Storage and cooking purposes.

■ Service of food and beverages, for example plates, knives, forks, cups.

■ Decor – napkins, tablecloths, slipcloths, banquet roll, place mats.

■ Hygiene – wipes.

■ Clothing, for example aprons, chefs' hats, gloves.

■ Packaging – for marketing and presentation purposes.

A considerable advance in the range of disposables available has been the introduction of disposables whose approximation to china and tableware is very close. For instance, they may have a high quality, overall finish and a smooth hard white surface. The plates themselves are strong and rigid with no tendency to bend or buckle, and a plasticising ingredient ensures that they are grease- and moisture-proof, even against hot fat and gravy. Oval luncheon plates, snack trays and compartment plates are all available to the caterer.

The advantages of disposables are:

■ Equipment and labour – disposables reduce the need for washing-up equipment, staff and materials.

■ Hygiene – usage improves the standard of hygiene in an establishment.

■ Time – disposables may speed up service, for example for fast food.

■ Properties – they have good heat retention and insulation properties.

■ Marketing – disposables can be used as a promotional aid.

■ Capital – usage reduces the amount of capital investment.

■ Carriage – they are easily transported.

■ Cost – disposables are cheaper than hiring conventional equipment.

The disadvantages of disposables are:

- Acceptability – customer acceptability may be poor.
- Cost – disposables can be more expensive than some conventional equipment.
- Storage – back-up quantities are required.
- Supply – there is heavy reliance on supply and delivery time.

## BAR AREAS

There are certain essentials necessary in the planning of bars. These are detailed as follows.

## Area

The bar staff must be given sufficient area of space in which to work and move about. There should be a minimum of 1 metre from the back of the bar counter to the storage shelves and display cabinets at the rear of the bar.

## Layout

Careful consideration must be given, in the initial planning, to the layout. Everything should be easily to hand so that the bar staff do not have to move about more than necessary.

## Plumbing and power

It is essential to have hot and cold running water for glass-washing. Power is necessary to provide the effective working of cooling trays, refrigerators and ice-making machines.

## Storage

Adequate storage should be provided, in the form or shelves, cupboard and racks, for all the stock required and equipment listed.

## Safety and hygiene

Great care must be observed so that the materials used in the make-up of the bar are hygienic and safe. Flooring must be non-slip. The bar top should be of a material suited to the general decor that is hard-wearing, easily wiped down and has no sharp edges. The bar top is usually of average working height – of at least 1 m (3 ft) – and a width of 0.6 m (20 in).

For the purpose of the Food Hygiene Regulations, all beverages are food. However, special exemptions are given to some of the provisions provided that only drink (i.e. beers, spirits, liqueurs and such like) is dispensed.

Some aspects of the provisions should be given particular attention. These are:

- Suitable overclothing.
- Possible contamination through smoking when handling food and drink.
- Inadequate glass-washing facilities together with the important process of glass-drying.
- Use of ullage and the possibility of contamination.
- Correct use of materials in bar design to facilitate easy cleaning.

## AUTOMATIC VENDING

In the broadest sense, automatic vending may be defined as 'time-saving selling by automation' for convenience. Vended goods have 24-hour availability and the units can be sited wherever required. It is a form of automatic retailing using one of the following:

- coin
- token
- banknote
- moneycard.

The types of service available may be broken down into two areas, namely service and facilities and consumables. Examples are listed in Table 5.4.

Within a catering framework, 'automatic vending' refers to the supply of a wide range of beverages, both hot and cold, through coin- or token-operated machines.

**Table 5.4   Vending service and facilities, and consumables**

| Service and facilities | Consumables |
| --- | --- |
| Television time | Hot and cold beverages |
| Gas | Meals |
| Water | Confectionery |
| Electricity | Tobacco |
| Shoe cleaning | Alcoholic drinks |
| Car parking | |
| Toilets | |
| Baggage store | |

## Types of machine

- *Merchandiser*  Sells its product as seen visually by the customer, for example confectionery machines.
- *Beverage vendor*  Mixes the ingredients in individual cups to which water is added.
- *In-cup system*  Ingredients are already in individual cups to which water is added.
- *Micro-vend system*  Provides a range of hot foods from which the customer may make a selection.

## Catering services

The catering services provided may come in the form of:

- Hot beverages, by use of powdered ingredients.
- Cold beverages, by use of post-mix syrup and water (carbonated or non-carbonated).
- Hot meals, by internal heating or with the use of microwaves and time cards or tokens.
- Meals and snacks, by means of refrigeration.

The numbers and types of machines required will depend on their location, the type and number of people they are providing a service for, the cost factor and the variety of food and beverage items required.

The machines required might be installed either individually or in small groups, to supplement the conventional catering establishment or to cover a small-scale demand that does not warrant the expense of employing the extra labour and plant. The opposite to this would be the installation of a complete vending service where demand is highly volatile, space is limited and the use of staffed operations would be uneconomical.

## Purchasing considerations

General factors, which should be considered prior to purchasing and in relation to vending equipment, may be summarised as follows:

- Cup sales (may be one to two drinks per person per day when charged but could double if offered free).
- Ingredient capacity – related to required periods of restocking.
- Number of selectors (items) available; this will often relate to the demand (anticipated number of customers).
- Hygiene – ease of cleaning.
- Extraction efficiency for heat/steam systems.
- Restocking – ease of filling.

- Maintenance – regular servicing contract.
- Physical dimensions/acceptability – will the machine fit into the environment and blend in with the decor?
- Siting – as close as is feasible to those using the machine, that is either on the workfloor or in a food service area so as to maximise use.
- Weight (floor loading) – ease of moving for cleaning and siting purposes.
- Availability of power and plumbing.
- Capital available – should the machine be leased, purchased or taken on a contract basis?
- Training – can staff be trained easily to replenish, clean and maintain machines?
- Policy – there must be clear guidelines linked to failure of a machine and insurance cover.

The potential disadvantages of vending are:

- It cannot accommodate rapid large-scale service.
- There is potential for vandalism and theft.
- Power failures will stop the equipment's functioning.
- It may be viewed by some customers as unsightly and remote, and lacking in true service elements.
- Some beverage units may require plumbing into mains water which may restrict their ideal siting.
- It may not be readily accessible to all who wish to use it.

## STAFFING

Staff have a critical influence on the success of a foodservice operation. Most businesses that fail to provide superior customer service do so because they have failed to recruit individuals that their customers would appreciate. The penalties are extreme, in terms of customer defection and loss of sales and profits.

Within a foodservice operation there are a range of roles. These include staffing for:

- food production
- food service
- beverage service
- marketing
- sales promotion

- merchandising
- financial and physical resource management
- people management
- supervisory management.

The true strength of a foodservice operation is the opportunity for human interface and the ability of its people to maximise that opportunity. Achieving this requires a systematic and analytical approach. When selecting customer contact personnel it is crucial to have people who are likely to be liked by customers and whose personal attributes include a positive attitude and a customer-orientated approach. Foodservice operations investing solely in greater efficiencies and mechanistic interactions can sacrifice the invigorative energies required to sustain positive and rewarding relationships with customers.

## Optimising human resources

The key selection attributes of enlightened food and beverage personnel are clear. What is needed is an intrinsic ability to help people; it is an inner genuineness and ability to satisfy the needs of others. Willingness to learn is also very important, as is a sense of urgency.

Staffing is a major resource, and maximising the potential of this resource requires the management of staffing to be at the forefront of the organisation and not within the traditional personnel (or human resources) department. It should be as prominent in the requirements of management responsibilities as are the management responsibilities for operations, finance and sales and marketing: it is a strategic partner with the organisation.

With more and more individuals entering the industry with improved educational qualifications, which is presenting its own challenges, it is easy to see that those individuals require higher maintenance. But in order to achieve a positive outcome, people need to be challenged and motivated through opportunity. Compensation through rewards and recognition should support this. Human resources should be the business' strength: the essence of the core competence.

The management of people is not, and should not be, primarily an administrative function. Managing people, developing teams and individuals, are all activities that are integral parts of the management of operations.

## Staff organisation

Staff organisation in food and beverage operations is focused upon having sufficient trained and competent staff on duty to match the expected volume of customer demand.

The staffing required will be as much dependent on the nature of the various methods being adopted – production method, service method, control method – as it is on determining the staffing levels to meet the expected volume of customer demand.

Customer demand, or throughput, can be determined from sales records. There is clearly also a relationship between the volume of customers served and the length of time they stay on the premises. The time that customers take in different types of operation varies.

There is also a relationship between the volume of customers and the opening times of the operation. For example, in a full-service restaurant the seating time of customers might average one and a half hours. If the restaurant is open for four hours, then it might be possible to fill the operation twice. If, however, the opening hours are only two and a half, then this would not be possible.

Opening times are determined by the consideration of:

■ local competition

■ local attractions, for example theatre

■ location of the premises, for example city centre/country/suburb

■ catchment area

■ transport systems

■ staffing availability

■ volume of business

■ local tradition.

Customer throughput can be calculated for different types of operation. Examples of how this can be determined for different types of operation are as follows.

### Table and assisted service operations

Since all customers are usually seated in both table and assisted service methods, throughput can be estimated for new operations as the level of throughput will be limited by the length of seating time and the opening hours of the operation. For existing operations, sales records will provide a guide to potential throughput. Staffing for each service period can then be estimated and allocated to specific duties. Staffing will also need to be estimated for preparation before and for clearing following service. Thus a restaurant open for two and a half hours at lunchtime may require staff for up to five hours.

To calculate the total staffing required:

1 Estimate the number of staff required for each range of duties per service period in one week.

2 Multiply the number of staff per service period by the number of hours to be worked in each period.

3 Divide total staff hours by full-time working week hours. This will give the full-time equivalent of number of staff required.

4 Mix full-time, part-time, casual, seasonal and temporary staff hours to cover all service periods.

5 Draw up staff rota which may need to be on a two- or three-week cycle to allow for days off and so on.

The number of staff to each service period can now be calculated and a rota drawn up. However, the actual staffing levels for these types of operation are determined taking account of various ratios. One such ratio might be covers per head, such as in determining the number of covers served by a station in a restaurant; another might be revenue per head.

## Cafeteria operations

There are five factors that influence potential throughput in cafeterias. These are:

- Service time – the time it takes each customer to pass along or by the counter and reach the till point.
- Service period – the time the cafeteria is actually serving.
- Till speed – the time it takes for customer to be billed and payment taken.
- Eating/seating time.
- Seating capacity.

The main criterion is seating capacity. The speed required in the queue is determined by the seating capacity and the average seating time. For example: a cafeteria with 186 seats and with a till speed of 9 per minute, will take 20.66 minutes to fill the cafeteria. If the customers' seating time is 20 minutes, then the cafeteria will be filled just after the first customers are leaving. A faster till speed will mean that the last customer through the till will have nowhere to sit. Too slow a till speed will mean the cafeteria is not being fully utilised. For one till, four to six people per minute is a maximum.

Generally, if the seating time is greater than the service period then the actual number of seats will need to equal the total number of customers. If the eating time is less than the time it takes to serve all the customers then the number of seats may be less than the actual number of people to be served. However, the queue may need to be staggered to avoid excessive waiting before service.

The staffing levels will take account of the number of till points that need to be open as well as the level of production, clearing and dishwashing required.

## Single-point service operations

Customer throughput in single-point service operations may be taken from records of till transactions. Increases and decreases in the throughput are provided for by increasing or decreasing the number of till points that are open (or in the case of vending, additional machines). If seating areas are provided, then similar calculations to those for cafeterias are carried out, assuming there is a known percentage of customers using the seating facility.

Again, staffing levels will take account of the number of payment points that need to be open as well as the level of production, clearing and dishwashing required.

### Specialised service

For hospital and airline tray methods there is a capacity limitation. For other forms of specialised service methods there are records or estimates of potential take-up of services in specific locations, for example hotel rooms, lounges or home delivery.

## Organising duties

All duties required within the foodservice operation can be broken down into a listing of tasks. These can then be rostered. The exact nature of a duty roster will vary depending on the type of establishment and according to the duties to be performed, the number of staff required, their time off, and whether a split/straight shift is worked.

The purpose of the duty roster is to ensure that all the necessary duties are covered in order that efficient production and service may be carried out. There is an old adage that 'everyone's responsibility is no one's responsibility'. It is crucial, therefore, in foodservice operations that all the required duties are covered and that all managers, supervisors and staff are responsible and accountable for specific tasks.

It is also important that a high level of discipline is observed during service periods. Losing a grip on the flow of the production and service through staff not knowing their responsibilities, or not carrying them out, or misguidedly trying to help others, can lead to chaos, which customers easily detect. Contingency plans should also be made, detailing action to be taken in the event of unexpected increases in business levels or shortages of staff.

Having properly detailed tasks and duty lists also provides the basis for staff training. Task and duty lists are drawn up for each task and duty, and these should identify the standards to be achieved.

## Defining responsibilities

In order for the catering cycle to be carried out efficiently, it is essential that all managers, supervisors and members of staff fully understand their responsibilities, have been trained to carry out their duties and also know the standards of performance which are expected of them. The basis for achieving this can be through having precise, agreed and written job descriptions.

Some examples of key roles within a foodservice operation are:

### Head chef

The head chef is responsible for the ordering, receiving, preparing and serving of all food to guests and staff where it may be required, including restaurant, bars, coffee shop and function rooms, in a hygienic manner.

Specific responsibilities might include:

- Food preparation and storage areas including kitchens, food and equipment stores.
- Food quality.
- Food preparation plant, equipment and utensils.
- Food supplies, cleaning materials.
- Food preparation, storage and wash-up staff including engaging, organising payment for casual labour.
- Petty cash.
- Goods inward bay, swill areas, corridors, wash-up area, stillroom.
- Hygiene standards in all the above areas.

Key targets might include:

- Gross profit in percentage and cash terms.
- Control of labour and other costs in percentage and cash terms.
- Specific customer satisfaction levels.

### Restaurant manager

The restaurant manager is responsible for the satisfactory service of all food and beverages to guests and staff, including the service of special function meals and buffet and cafeteria service.

Specific responsibilities might include:

- Restaurant, dispense bars, cloakrooms.
- Banquet and restaurant furniture and equipment.
- Linen, glass, cutlery and stationery.
- Restaurant floats, takings, petty cash and casual wages for restaurant and function waiting.
- Engagement and organisation of payment of casual staff.
- Uniforms in dining room.
- Transport for late staff.
- Hygiene standards in all the above areas.

Key targets might include:

- Restaurant labour cost in percentage and cash terms.
- Liquor sales in percentage and cash terms.
- Revenue targets and average spend per head figures.
- Specific customer satisfaction levels.

### Bars manager

The bars manager is responsible for the ordering, receiving, preparing and serving of all beverage items to guests and staff where it may be required and the maintenance of satisfactory standards of safety, hygiene, service and customer relations.

Specific responsibilities might include:

- Bars, liquor and tobacco sales areas.
- Bar glassware, equipment and utensils.
- Stocks of alcoholic and associated beverages, tobacco, food and sundry supplies sold in the bars.
- Bar floats and takings.
- Permanent and temporary bar staff.
- Enforcement of licensing, hygiene and safety regulations.

Key targets might include:

- Bar labour and other costs in percentage and cash terms.
- Liquor sales in percentage and cash terms.
- Gross profit in percentage and cash terms.
- Revenue targets and average spend per head figures.
- Specific customer satisfaction levels.

### The sommelier

Sommeliers are specialists in wine service charged with assisting guests in making choices and then ensuring correct service. Alternative terms for a sommelier are wine waiter, wine butler, wine captain, wine steward or, in larger units where they also have responsibility for other personnel, cellar-master. In short, the sommelier is responsible for the satisfactory service of all wine and other drinks to guests and staff including the service of special function meals and buffet service.

Specific responsibilities might include:

- Selecting and ordering wines and spirits.
- Organising the cellar layout and maintenance of the cellar.
- Setting up and maintaining control systems for beverage inventory and inventory tracking.
- Sales tracking.
- Training.
- Cellar, dispense bars.

- Furniture and equipment.
- Staff organisation including the engagement and organisation of payment of casual staff.
- Hygiene standards in all the above areas.

Key targets might include:

- Labour cost in percentage and cash terms.
- Liquor sales in percentage and cash terms.
- Revenue targets and average spend per head figures.
- Specific customer satisfaction levels.

### Storekeeper

The storekeeping duties of any foodservice operation are a crucial part of the business. Effectiveness in the storekeeping has a direct impact on the profitability of the operation.

Many departments draw supplies from stores, including: ancillary services, banqueting, bar(s), lounge(s), kitchen, restaurant, room/floor service and stillroom.

The storekeeper will hold a listing of departments serviced from the stores with each department head and any other authorised signatory's signature.

In short, the storekeeper is responsible for the ordering, receiving, storing and issuing of all stores items where they may be required and the maintenance of satisfactory standards of safety, hygiene, service and interdepartmental relations.

Specific responsibilities might include:

- Control of quality purchasing.
- Ensuring correct procedures are followed in all requisitioning.
- Handling, care and organisation of stock.
- Liaison with a multitude of other departments and their heads.
- Management of the inventory control system.
- Maintenance of vendor relationships.
- Monitoring of market price fluctuations.
- Maintenance of quality standards.
- Recordkeeping.
- Enforcement of hygiene and safety regulations.

Key targets might include:

- Stock and other costs in percentage and cash terms.
- Wastage in percentage and cash terms.

## Staff training

Training is the *systematic development of people*. The general objectives of training are:

- To increase the quantity and quality of output by improving employee skills.
- To reduce accidents.
- To increase the return to the employee in personal rewards, i.e. increase pay, recognition and other benefits which the employee wants from the job.
- To make the operation more profitable by reducing the amount of equipment and material required to produce or sell in a given unit.
- To make it possible for the supervisor to spend less time in correcting mistakes and to spend more in planning.
- To minimise discharges because of inadequate skills.
- To improve morale and achieve a more satisfactory working environment.
- To enable new employees to meet the job requirements and enable experienced employees to accept transfers, adapt to new methods, increase efficiency and adjust to changing needs.
- To encourage willingness, loyalty, interest and the desire to excel.

A training need is present when there is a gap between:

- the knowledge, skills and attitudes displayed by people in their jobs, and
- the knowledge, skills and attitudes needed for them to achieve the results the job requires both now and in the future.

The advantages of well-produced training programmes include:

- Standards of performance required being identified.
- Improved ability of staff.
- Availability of a means of measuring ability.
- More efficient working.
- Clearer responsibilities.

The role of the manager/supervisor in training is to:

- Ensure that staff are competent to carry out the duties required of them.
- Ensure that legal and company requirements are met (for example, no staff under 18 on dangerous machinery).
- Develop and train staff as required.
- Develop existing staff to train others.

- Identify training needs of staff now and in the future.
- Develop the necessary skills in order to achieve the points made on the advantages of well-produced training programmes.

## Health and safety

There are common law duties on employers, which are:

- To select reasonably competent staff (or provide training to bring new recruits up to a reasonable standard of competence).
- To provide adequate materials required for the job.
- To provide a safe system of working (this duty has been taken over to a large extent by the provisions of the Health and Safety at Work Act 1974).

Employees may claim damages from the employer for any injury sustained as a result of any breach of these requirements. Even if there has been no injury, where the employer's breach has created a potential hazard, the employee could be justified in resigning without notice and making a successful claim of unfair constructive dismissal.

**SUMMARY**

This chapter has considered the broad and some detailed considerations in the planning, design, equipping and staffing of foodservice operations. The broad systematic consideration takes into account the market needs, the operational needs, the space allocation requirements, finance availability and hygiene health and safety matters. The detailed considerations have demonstrated how the choice of design and equipment needs to make a contribution both to the customer needs in terms of the whole meal experience and the operational needs of being able to provide customer services. Finally, consideration has been given to some aspects of determining staffing levels for various types of foodservice operation and the importance to the success of the business of defining responsibilities and carrying out training.

**FURTHER READING**

Cracknell, H. L., Kaufman, R. J. and Nobis, C. (2000) *Practical Professional Catering Management*, London: Macmillan.
Fellows, R. and Fellows, J. (1998) *Buildings for Hospitality*, Harlow: Longman.
Jones, C. and Jowett, V. (1998) *Managing Facilities*, Oxford: Butterworth Heinemann.

Jones P. and Merricks, P. (eds) (1994) *The Management of Foodservice Operations*, London: Cassell.

Kinton. R., Cesarani, V. and Foskett, D. (1999) *The Theory of Catering*, London: Hodder and Stoughton.

Lawson, F. (1995) *Restaurants, Clubs and Bars: Planning, Design and Investment for Food Service Facilities*, Oxford: Butterworth Heinemann.

Lillicrap, D., Cousins, J. and Smith, R. (1998) *Food and Beverage Service*, London: Hodder and Stoughton.

Mullins, L. J. (1998) *Managing People in the Hospitality Industry*, 3rd edition, Harlow: Longman.

Riley, M. (2000) *Managing People*, Oxford: Butterworth Heinemann.

# CHAPTER SIX

# FOOD AND BEVERAGE SERVICE

## AIM

This chapter considers various aspects in the management of food and beverage service.

## OBJECTIVES

This chapter is intended to support you in:

■ developing your understanding of the service sequence and the service process

■ identifying and categorising food and beverage service methods

■ exploring the relationship between operational choices in food and beverage service and resource productivity

■ developing approaches to the maintenance of good customer relations

■ dealing with the management of the volume in food and beverage service

■ identifying and applying sales promotion principles

■ managing the seven stages of the service sequence

■ controlling revenue.

## FOOD AND BEVERAGE SERVICE AS TWO SYSTEMS

Food and beverage service has traditionally been seen as a delivery system. However, as we saw in Chapter 1 (page 2), food and beverage service actually consists of two separate systems, which are being managed albeit at the same time (Cousins 1988). These are:

- *The service sequence*, which is primarily concerned with the delivery of food and beverages to the customer.
- *The customer process*, which is primarily concerned with managing the experience of the customer.

Separating the service process into these two systems provides for a better understanding of the processes as well as some indication of potential options in the organisation of food and beverage service.

## The service sequence

The service sequence consists of seven stages (Lillicrap *et al.*, 1998). These are:

1 preparation for service

2 taking orders

3 the service of food and drink

4 billing

5 clearing

6 dishwashing

7 clearing following service.

Within these seven elements, there is a variety of alternative ways of achieving the service. The service sequence is in essence the bridge between the production system, beverage provision and the customer experience (or process). The choices on how the service sequence is designed, planned and controlled are made taking into account a number of organisational variables. These include:

- customer needs
- level of customer demand
- the type and style of the food and beverage operation
- the nature of the customers (non-captive, captive or semi-captive)
- prices to be charged
- production process
- volume of demand

- volume of throughput
- space available
- availability of staff
- opening hours
- booking requirements
- payment requirements
- legal requirements.

## The customer process

If food and beverage service is viewed as primarily a delivery process, then the customer can often be seen as a passive recipient of the service. As a result, systems and procedures tend only to be designed from the delivery perspective. However, as has been indicated in Chapter 1 (page 32), a customer service specification cannot be achieved if it does not take account of both the infrastructure supporting the specification as well as the ability to implement standards within the interactive phase.

If the whole issue of quality is to be taken seriously, then the customers' involvement in the process must be considered. Customers are not passive but provide the impetus for the operations in the first place. In addition, the customer receiving the food and beverage product is required to undertake or observe certain requirements. It therefore makes sense to ensure that this process through which the customer must go is considered and managed.

In food and beverage operations, fifteen separate service methods can be identified if the delivery system, or service sequence approach, is taken. However, this number is reduced when the analysis is taken from the customer process perspective. Four basic customer processes can be identified based on what the customer has to be involved in. These are:

**A**  Service at a laid cover.

**B**  Assisted service – part service at a laid cover and part self-service.

**C**  Self-service.

**D**  Service at a single point (ordering, receipt of order and payment).

In these four service processes, the customer comes to where the food and beverage service is offered and the service is provided in areas primarily designed for the purpose. However, there is then a need for a fifth process where the customer receives the service in another location and where the area is not primarily designed for the purpose. This can be called:

**E**  Specialised service or service in situ.

A summary of the five customer processes is shown in Table 6.1.

**Table 6.1** Simple categorisation of the customer process

| Service method | Food and beverage service area | Ordering/ selection | Service | Dining/ consumption | Clearing |
|---|---|---|---|---|---|
| A Table service | Customer enters area and is seated | From menu | By staff to customer | At laid cover | By staff |
| B Assisted service | Customer enters area and is usually seated | From menu, buffet or passed trays | Combination of both staff and customer | Usually at laid cover | By staff |
| C Self-service | Customer enters | Customer selects own tray | Customer carries | Dining area or takeaway | Various |
| D Single-point service | Customer enters | Ordered at single point | Customer carries | Dining area or takeaway | Various |
| E Specialised or in situ | In situ | From menu or predetermined | Brought to customer | Where served | By staff or customer |

Within the A–E categorisation, all fifteen food and beverage service methods can be shown as follows:

**Group A: Table service**
Service to customers at a laid cover:

1 Waiter:
   (a) silver/English
   (b) family
   (c) plate/American
   (d) butler/French
   (e) Russian
   (f) guéridon.

2 Bar counter

**Group B: Assisted service**
Combination of table service and self-service:

3 Assisted service ('carvery' type operations and buffets)

**Group C: Self-service**
Sell-service of customers:

4 Cafeteria:
  (a) counter
  (b) free flow
  (c) echelon
  (d) supermarket.

(*Note*: some 'call order' production may be included in cafeterias.)

## Group D: Single-point service
Service of customers at a single point – consumed on premises or taken away:

5 Take away
6 Vending
7 Kiosks
8 Food court
9 Bar.

## Group E: Specialised (or in situ)
Service to customers in areas not primarily designed for service:

10 Tray
11 Trolley
12 Home delivery
13 Lounge
14 Room
15 Drive-in.

(*Note*: 'Banquet/function' is a term used to describe food and beverage operations that are providing for a specific number of people at specific times in a variety of dining layouts. Service methods also vary. In these cases, banquet/function catering refers to the organisation of service rather than a specific service method.)

With the exception of group E, the customer process in all other groups is similar within the service methods found in each group. Additionally, the skills, knowledge, tasks and duties required are similar within each group, with group A being the most complex and group D least complex. Group E has a special set of requirements, some of which are different from those found in the other groups. Taking the service sequence, it is possible to identify the commonality of tasks and duties and therefore organisational needs as well as staff development needs, within each service method group.

Viewing food and beverage service from the customer process approach not only ensures a customer-service-based perspective but also allows the management to consider alternatives. It is possible, for instance, to alter the delivery of the service without essentially changing the customer process, by moving between service methods within each group. Thus, the change from full silver service to a plate service delivery system does not essentially alter the customer process. It will, however, have effects on the way the service sequence is organised and possibly the production system. On the other hand, changing between service method groups substantially changes the customer process. If, for instance, the service method changes from one in group A to one in group C, the effects on the requirements placed on the customer are very different, as indicated in Table 6.1.

## CUSTOMER SERVICE AND RESOURCE PRODUCTIVITY

On the one hand a food and beverage operation is designed to provide customer services and on the other the achievement of profit is determined largely by the efficiency of the use of resources. Customer service can be defined, as in Chapter 1, page 30, as being a combination of five characteristics. These were presented in the model together with the resources being managed, as shown again here in Figure 6.1.

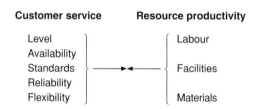

**Figure 6.1** Customer service versus resource productivity

In determining the customer service specification for a particular operation, it is necessary to consider the effect that the achievement of the service specification will have on the productivity of the resources. The effects of variation in the five customer service characteristics and the resource utilisation can be considered as follows (Cousins 1994):

- *Service level* As the level of personal service increases, the labour costs will increase as the number of staff required will increase as well as the level of staff professionalism. Mealtimes are likely to become longer and therefore the potential capacity of the operation will reduce. In addition, in the higher levels of food and beverage service, the equipment used tends to be of higher quality and the amount of equipment needed increases.

- *Availability of service* Increasing the availability of the service will potentially increase labour and material costs and will reduce the efficiency of the facilities used. In these cases it is necessary to endeavour to match the labour and materials being used to the expected volume of business which will vary over a given period.

- *Level of standards* Increasing the level of standards in the food and beverage operation will increase the cost of materials as better-grade materials are used and will increase the cost of labour, as the level of staffing and the staffing professionalism will need to be higher. In addition, the provision of the facilities will also have a higher cost again because of the higher grade of finishes being used.

■ *Reliability of the service*  In order to ensure a high reliability in the provision of the service, again the labour and material costs will increase because, in order to protect the reliability of the product, it will be necessary to have a higher proportion of equipment, labour and materials available.

■ *Flexibility of the service*  Moving away from a limited standard range of product and service will increase material and labour costs and will reduce the efficiency of the facilities being used.

In all cases, the opposite of the examples given above will potentially increase the efficiency of the resources being used. The development of the customer service specification should take account of the five characteristics above and will therefore predetermine the level of resource utilisation and thus the level of efficiency possible. In summary, the higher the level of customer service, then the greater the potential for lower efficiency in the resource utilisation. However, it is possible through changes in the service process to effect greater efficiency without fundamentally altering the customer process: moving from full silver service to plate service, for example.

## CUSTOMER RELATIONS

The existence of good customer relations is as much a part of the food and beverage product as any other aspect. Developing and maintaining good customer relations can be achieved if people working in the food and beverage operation have:

■ The ability to *recognise the symptoms* of a deterioration in customer relations.

■ The ability to *minimise the causes* of customer relations problems.

The *symptoms* of potential customer relations problems are:

■ Increasing number of complaints generally.

■ Increasing number of complaints specifically about staff.

■ Increasing number of accidents.

■ Regular mistakes by staff in orders.

■ Customers arriving without previous bookings' being noted.

■ Breakages.

■ Shortages of equipment.

■ Arguments between staff.

■ Poor morale of staff.

■ High turnover of staff.

*Minimising the causes* of customer relations problems is concerned with ensuring that the conditions that staff work under are likely to support the maintenance of good standards of interpersonal skills. There are four requirements to be considered when attempting to achieve this:

■ The existence of *agreed procedures* for dealing with a range of customer service issues.

■ The customer service specification being able to be supported by the *physical capabilities* of the operation.

■ The customer service specification being able to be supported by the technical, interpersonal skills, product knowledge and team working *abilities of the staff.*

■ The identification of the likely *customer satisfaction* or otherwise that customers are likely to receive from the food and beverage experience.

These four requirements are examined further below.

### Agreed procedures

Example of situations where there is a need for agreed procedures are:

■ modes of address of customers

■ wrong orders

■ complaints about food and beverage items

■ lost property

■ guest illness

■ alcohol overconsumption by guests

■ enforcement of dress codes

■ enforcement of mobile phone and smoking codes

■ dealing with children (and lost children)

■ dealing with customers who:
    – have limited mobility
    – are blind or partially sighted
    – are deaf
    – do not speak English

■ emergencies such as power cuts, fire alarms and bomb threats

■ unacceptable guest behaviour.

Procedures for all these types of situation should be agreed and operated, and then reconsidered on a regular basis as part of training sessions and staff feedback sessions.

### Physical capabilities

Limitations in the physical capabilities of the operation to meet the requirements of the customer service specification will always be the cause of difficulties. This is why the customer service specification itself should only be agreed by taking account of the physical capabilities of the operation.

### Abilities of the staff

Limitations in the capabilities of the staff to support the intended customer service specification will also always be the cause of difficulties. Again there has to be a balance between the technical and interpersonal skills, product knowledge and teamworking capability of the staff and the requirements of the customer service specification. As well as interaction with customers, service staff also are interacting with staff outside of the service areas, for example kitchen staff, bill office staff, dispense bar staff, stillroom staff. It is important that the provision of the food and beverage product within an establishment is seen as a joint effort between all departments, with each department understanding the needs of the others in order to meet the customers' demands. If there is imbalance then either the staff capabilities have to be modified or customer service specification altered so that the two are in harmony.

### Customer satisfaction

Knowing what is the potential for customer satisfaction from the food and beverage product can help to ensure that there are procedures in place for dealing with any difficulties that might arise. The potential for satisfaction should already have been built into the design of the product so that it meets the needs the customers have at the time. There is, though, also the potential for dissatisfaction. In Chapter 1 (page 12) we identified that the potential dissatisfactions fall into two categories: those which are controllable by the establishment, such as scruffy, unhelpful staff, or cramped conditions; and those which are uncontrollable, such as behaviour of other customers, the weather or transport problems. Being able to identify all of these possibilities will enable an operation to have procedures in place to deal with them when they occur.

In minimising the potential for customer relations problems, then, there has to be equal concern over the physical aspects of the service, the way in which the service is operated, and with the interpersonal interaction between customers and staff.

## MANAGING VOLUME

Business volume inevitably varies throughout any trading period whether this be a year, a month, a week or even an hour. Operating at less than full capacity for any period can lead to a disproportionate increase in costs and therefore a reduction in the overall profit contribution. The management of a foodservice operation, therefore, is also about matching the ability of the operation to provide services to the expected volume of demand.

Knowles (1996) identifies seven specific dimensions that should be taken into account when considering the hospitality product (see page 8). One of these dimensions is the 'perishability' of the product. This is a key dimension of the food and beverage product: it cannot be stored. For instance, seats in a restaurant, which are not sold at one meal-time, cannot be compensated for by additional sales at another time. In other words, the sale of food and beverage is limited by the capacity of the operation. Therefore, in food and beverage operations it is necessary to consider how the capacity of the operation for customer sales can be managed in order that the goals of the business may be achieved.

## Measuring capacity

The capacity of a food and beverage operation is measured by considering not only the maximum capacity of customers at a given time but also the capacity that can be achieved over time. For example, a restaurant operation with a maximum seating of 100 covers can achieve a much higher actual capacity for a given meal period if the seats can be used more than once during the period. The potential for this will, however, vary according to the type of operation. A banqueting room, for example, can usually be filled only once during a meal period and therefore the size of the function in terms of covers served will determine the capacity achieved at that time.

## Volume and service organisation

One of the key differences between the management of food and beverage production and the management of food and beverage service is that as the volume of business increases, the production process will require fundamental alteration whereas the service process may simply be multiplied (Cousins 1988). As the volume of food production increases, the way in which the production is organised has to change. This change can be either where the process is separated into various parts of the menu required, which is the basis of the *partie* system, or where the production system is based on the types of process being used. For food and beverage service, as the volume increases, additional service is provided through, for instance, increasing the number of stations in a restaurant. This is much the same as the opening of additional checkouts in a supermarket or increasing the number of tellers available in a bank as the level of demand increases.

Whilst in food service there is the possibility of changing the service methods, such changes are usually driven by needs to improve resource efficiency rather than by the need to provide for higher volumes of business. An example is breakfast service. This can be provided through conventional table service at any volume of business but the need to reduce costs, especially staff costs, is the main reason behind moving to a buffet system.

## Increasing throughput

A way of increasing the potential volume of demand that can be accommodated is to consider ways of increasing the throughput of the number of customers. The desirability of this, and the extent to which it can be achieved, varies with the type of operation.

There are various norms, which exist for seating times. For instance, in a fine dining restaurant this might be two hours, through to a fast food operation with seating being ten minutes. Some approaches to increasing throughput might be as follows:

■ For bar operations, efficient clearing will encourage further sales or discourage lingering. People feel uncomfortable sitting at an empty table or bar. This approach can also be adopted in lounge areas and for cafeterias.

■ For areas where table meals are served, the type of operation will have an effect on the potential to increase the throughput. The higher the level of service – and usually the higher the price – then the more negative is the customer's reaction likely to be to attempts to limit the length of the meal, especially where the meal out is the sole purpose of an evening. Initial alternatives could be to extend opening hours, set sitting times or be able to separate the customer who might accept this approach from those who will not. Combinations of these approaches are often found.

■ Both brighter lighting and less comfortable seating, used in appropriate settings, can encourage increased throughput.

■ For some operations, encouraging customers to share tables can also be a way of increasing throughput. The acceptability of this to customers substantially decreases in operations with higher levels of service and higher prices. However, this possibility is also becoming far less acceptable in any type of operation.

Other approaches include limiting the need for increasing the throughput of customers, such as setting minimum charges for peak demand periods thus attempting to ensure maximum revenue from the customers who are being accommodated. Reduced menu alternatives with quick service promises can also be considered. Additionally, restaurant operations offering an alternative seating area for coffee and drinks can free up tables in the dining area.

## Limiting demand

Where demand is significantly higher than the capacity of the operation, consideration must be given to methods of limiting the volume of demand. Depending on the type of operation, this issue varies in significance. An à la carte restaurant operating at a high customer service specification will tolerate fluctuations in demand and seek to ensure availability and flexibility to meet all the expected demand. On the other hand, a cafeteria operation will seek to maximise demand during the service period.

Limitations in demand can be achieved through pricing policies. In city-centre hotels, for instance, the demand for full breakfast is limited in this way through disproportionately higher pricing for a full breakfast compared to other alternatives. Meal packaging is also a way of reducing the variations in the range of demand being met.

## Using queues

Queues can be used to ensure that the operation is working to full capacity. Examples of this approach are found in, for instance, fast food operations where, although the queue is controlled by a time limit for the customers to queue, it does provide constant demand at the service point. Another example is, for instance, TGI Fridays, where the queue for food service is the central bar area. In this operation, the queue becomes part of the meal experience and also provides for revenue from the queue, through drink sales, whilst waiting for meal service. In managing the queue requirement there are a number of factors to be taken into account so that the process of waiting in the queue does not become a negative part of the service process from the customers' perspective. The factors which affect customer satisfaction and some of the actions that the food service operation can consider, are summarised in Table 6.2.

## Banquet/function operations

In the organisation of banquet/function operations, there are special considerations in respect of capacity issues. Clearly, the capacity of the function rooms will determine the maximum numbers that can be accommodated at a particular time. However, variations in the service methods and the dining layouts can alter both the maximum numbers which can be served and also the volume which can be achieved over time. Selling functions that are similar in service method and layout, for instance, can reduce the preparation for service and the clearing after service periods.

In addition, the capacity of function rooms is affected by the combination of the bookings taken. The taking of certain types of function will reduce or preclude the taking of others. Noisy presentations will, for instance, limit the use of adjoining rooms. If the intention of the operation is to be flexible, then this is inevitable. If the operation wants to specialise (and therefore reduce the flexibility), it is possible to increase the volume throughput. This supposes, however, that the volume of business requiring more standardisation is available.

## The complexity of managing capacity

Managing capacity in food and beverage operations is not a simple issue. The provision of food and beverages is highly complex, with a variety of stages in both the production and the service processes, all of which have an effect on the volume of business that can

**Table 6.2** Service considerations in minimising queuing dissatisfaction

| Factor | Service consideration |
| --- | --- |
| Unfair vs fair wait | Try to ensure that the wait the customer undertakes is perceived as fair; design queuing systems to ensure strict rotation |
| Uncomfortable vs comfortable wait | Consider the impact of the waiting environment; seek to maintain a high level of comfort |
| Unexplained vs explained wait | Provide reasonable explanations for the wait and update regularly; try to avoid the customer's seeing underused capacity |
| Unexpected vs expected wait | Accept responsibility; provide reasonable explanations for the wait and update regularly |
| Unoccupied vs occupied wait | Provide distractions, which either increase the efficiency and effectiveness of the service sequence or involve the customer more in the service sequence |
| Initial vs subsequent wait | Design the service sequence so that the customer has early contact with the servers; try to spread the total wait time across a number of the stages of the service sequence |
| Anxious vs calm wait | Assess the general level of anxiety of the customers; be aware of the needs of customers for staff contact and reassurance |
| Solo vs group wait | Recognise that solo waits feel longer than group waits; consider ways of ensuring that the wait is more pleasant through providing distraction |
| Valuable service vs less valuable service | Recognise that cusomters will wait longer the higher the value of the service, but still try to minimise the wait time |

*Source*: based on proposals by Davis and Heineke (1994)

be met. In addition, the limitations posed by the physical facilities are not always the key determinant of the potential capacity that can be achieved. In many cases the customer service specification will determine that efficiency in the use of the facilities will be out-weighed by the need to provide a certain level of service. In addition, the control of labour and material costs must be taken into account in determining the potential volume of business which can he handled within the predetermined customer service specification.

**SALES PROMOTION AND MERCHANDISING**

## Sales promotion

According to Buttle (1996) and Kotler (1999), sales promotion is about offering short-term incentives, which are designed to change the buying habits of customers and to increase the revenue of the operation. In order to do this, sales promotions are geared to directly encourage the customer to purchase, often through short-term improvements in the cost/value ratio.

Sales promotions as a marketing tool requires planning, monitoring and careful evaluation, so that mistakes are not repeated, successes are, and these are then built upon. Additionally, by their very nature, sales promotions are designed to attract attention; consequently the operation must be geared up to meet the additional demand that the promotion is likely to generate.

Sales promotions are orientated towards changing the customer's short-run purchasing behaviour through:

- Increasing average spend and therefore sales revenue.
- Invigorating slow-moving product(s).
- Promoting a new menu, product or product range.
- Influencing impulse purchasing in a certain fashion.
- Amalgamating items for sale.
- Attracting attention to the business in slower months.
- The celebration of special event(s).
- Increasing customer visits.
- Adding variety and interest to bars, restaurants and so on.
- Establishing or enhancing awareness in potential customers' minds of the business and its products.
- Stimulating purchasing by facilitating communication of product/business features and benefits.
- Positively altering customers' opinions and attitudes.
- Informing in order to entice business.
- Increasing product/service profile.

The essential feature of sales promotions is to move or incentivise the sale of the product today, or for a specific period, and not at some future point. This is achieved through offering additional value, financial inducement to purchase and try, advertising campaigns and so on. Sales promotions can also be linked to public relations and sponsorship strategies.

## Merchandising

Merchandising revolves around attempting to increase spend per head. Its basis is often associated with heightening the values, beliefs, attitudes, ideas and other meaningful values adopted by customers. In food and beverage operations, merchandising is about helping customers to interpret and evaluate what is being sold through a variety of verbal and non-verbal reassurances of the quality of the offering. All of this has to be consistent with the expectations the intended market might have, especially where, in attempting to be competitive, the foodservice operation is increasing the likelihood of increasing competition from competitors.

The aims of merchandising are to:

- Identify real opportunities to promote sales.
- Recognise and promote customer benefits.
- Maximise the value and sales.
- Appeal to the senses, and the customers' identification of 'self'.

The four principal ways of achieving this are through:

- Starting to appeal to more customers.
- Charging existing customers more money.
- Spurring existing customers to spend more money.
- Investing what is sold with cultural cachét and clearly expressed benefits.

In order to be able to adopt any of these approaches the food and beverage operation needs to attract customers to the business, encourage them to spend and also to encourage repeat business.

Merchandising can be most effective where it is based on a genuine understanding of customer needs. Merchandising which is empathetic towards the customer is based on an awareness and understanding of the emotions and feelings of other individuals.

The aim of merchandising is to identify a range of opportunities to promote sales, thereby maximising volume and revenue. If guest contact personnel are involved in conceiving approaches to merchandising, such approaches will be better targeted as they will utilise the knowledge that these staff have of their guests and their understanding of the specific needs and desires of their customers. Merchandising techniques developed in this way can provide 'targeted' quality products, which are more likely to lead to total satisfaction and repeat business.

In effect, operations are then able to recognise and promote specific customer benefits from a position of depth knowledge. In empathetic merchandising the operation is more able to target merchandising to communicate social and economic status and worth, group affinity and distinction, symbolic association, self-image and shared value. Table 6.3 provides a summary of merchandising approaches and possible sample outcomes.

**Table 6.3**   Merchandising approaches and sample outcomes

| Merchandising approaches | Sample outcomes |
| --- | --- |
| Marketing | Identifies demand with the ultimate aim of expanding the customer base by creating and keeping customers |
| Advertising | Attracts the customer through visual merchandising, sensory merchandising and service merchandising |
| Selling | Through point-of-sale and active promotion of product |
| Profitability | Ensures business success and strengthens and prolongs the life cycle of the business |
| Perception, experience and mood – staff recognition of immediate needs through reading the guest | Recognition that no two people are the same and perceive stimulus differently at differing times |
| Design | Building strong emotional and psychological links between the business environment and the customer |
| Personality – traits, behaviours and experiences making the customer distinctive and unique | Recognition of customer traits or characteristics reflected back ensuring the customer realises they are in the right environment |
| Emotional value and connectivity | Ensures customers are valued and have an orientation with the business' success |
| Customer satisfaction and self-actualisation need | Ensures the continuation of the process and meets the customer's esteem needs (rising from notions of 'wise choice' and other positive character elements) |

### Menu and beverage list merchandising

The menu and beverage lists are vitally important sales tools. Menu and beverage list merchandising is concerned with the way in which the menu and beverage lists can be most efficiently utilised as catalysts for optimising sales. It is necessary therefore for all menus and beverage lists to be correct against a checklist of operational compatibility, overall design and layout, clarity of expression, legibility, trades description, size and cleanliness.

## Creative merchandising

Displaying products in an effort to enhance sales applies as much to food and beverage operations as it does in general retail operations. The illuminated fascias above fast food service counters, which graphically exhibit the menu, illustrate this well. However, it is equally important for fine dining restaurants, for instance, to set the scene with display materials. These can include own-brand merchandising like champagne, wines, or the chef's own chocolate truffles, sauces and preserves.

Merchandising stimuli for foodservice operations can include:

■ aromas

■ audio visual displays

■ bulletin/blackboards/floor stands

■ directional signs

■ display cards/brochures

■ displays of food and drinks
- trolleys (sweet, liqueurs and so on)
- buffets/salad bars
- self-service counters – bar displays, flambé work and so on

■ drinks mats and place mats

■ fascia boards

■ illuminated panels

■ other customers' food and drink

■ posters

■ production areas being able to be seen

■ tent cards

■ using service storage, as for instance, in wine racks, as part of the design concept.

Merchandising should not be difficult. In promoting sales, the basis of the promotion should be on providing customers with well-researched, quality products which will potentially match the customers' perceived value of those products and their need for them. This is an extension of the consumer–product relationship (as discussed in Chapter 2) which the foodservice operation is intending to develop and maintain.

In order for merchandising to be successful it has to be supported by corresponding well developed personal selling and interpersonal skills of the staff (see 'Taking food and beverage orders', page 209). If staff training includes the examination of the profiling of the operation's target groups, then staff will be aware of:

■ The nature of the demand being met.

■ The people and organisations buying the product.

■ The frequency of their custom.

■ Their use of other businesses and why.

■ Their use of disposable income.

■ Their desire to express their unique identity.

■ Their desire for greater variety tailored to their individual needs.

Excellence in food and beverage management comes from having a good knowledge of the markets being served, the nature of the demand being met and the application of exemplary merchandising principles in order to establish and maintain custom.

## MANAGING THE SERVICE SEQUENCE

In developing the customer service specification, the capability of the operation needs to be considered. Similarly, once the customer service specification has been determined, then the service sequence can be designed or redesigned and managed in order to ensure that the customer service specification is achieved. Aspects of managing the seven stages of the service sequence (Lillicrap *et al.* 1998) are considered below.

### 1   Preparation for service

Within the service areas, there are a variety of tasks and duties which need to be carried out in order to ensure that adequate preparation has been made for the expected volume of business and the type of service which is to be provided. This should also include the briefing of staff to ensure that they have adequate knowledge of the product.

One of the preparatory tasks is the taking of bookings. Systems need to be developed to ensure that bookings are taken in a way that ensures the efficiency of the operation. This includes consideration of overbooking systems in operations where bookings are taken. There are, however, risks with this approach. It is also necessary to take into account the law on contract.

A contract is made when one party agrees to the terms of an offer made by another party. In food and beverage service, there are in essence two types of customer: those who pre-book and those who do not (often called chance or casual customers). For those who pre-book, the offer is made by them, say a requirement for a table for four at 1 p.m. If the restaurant suggests an alternative, for example 'We do not have a table at 1 p.m., but we have one at 1.30 p.m.', then the offer is made by the restaurant.

There is a requirement for a price list to be shown (see page 23). In operations where the customer may not have pre-booked or is not required to pre-book (for example, fast-food operations) it is likely to be considered, in law, that the price list constitutes an offer.

If customers fail to turn up on time, then the table need not be held. Similarly, if the party is only two and not the four previously booked, then restaurants may seek compensation. Alternatively, if the food and drink are not as expected, then the customer can refuse to pay but must provide proof of identity and their home address. Only if fraud is suspected may the police be involved, as fraud is a criminal offence.

However, contracts may be broken if one party is induced to enter into a contract by false statement, for example, if promised a menu which is not available. In this case there is no obligation for the customer to continue with the contract. Also, if either party is unable to meet the terms of the original contract owing to unforeseen circumstances, such as illness of customer, or the restaurant's burning down, then the contract becomes frustrated as it cannot be fulfilled.

Care should be taken with minors: contracts cannot be made with persons under 18 unless it is for 'goods and services suitable to the minor's needs and his/her station in life'.

### 2   Taking food and beverage orders

Taking orders from customers for the food and drink they wish to have, takes time. Limiting the choice can reduce this time but this possibility depends on the particular operation. The order-taking process, though, is part of a longer process, which feeds information to the food production or bar areas and provides information for the billing method. Whatever type of system is used, whether manual or electronic, it will be based on one of the three basic order-taking methods. These are:

- *Duplicate*   Order taken and copied to supply point and second copy retained by server for service and subsequent billing.
- *Triplicate*   Order taken and copied to supply point and cashier for billing; third copy retained by server for service.
- *Service with order*   Taking order and serving to order, as used, for example, in bar service or takeaway methods.

Within the order-taking procedure there are many opportunities for exploiting the potential for personal selling that can be carried out by service staff. Personal selling refers specifically to the ability of the staff in a food and beverage operation to contribute to the promotion of sales. This is especially important where there are specific promotions being undertaken. The promise of a particular type of menu or drink, a special deal or the availability of a particular service can often be devalued by the inability of the staff to fulfil the requirements as promised. It is therefore important to involve service staff in the formulation of particular offers and to ensure that briefing and training are undertaken so that the customer can experience what has been promised.

However, personal selling does not solely relate to supporting special promotions. The contribution of staff to the meal experience is vital. The service staff contribute to the customers' perception of value for money, hygiene and cleanliness, the level of service and the perception of atmosphere that the customer experiences. Within the context of selling the service, staff should therefore be able to:

■ Detail the food and drink on offer in an informative way and also in such a way as to make the product sound interesting and worth having.

■ Use opportunities to promote specific items or deals when seeking orders from the customer.

■ Seek information from the customer in a way that promotes sales. For example, rather than asking if drinks are required with the meal ask which drinks are to be required with the meal.

■ Use opportunities for the sales of additional items such as extra garnishes, special sauces or accompanying drinks such as a dessert wine with a sweet course.

■ Provide a competent service of the items for sale and seek customers' views on the acceptability of the food, drinks and the service.

### 3 The service of food and beverages

The various service methods available are given on pages 193–4 of this chapter. The choice of service method will depend as much on the customer service specification as on the capability of the staff, the operation and the equipment available. Differing service methods will also determine the speed of service and the time the customer takes to consume the meal, which in turn will have an impact on the throughput of customers.

Within food and beverage service there is a variety of rituals or conventions that are usually observed. These rituals exist to help the service process go well, and all of them have logical operational reasons for their existence. Some of these are listed together with their rationale in Table 6.4.

Table 6.4 is not exhaustive. Other conventions include: all staff passing each other by always moving to the right – which avoids dancing in a corridor and reduces the risk of accidents – or never leaving or entering a room without also carrying something – otherwise what is the point of leaving or entering a room?

Food and beverage service is a difficult job. Whilst there have been changes in food and beverage service, with less emphasis on the high-level technical skills (mistakenly bemoaned by some as deskilling), what was not being recognised was that other parts of the job are just as, if not more, important. The other fact that was not initially recognised was that good service did not have to be confined to a particular type of restaurant and a particular type of service style. In other words, good service is not defined by the use of a narrow range of high-level technical skills.

For food and beverage service the key requirements for staff are:

■ sound product knowledge

■ competence in technical skill

■ well-developed social skills

■ the ability to work as part of a team.

**Table 6.4   Some service rituals and the rationale for them**

| Service rituals | Rationale |
| --- | --- |
| Using standard lay-ups | The lay-up on a table gives an indication of the type of meal being taken, the sequence of courses or what stage customers are at within a meal. There is a standard convention that lay-ups are placed as if for right-handed people and most techniques for service are based on this principle. It makes for neatness and consistency but there is no implied discrimination here |
| Using order notation techniques | Helps with identifying, for any server, which member of a party is having what items of food or drink. Saves confusion |
| Taking orders through hosts | This is common courtesy – the host is usually paying for the meal and agreement needs to be obtained for any items that are to be served |
| Service of a party from the right of the host with the host last | Honoured guests are usually seated on the right of a host at a function |
| Service of food from the left of a guest | This means that the service dish is nearer the plate for ease of service and to prevent food being spilt on to the customer, customers can more easily see the food being served, and make choices if necessary, and service staff are also able to see and control what they are doing |
| Clearing from right of a guest | This means that the plates can be removed from the guest with the right hand and the stack of plates is then behind the customer's chair in the left hand. It is neater, and if there is an accident it goes to the floor rather than over the customer |
| Service plated food from right of a guest | Same reasons as clearing from the right. The additional plates to be served are held over the floor behind the customer. It is neater and reduces the risk of the food being dropped on the customer |
| Service beverages from the right of a guest | Glasses are usually placed on the right-hand side and therefore the service of beverages follows from this. Also, for individual drinks and for other beverages any tray is behind the customer's seat in the server's left hand |
| Not leaning over customers | Mainly this is courtesy and respect for physical space. It is also worth remembering that no matter how clean service staff are, food smells tend to cling to service uniforms |

**Table 6.4**  (*cont'd*)

| Service rituals | Rationale |
| --- | --- |
| Serving cold food before hot food | When the hot food is served the service is complete and customers can enjoy the meal without waiting for additional items. For the same reason, accompaniments should be automatically offered and served at the same time as the food |
| Serving wine before food | Similar to above. Customers do not want to wait for wine service with hot food going cold and they want to enjoy it with the meal |
| Sequencing of banquet/function staff line-ups | The people serving the main guests and the stations furthest from the service door should be into the room first. This is courtesy and operational sense otherwise people can fall over each other |
| Separating service from food/drink collection and station clearing | This ensures that there is always someone in the room to attend to guests and to monitor the service overall whilst others are clearing and bringing in food and drink orders. This approach also allows for the training of new staff and ensures that customer contact is primarily through experienced staff |

Good food and beverage service is achieved where management continually reinforces and supports service staff in the maintenance of high standards of achievement in these aspects. Additionally, the provision and maintenance of good service is primarily dependent on teamwork, not only amongst service staff but also amongst and between staff in other departments.

For managers within the foodservice operations, skills in marketing, staff management, team development, training, customer relations, financial management and operational management are necessary for the management of the service sequence and, ultimately, for the survival of the business.

### 4  Billing

The various billing methods found in food service operations are as follows:

- Bill as check – second copy of order used as bill.
- Separate bill – bill made up from duplicate check and presented to customer.
- Bill with order – service to order and billing at same time, for example, bar or takeaway methods.
- Prepaid – customer purchases ticket or card in advance either for specific meal or specific value.

- Voucher – customer has credit issued by third party, for example, luncheon voucher or tourist agency voucher, for either specific meal or specific value.
- No charge – customer not paying.
- Deferred – refers to function-type catering, for example, where bill is paid by organiser.

The choice of billing method will be dependent on the type and style of the operation. However, the billing system is also part of a longer process linked first to the order-taking method and second to the revenue control procedures (see 'Revenue control' below). In managing the billing method, it is necessary, therefore, to ensure that the method chosen supports both the order-taking method and the revenue control requirements. The range of acceptable payment methods, for example, needs to be predetermined, as well as the level of discretion which is to be allowed to different individuals or groups of staff. Consideration also needs to be given to the use of electronic point-of-sale (EPOS) control systems.

## 5  Clearing

The various clearing methods found in foodservice operations may be summarised as follows:

- Manual 1 – the collection of soiled ware by waiting staff to dishwash area.
- Manual 2 – the collection and sorting to trolleys by operators for transportation to dishwash area.
- Semi-self-clear – the placing of soiled ware by customers on strategically placed trolleys within dining area for removal by operators.
- Self-clear – the placing of soiled ware by customers on conveyor or conveyorised tray-collecting system for mechanical transportation to dishwash area.
- Self-clear and strip – the placing of soiled ware into conveyorised dishwash baskets by customer for direct entry of baskets through dishwash.

The choice of clearing method, whether manual by staff or involving customers, will be dependent not only on the type of operation but also on the nature of the demand being met. In captive situations, for instance, it is possible to have greater customer involvement.

## 6  Dishwashing

The capacity of the dishwashing system should always be greater than the operational maximum required. This is because slow dishwashing increases the amount of equipment required to be in use at a particular time and increases the storage space required in service areas.

The various dishwashing systems are as follows:

■ Manual – the manual washing by hand or brush machine of soiled ware.
■ Semi-automatic – the manual loading by operators of dishwash machine.
■ Automatic conveyor – the manual loading by operators of soiled ware within baskets mounted on conveyor for automatic transportation through dishwash machine.
■ Flight conveyor – the manual loading by operators of soiled ware within pegs mounted on conveyor for automatic transportation through dishwasher.
■ Deferred wash – the collection, stripping, sorting and stacking of ware by operators for transportation through dishwash at later stage.

The potential volume that can be accommodated increases, as does potential efficiency, from the manual method to the flight conveyor method, and the choice of method will be largely dependent on the scale of the operation. It is often necessary to employ more than one method. The deferred wash system can be used as a cost-saving approach as wash-up staff do not have to be employed until the end of a service period, especially when this is late at night.

## 7  Clearing following service

After the service periods there is a variety of tasks and duties to be carried out, partly to clear from the previous service and partly to prepare for the next. The efficient management of the clearing stage can have a dramatic impact on the potential reuse of an area.

Included in this stage of the service sequence is the requirement for the management of cleaning programmes. Detailed cleaning schedules need to be developed to ensure that all cleaning activities are coordinated. These can be daily, weekly, monthly and for other periods. Alongside these cleaning schedules, it is desirable to incorporate maintenance checks. These, together with the operation of cleaning schedules, can help to ensure that equipment and facilities are always available and in working order.

## REVENUE CONTROL

Revenue control encompasses the sale of all food and beverage and is essential to ensure maximum return. Particular attention must be paid to the key factors influencing profitability. Crucial controls have to be assigned for the main factors affecting the revenue of the business, such as the menu, wine list and other beverages, the total volume of food and beverage sales, the sales mix, the average spend of customers in each selling outlet at different times of the day, the number of covers served and the gross profit margins.

## The control system

The revenue control system should be simple, manageable and ensure control:

- at all locations of the operation where selling takes places
- for all items internally issued from the various departments.

The aims of the revenue control system are to:

- reduce pilfering
- eradicate wastage
- protect revenue.

The type of control system varies with the size of the operation. There needs to be accountability for what has been served to the customer and payment for what has been issued from the kitchen or the bar. Accurate billing should be standard and the outcome should be that the system can provide a detailed breakdown of sales and revenue sources in order that adjustments and improvements may be made.

Payment for food and beverage may be made in many forms such as cash, cheques, foreign currency, credit cards, debit cards, Eurocheques, travellers' cheques and so on. All staff handling cash and other payment methods should be adequately trained in the policies of the operation and the procedures to be followed with the aim of ensuring that revenue security is efficiently carried out at all times.

Whatever revenue control system is used, it should be able to generate information for a variety of performance measures. These can include:

- Reconciliation of total payments against orders served.
- Average spend per head on food or beverages.
- Average bill.
- Sales mix data.
- Payment method breakdowns.
- Seat turnover – the number of times a seat is used in a service period.
- Sales per member of service staff.
- Sales per period – can be monitored on an hourly basis such as in fast food operations or in bar operations.
- Sales per seat.
- Sales per square metre or square foot.

The nature of, and the relationship between, revenue, costs and profits are explored in detail in Chapter 7, pages 224–52 together with an examination of the various performance measures.

## Common malpractices

Although one of the aims of control systems is to eliminate dishonesty, this cannot always be achieved, but the control system can make such malpractice much more difficult. When designing control systems it is worth investigating possible malpractices. Some of the common ones are listed in Table 6.5 together with advice on detection and also a value of the difficulty of detection, rated 1 to 3, with 3 being the hardest to detect.

Information on possible malpractices should be shared through trade and professional association meetings so that up-to-date knowledge of potential malpractices can be obtained.

**Table 6.5** Some common malpractices in food and beverage service operations

| Malpractice | Detection | Value[a] |
|---|---|---|
| Dilution of liquor | A hydrometer will detect dilution, but a control test should also be performed from a new bottle as air temperature can affect the result. However, this test is easy to make | 1 |
| Short measures | Cocktails and other mixed beverages are vulnerable here. Can be detected by observation, usually signalled by a complaint | 3 |
| Overcharging of customers | Not easily checked in a busy bar or restaurant. If done frequently enough, the thief can end up with spare bottles or other items of unrecorded stock. Nowadays a receipt should always be proffered | 2 |
| Undercharging of friends | Not easily checked in a busy bar or restaurant. If this appears to be taking place, a careful watch is necessitated. General control procedures should detect this with checking systems and under due diligence a camera can be focused on cash registers | 3 |
| Management pilferage | Difficult to detect as managers have greater freedom of access. Missing produce/product can be written off as waste without ever being detected as pilferage. All management should have ledger accounts for all entertaining, comping and writing off. The existence of this type of control provides for open identification of potential abuse | 3 |
| Kickbacks to managers | Here it is necessary to know what was purchased etc. A supplier can make kickbacks directly to manager(s) ensuring the supplier's product is adopted above others. | 3 |

**Table 6.5** (*cont'd*)

| Malpractice | Detection | Value[a] |
|---|---|---|
| | Free products, which could reduce operational costs, may be kept as incentive for buying goods from one supplier over another. Goods offered as 'incentive' may also never actually arrive at the property and may be delivered to the member of staff or manager's home address. Kickbacks are always brought to light by lengthy and in-depth analysis | |
| Part-time banqueting personnel removing food, beverages and light equipment from the establishment | Utilise establishment security personnel to have a high-profile presence and randomly search personnel. Provide clear polythene bags for all personal items brought into the premises so as to be able to recognise the content on exiting the premises. In banqueting, for example, agreed limits of an average of $1/2$ bottle per guest can still lead to whole bottles being misappropriated or creamed off the top. Corks could be counted back, although corks can also be stored and brought into the premises. Again, vigilance is important | 3 |
| Cellar/stores personnel | Items can be booked out to bars but not delivered. In this case they are lost at cost price. The blame can later be placed on the bars as having lost the items. Good control procedures should be able to detect this over time | 2 |
| Cash registers taken off-line | A register or point-of-sale machine may be taken off-line, and assigned to only a couple of personnel to use it. The server's sales can be tracked off-line, albeit the machine is still tied into remote kitchen printers. Sales are recorded separately and the proceeds stolen by the member of staff or manager. This individual can make the adjustments the next day or at close of shift. Good control procedures and random checks can detect this over time | 2 |
| Complimentary meals | Managers can void bills by using their management keys on point-of-sale machines. They can also give complimentary meals. Transactions handled can be voided or recorded as complimentary and the revenue stolen by the manager. See possible approach to control under management pilferage above. | 2 |

**Table 6.5** *(cont'd)*

| Malpractice | Detection | Value[a] |
|---|---|---|
| Utilising differentiated gross profit percentages | Items can be recorded as being sold in a department where the gross profit is lower than in the department where the items are actually sold, e.g. optic liquor as off-licence liquor sales. Can be detected over time through control procedures and by examining sales patterns for anomalies | 3 |

[a] Refers to difficulty of detection; a value of 3 denoting the most difficult to detect

## SUMMARY

This chapter has considered and explored the concept of two distinct systems being managed within food and beverage service, albeit at the same time. This approach recognises the importance not only of the management of the service sequence (or delivery system) but also of the customer experience or process. This approach can assist in developing customer service specifications, especially where the implications of various decisions are understood within the context of the impact that such decisions can have on resource utilisation and efficiency.

Managing the seven stages of the service sequence becomes better informed by taking into account the effects that can be experienced by the customer, through the development and maintenance of good customer relations, the maximisation of the opportunities for merchandising and sales promotion, and taking account of the need to manage the volume of demand. The importance of revenue control has also been highlighted.

## REFERENCES

Buttle, F. (1996) *Hotel and Food Service Marketing – A Managerial Approach*, London: Cassell.

Cousins, J. (1988) 'Curriculum development in operational management teaching in catering education' in *The Management of Service Operations*, Johnson, R. (ed.), Bedford: IFS Publications, pp.437–59.

Cousins, J. (1994) 'Managing capacity' in *The Management of Foodservice Operations*, Jones, P. and Merricks, P. (eds), London: Cassell, pp.174–87.

Davis, M. M. and Heineke, J. (1994) 'Understanding the roles of the customer and the operation for better queue management' *International Journal of Operations and Production Management* **14** (5) pp.21–34.

Knowles, T. (1996) *Corporate Strategy for Hospitality*, Harlow: Longman.

Kotler, P., Bowen, J. and Making, J. (1999) *Marketing for Hospitality and Tourism*, 2nd edition, Hemel Hempstead: Prentice Hall.

Lillicrap, D., Cousins, J. and Smith, R. (1998) *Food and Beverage Service*, London: Hodder and Stoughton.

# CHAPTER SEVEN

# APPRAISING PERFORMANCE AND MAKING STRATEGIC DECISIONS

This chapter aims to identify and evaluate the techniques of measuring and appraising the performance of food and beverage operations and to consider and apply approaches to strategic decision-making.

This chapter is intended to support you in:

- considering the basis for performance appraisal

- identifying the aspects of foodservice operations which are commonly appraised

- developing skills in the application of a range of performance measures and appraisal techniques to individual aspects of food and beverage operations, the product and the whole operation

- determining the usefulness and limitations in the various quantitative and qualitative appraisal techniques and their application to food and beverage operations

- identifying the components of strategic planning as a systematic process

- identifying and applying approaches to business analysis and evaluation

- selecting and applying strategic planning models and approaches appropriate to foodservice operations.

The appraisal of a food and beverage operation is a set of tasks, the first of which involves the individual consideration of a range of operational variables, and the second the consideration of the operation as a whole. The completion of these tasks then provides the basis for making strategic decisions about the operation and the business.

In order to systematically appraise an operation it is necessary to identify the component parts of an operation and to appraise them separately before bringing them all together and appraising the operation as a whole. For a food and beverage operation the first component parts for performance appraisal are:

- revenue
- costs
- profits
- the product.

The nature of revenue, costs and profits is complex. Each of these component parts is considered in detail in this chapter together with the approaches that might be used to appraise them. The key points in their appraisal are identified at the end of the sections where they are examined.

The appraisal of the product is then considered taking account of the data which the appraisal of the revenue, costs and profits might provide. Once this has been completed it is possible to bring the various strands together in order to complete the appraisal of the operation as a whole and to give consideration to making strategic decisions about the operation and the business.

## Fundamentals of appraisal

Appraisal is the action of placing a value on a measurement or collection of measurements. The measurements taken in a food and beverage operation are concerned predominantly with performance, and are therefore often referred to as performance measures. However, a measure alone has no value. In order to be able to place a value on a performance measure, there will need to be an identified objective to measure it against. For example, an actual revenue measurement of £1200 has limited value until it is compared with a revenue objective of £1000. The revenue can then be appraised as surpassing the objective by £200, or 20 per cent.

Other measurements and objectives are needed in order to explore or value the revenue measurement further. If cost objectives and actual costs are known, it is possible to explore or value the revenue measurement in a more meaningful way, i.e. the amount of profit (or loss) can be measured. Subsequently, a profit objective can also be applied and a further value placed on the achievements of the operation.

In order to begin to appraise a food and beverage operation it is therefore a prerequisite to identify the goals and objectives of the operation. Knowing the operation's goals and objectives will enable the appraiser to focus on those parts of the operation which most significantly impact on the achievement of the goals and identified objectives.

In Chapter 1 (page 24) we identified that goals, or aims, are the broad intentions of an organisation whilst objectives are the measurable outcomes which will indicate the progress being made by an organisation towards meeting its specific goals. Operational appraisal, then, is concerned with measuring achievement against the objectives.

There may, however, be circumstances where the operation's objectives are not clear. In these situations it will be necessary for the appraiser to take a proactive role. This proactive role will vary depending on the responsibilities of the appraiser. For example:

- Area managers, managers, department heads and others with responsibility for revenue, costs, profits and product quality, who are unclear as to their objectives, need to be proactive by consulting with other members of their organisation (usually their immediate line manager), in an attempt to establish what the objectives are.

- An owner-operator with no clear objectives should consider what their objectives are. This can be done either by the owner or in consultation with others: their staff and/or a consultant, for example.

The formulation of objectives is an important part of any business in order to try to ensure that resources are being directed efficiently and that the goals will be met. As objectives are dynamic and vary according to circumstances, the setting and revising of objectives is a continuous process. Appraisal is part of this process as it measures the extent to which the objectives are being met. The resultant appraisal will help in confirmation or revision of the appropriate goals for the organisation, which in turn will lead to the setting, or revising of the organisation's objectives.

## The basis for effective operational appraisal

Effective appraisal can be achieved only if there are established objectives for the food and beverage operation. These objectives are usually in the form of budgets and statements of other standards against which actual performance can be measured and appraised. The time and resources devoted to identifying, establishing and communicating objectives will vary between operations, depending on the perceived importance of this process. In operations where the objectives are not clear, staff and management should be proactive in order to identify and establish what their objectives actually are.

### Budgets

Some of the measurable objectives of a food and beverage operation are commonly expressed in the form of budgets. Examples of measurable budget objectives are revenue, costs, profits, average spend per head, number of customers. These objectives are used in a number of ways:

- Budget objectives are compared to actual performance and therefore help to appraise that performance, for example revenue budgets.
- Budget objectives help to effect control over the operation, for example cost budgets.
- Budget objectives help to predict the future, for example cash flow and profit forecast budgets.

Operators will use budgets mainly to assist in making reasoned and objective evaluation of the performance of the operation, so that informed decisions can be made regarding their business. However, budgets can be used for other reasons.

Budgets are often thought to act as a motivator. Sometimes the ability to achieve the budget is related to remuneration and bonuses, or, if budgets are not met then employment of those thought to be responsible may be terminated. This 'stick and carrot' use of budgets can act as a motivator if the budgets are perceived to be achievable, or conversely a demotivator if they are perceived to be unobtainable. For this reason, budgets are not necessarily a statement of required results but are very often set with a view to motivate.

Evidence from Shortt (1992) identifies this to be the case in the situation where an operations manager for a small group of hotels sets budgets that are more difficult to achieve than the actual desired or possible budget. This was done in order to 'keep managers on their toes'. The argument against this is that managers may know that these budgets are being set so as to be too difficult to achieve, and the desirable motivation can therefore be negated.

In order to avoid this potential conflict, budgets may be set with the agreement of all the participating parties. In large organisations this is clearly impractical, as a board of directors is unable to agree budgets with all the individuals involved in achieving those budgets. Instead, budgets are agreed between layers of the organisation, for example between the board of directors and the operations director, then the operations director and the regional managers, and so on until agreement between the unit managers and the department heads. In smaller and owner-operated food and beverage operations, this agreement between the parties is potentially easier to achieve.

Even with such a 'consultative' approach to budget-setting it is still possible for there to be conflict, with one side wishing to increase budget sales and reduce budget costs (often the position of the more senior manager, the budget-setter), whilst the other party is trying to reduce budget sales and increase budget costs (often the position of the more junior manager, the budget-taker).

Nevertheless, however they are set, it is still possible for budgets to be ill-conceived and badly or falsely communicated. If the desired operational objective is to be identified through the budget, then the setting of the budget itself should be examined for its possible limitations, and how these limitations might affect the use of budgets as an appraisal or valuation of the actual achievement.

In summary then:

■ Budgets which are set in measurable and achievable terms, and which need to be achieved in order that the organisation can realise its goals, are true objectives.

■ Budgets which are set as intentions for the organisation and bearing little relationship to the goals of the organisation are not true objectives. These are merely board intentions, which are being used for other purposes, such as being the basis for determining bonus payments for managers.

In measuring performance against budgets, it is worth first considering the true nature of the budgets as this will determine the extent to which the performance appraisal is a measure of the effectiveness of the organisation in meeting its goals.

## Standards

Other measurable objectives of a food and beverage operation are often expressed as standards. Examples of measurable standards objectives are: portioning, purchasing specifications, staff uniform, temperature, time. These standards are seen to be useful to operators in a similar way to budgets:

■ Standards are compared to actual performance and therefore help to appraise that actual performance, for example portioning.

■ Standards help to effect control over specific parts of the operation such as staff uniform and hygiene.

■ Standards can contribute to ensuring a consistent product, for example the same service, the same meals and the same atmosphere at all times and in all locations.

Some operators will write these standards down in the form of training manuals, with many branded retail foodservice operations[1] being extremely detailed in their approaches. The manuals will attempt to prescribe precisely each task and duty to be performed, often supported by the use of diagrams, photographs and videos. These manuals are generally used for three main purposes:

---

[1] Chain restaurants have been seen to take a relatively high-profile position in terms of their location (high streets, shopping areas, European ferries, motorway services, hospitals, workplaces and educational establishments), and place great importance on their image through the use of concepts. These foodservice operations apply many of the management methods employed by retailers, as do other service industries such as banking and printing, with the change of emphasis being focused on how best to provide an improved customer experience. The branding of foodservice operations might also be seen to have developed from approaches used in the retail industry, and provides marketing advantages as well as some economies of scale in purchasing, training and distribution. For these reasons, the term 'branded retail foodservice operations' is generally used to describe these types of establishment.

■ Manuals can provide a way for management to communicate the prescribed perform-ance of various tasks and duties necessary to produce and control their product.

■ Manuals help to ensure consistency of product throughout all the food and beverage operations in a group or chain.

■ Manuals can act as a set of objectives against which to appraise performance.

As with budgets, not all food and beverage operations will have written standards, and similarly, operators and managers should be proactive in trying to identify and establish what these standards are.

In general terms, the existence of agreed standards can be seen to make a useful con-tribution to the maintenance of consistent product delivery for an operation. We have, though, already drawn a distinction (in Chapter 1, page 29) between different types of standard. Product quality (in terms of technical standards) and service quality (in terms of service standards) are, by their very nature, different. Technical standards can be iden-tified, measured and compared. Also, procedural service standards can often be usefully identified. Service, though, is highly varied and there is some doubt about the extent to which it is possible to prescribe useful service standards beyond defining a relaxed frame-work (especially for convivial standards) or whether, for some operations, prescribing service standards is desirable at all.

## APPRAISING REVENUE

Food and beverage operators view revenue as perhaps the most important measure in the operation. Revenue is also called 'turnover', and is often quoted as a measure of the size of a business. But high revenue does not necessarily equate with high success: operations with high revenue can, and do, fail. However, to be successful, revenue is a prerequisite, and most operators would put revenue achievement at the top of their list of objectives.

Revenue is a consequence of two variables: price and volume. Changes in one or both of these variables will affect the level of revenue over time. Table 7.1 demonstrates how changes in the price and volume variables can affect the revenue.

In Table 7.1:

■ Example 1 is the starting point or baseline.

■ Examples 2–6 show revenue increasing.

■ Examples 7–11 show revenue decreasing.

■ Examples 3 and 5 produce increased revenue even though one of the variables has decreased.

■ Examples 10 and 11 produce decreased revenue even though one of the variables has increased.

**Table 7.1** The effect of price and volume on revenue

| Example | Covers/volume | Price/ASPH (£) | Revenue (£) |
| --- | --- | --- | --- |
| 1 | 100 | 10.00 | 1000.00 |
| 2 | 120 | 10.00 | 1200.00 |
| 3 | 120 | 9.00 | 1080.00 |
| 4 | 100 | 12.00 | 1200.00 |
| 5 | 80 | 15.00 | 1200.00 |
| 6 | 120 | 12.00 | 1440.00 |
| 7 | 80 | 10.00 | 800.00 |
| 8 | 80 | 9.00 | 720.00 |
| 9 | 100 | 9.00 | 900.00 |
| 10 | 80 | 11.00 | 880.00 |
| 11 | 110 | 9.00 | 990.00 |

ASPH = average spend per head

In order to appraise the revenue of an operation over time it will therefore be necessary to collect information on both the price and the volume variables.

Most food and beverage operations will measure volume by the number of customers served. In a table-service restaurant operation this is a fairly simple matter of referring to copy customer bills, kitchen order checks or electronic data collection from the cash register. In a counter-service food and beverage operation such as a fast food outlet it is not so easy to know the number of customers that have been served, and therefore the number of transactions may be recorded. In some food and beverage operations, for example a bar, it is not seen as necessary to know the number of customers or the number of trans-actions. In this situation the revenue is still a product of the price and the volume, but it will not be possible to identify the reasons for any revenue variations so accurately.

The prices of an operation can be taken from the menus, wine and drinks lists and other methods of 'product offer' communication. However, price can also be measured by how much a customer is spending. Many operations use average spend per head (ASPH), or average check, as a way of determining the price variable.

## Using price and volume data

If an operation knows its total revenue and the number of customers or number of checks over a specific period, then it is possible to calculate the ASPH and the average check figures. For example, if:

| | |
| --- | --- |
| Total revenue | £1000 |
| Total number of customers | 500 |
| Total number of transactions | 100 |

then:

> ASPH = £2.00 (total revenue ÷ number of customers)
> Average check = £10.00 (total revenue ÷ number of transactions)
> Average group size = 5 (total number of customers served ÷ number of transactions)

This example also shows the calculation used to determine the average size of a group of customers. This can be useful information. Knowing that larger or smaller groups of customers make up a significant part of the market can help in the planning of the restaurant and kitchen layout for example, or to focus advertising and promotion.

## Interpreting calculations

An ASPH or average check amount can be misleading because 'averages' do not give the whole picture. An ASPH of £12.50 could be the result of all customers spending £12.50; or half the customers spending £6.25 and the other half spending £18.75. The same mis-interpretation can be applied to the average group size measure, and also to, for instance, the average number of customers per hour, day or week. Numerous combinations are possible and it is therefore important to take into account the limitations of averages.

It is often useful to generate figures that show the ASPH for different quartiles. This will give information on, for instance how many customers are spending within the highest 25 per cent of spend, the bottom 25 per cent of spend and the middle two 25 per cents. This can also be useful over specific service times such as main meals times where minimum charges can be introduced to force up the level of the ASPH.

These measurements and others are seen to be more useful when they are used for cross-sectional and time-series analyses.

- *Cross-sectional analysis* This is (a) to compare one section of an operation with another section of the same operation, or (b) to compare one operation or part of an operation with another in the same or similar sector of the food and beverage operations business. For example, comparing the revenue of one steakhouse restaurant with that of another in the same chain, or comparing the revenue of one fast food chain with that of another chain.

- *Time-series analysis* This is to compare a measure over a period of time, for example comparing the revenue of a unit for one week with the revenue of the same unit for the previous week or with the revenue from the same week one year ago. Comparing present with past performance helps place some value on the revenue measure, although it is important to take into account any circumstances that may have changed.

## Taking account of price changes and inflation

When comparing revenue for different trading periods it is important to take account of price changes and inflation in order to get a truer picture of the performance of the operation. For example, a restaurant that had a revenue of £100 000 in year 1 and a revenue of £120 000 in year 2, is seen to have increased its revenue by £20 000 or 20 per cent. Let us assume that the number of customers has remained static and that prices were increased by 10 per cent. (In this particular example we will assume that the annual rate of inflation was 10 per cent, although this by itself may not be the only reason why prices were increased or changed.) Taking into account the price rise it might be said that the value of the increased revenue is not £20 000 but only £10 000. In general terms one would have expected the restaurant to increase its revenue to £110 000 in the second year just to remain at the same revenue level, i.e. £100 000 plus the rate of inflation/rate of price increase at 10 per cent (£10 000) would be £110 000. Although the restaurant had an actual revenue of £120 000, taking account of the effect of inflation will mean that revenue has increased only by £10 000, or 9.1 per cent in real terms. (To take account of inflation the revenue should have been £110 000. Actual revenue was £120 000, the percentage increase is therefore 9.1 per cent [£10 000/£110 000 × 100].)

When comparing revenue for different time periods, it is therefore important to know if price rises and inflation have been taken into account.

## Comparing like with like

Revenue comparisons between food and beverage units should also be made with some caution and in relation to the circumstances. Two roadside restaurants in the same chain will have identical menus and prices, and may even have the same seating capacity, but their revenues may be different. This difference in revenue will still be a product of the volume and price variables, but factors outside the control of the unit management, such as location and spending power of their market, will affect revenue levels, and therefore the revenue budgets need to allow for these differences. Revenue comparisons between food and beverage businesses also need to be made with caution because the objectives and/or costs of the two businesses may be different. The performance of any operation therefore cannot be made using revenue alone.

In order to make effective comparisons between food and beverage operations other forms of revenue measurements can be made. Revenue per customer/seat/square metre/staff member and so on can be measured and compared with that of similar operations. These measures can also be performed over time on the same business or unit. The real question when these types of measurement and comparison are made is: are they useful? It is not always clear if these measurements and comparisons will be useful until they are actually measured and compared. If the time and data are available to make these types of detailed measure and comparison, then it may be worth doing.

## Comparison over time

Perhaps the most useful form of revenue appraisal is over time. Average spend per head, average revenue per customer, number of customers, revenue per member of staff, revenue per square metre and so on can all be measured on an ongoing basis and compared. It will therefore be possible to identify changes and perhaps trends, and if any significant changes in these measures are noticed, remedial action can be taken.

When comparing over time, comparisons are often made between the same periods of different years, for example January this year with January last year. This can have problems. The number of Sundays for instance can have an effect on the potential of the business let alone the actual achievement. The operations may be closed on a Sunday. For this reason, rolling totals of twelve months are often used. Thus the total revenue and other measures for the twelve months to the end of January are compared with the total revenue and other measures for the twelve months to the end of December. This type of comparison over time gives a far better indication of actual trends than simply taking a comparison of month to month.

## Key points of revenue appraisal

- Revenue is a product of price and volume. An appraisal of revenue will need to take account of changes in both of these variables.

- Averages of price, volume and revenue do not always accurately reflect the complete situation and are prone to misinterpretation.

- Inflation and price rises need to be taken into account when comparing different trading periods.

- Different businesses, operations and units may have different objectives, and direct comparisons may not be comparing like with like.

- Comparison over time can be useful, and it is worth considering with rolling twelve-month totals providing a useful basis for determining true trends and performance.

- Revenue cannot be fully appraised without reference to other operational variables such as cost and profit.

## APPRAISING COSTS

Whilst it is important for the operation to obtain revenue, costs are seen as the most important item for the operation to *control*. Costs are usually divided into fixed, variable and semi-variable costs:

- *Fixed costs* remain constant over a set period of time even though the level of business fluctuates. Such costs include rent, rates and insurance premiums.

- *Variable costs* are proportional to the level of business and might include meal ingredient costs and beverage costs.

- *Semi-variable* costs are part fixed and part variable, for example staff and fuel.

However, it is more important to know how and why any costs are incurred, and how to measure them accurately, than to argue if they are fixed, variable or semi-variable.

Most *fixed costs* (and some *variable costs*) can be negotiated with the supplier. Rent, insurance and even interest rates (the cost of borrowing money) are services that are supplied within a competitive market and it is therefore worth considering opportunities for alternative, and possibly cheaper, sources of these services. Once the costs of these services are established, they are then fixed for the duration of the contract period, which is usually one year (although interest rates and some other costs can fluctuate more often).

*Variable costs* and *semi-variable costs* can be appraised in absolute terms, but are more commonly appraised as a proportion of revenue. Putting aside the fixed part of the semi-variable costs (for example the standing charge for electricity), these variable costs are proportional to the volume of business and therefore revenue. A food and beverage operation will measure the costs of food, beverages, staff, linen, disposables, marketing, maintenance and other variables as a percentage of revenue, usually on a weekly basis.

## Identifying and measuring costs

Appraising these fixed and variable costs objectively can be performed as follows.

- *A cross-sectional analysis* This can be performed by comparing the costs incurred by one food and beverage operation with those incurred by similar types of food and beverage operation, thereby allowing a 'value for money' appraisal to be performed. Publications such as Keynote and Mintel reports and trade magazines such as *Caterer & Hotelkeeper*, *Restaurant Magazine* and others, provide useful information in this area, so that comparisons can be made. However, the cost structures of food and beverage operations can vary in a way which makes comparisons difficult. For example, one restaurant may be owned and operated by a family partnership which owns the premises outright (the debt having been paid off over a long period of time), whilst another restaurant is paying high rent or interest charges. The fixed costs of these two similar restaurants will be very different, resulting in a much lower break-even point (the point at which the operation starts making a profit) for the restaurant with the lower fixed costs. These cost structures are often seen to change over the life cycles of most businesses.

- *Relating one cost to other costs* Costs are almost certain to increase in absolute terms year on year, owing to inflation and the changing cost structure of the business, but by appraising costs as a proportion of total costs, or as a proportion of total revenue, a comparative measure can be established. For example, if fixed costs in year 1 are 25 per cent of total costs and 7 per cent of total sales, and in year 2 are 30 per cent and 9 per cent respectively, then a relative dimension is added to cost appraisal. These changes in costs can be calculated to provide a relative measure, which helps in their appraisal. This relative measure is sometimes miscalculated, as there may be confusion as to how percentage changes are measured. Table 7.2 gives an example of how these measurements are made.

**Table 7.2** Calculation of change in costs and revenues

| Costs/revenues | £ |
| --- | --- |
| Last period's cost | 1 000 |
| Present period's cost | 1 200 |
| Last period's revenue | 10 000 |
| Present period's revenue | 11 000 |
| Absolute change in cost | 200 |
| **Percentages** | **%** |
| % change in absolute cost | 20 |
| Last period's cost as a percentage of revenue | 10 |
| Present period's cost as a percentage of revenue | 10.9 |
| % change in cost as a percentage of revenue | 9 |

■ *A time-series analysis* Comparing costs over a period of time, usually year on year, is the basis for this type of analysis. The absolute and the percentage change in these costs can be measured and a comparison made with the previous year's changes. One common budget or standard objective measure in these circumstances is the current rate of inflation or retail price index. Changes in staff costs (rates of pay) are often related and calculated in this way. However, if some costs are seen to rise significantly more or less than the current rate of inflation, or significantly more or less than in previous years, consideration should be given to changing the operating systems of the food and beverage business to take advantage of, or counter, this changing cost structure. Changing from electricity to gas or changing from silver service to buffet service, in order to reduce fuel or staff costs, would be examples of changing operating systems in order to reduce these costs in real and proportional terms.

Again in this approach it is often that comparisons are made between the same periods of different years. As was considered under revenue above (page 227) approaching comparisons in this way can have problems. Therefore consideration should also be given to the comparison of rolling twelve-month totals over time.

Table 7.2 indicates how the percentage change in absolute terms is calculated by dividing the difference between the costs in this period and the period before (£1200 − £1000 = £200), by the original or last period's cost (£1000), and multiplying by 100:

$$\frac{1\,200 - 1\,000}{1\,000} \times 100 = 20\%$$

Costs can be said to have risen 20 per cent in absolute terms. However, as a percentage of revenue, costs have been seen to rise from 10 per cent to 10.9 per cent. The percentage change in these cost percentages is calculated as follows:

$$\frac{10.9 - 10}{10} \times 100 = 9\%$$

The percentage change in costs as a percentage of revenue is 9 per cent. The percentage change between 10 per cent and 10.9 per cent is *not* 0.9 per cent. It is critically important to know the difference between these measurements, 20 per cent being the absolute cost change percentage, and 9 per cent being the relative change in the cost as a percentage of the revenue. It might perhaps be more accurate to say that costs have risen by 9 per cent (relative to revenue) than by 20 per cent (in absolute terms).

If the figures here were representing rolling twelve-month totals, the same issues would apply. However using a twelve-month rolling total gives a truer indication of trends and how the operation is doing over time. It is worth considering.

## Industry norms

There is no one standard or budget percentage for the various costs. Food costs of between 20 and 60 per cent are often quoted as acceptable for particular types of operation, as are staff costs of between 11 and 35 per cent and marketing costs of between 1 and 2 per cent. Some examples of food, liquor and labour costs for different types of operation are given in Table 7.3. However, these figures should be used only as a guide because the actual percentage of the cost will vary depending on the specific objectives of the food and beverage operation.

It might be assumed that some sectors of the industry will share similar cost percentages, but there is no evidence to support this assumption. An up-market restaurant with an average spend per head of around £50–£70 may have the same food cost percentage as a roadside food and beverage operation with an average spend per head of around £5. The two operations may also have similar staff cost percentages. Conversely, two very similar operations may have widely differing cost percentages, for example staff cost percentages being low, say 15 per cent of total revenue in an operation run and staffed by a

**Table 7.3** Examples of food, liquor and labour cost percentages for differing types of foodservice operation

| Type of operation | Food cost (%) | Liquor cost (%) | Labour cost (%) |
|---|---|---|---|
| Public house | 40–60 | 45–60 | 15–30 |
| Restaurant | 30–50 | 35–55 | 25–35 |
| Banqueting | 30–45 | 30–45 | 18–32 |
| Fast food | 20–35 | – | 11–18 |
| Popular catering | 30–45 | 45–60 | 15–35 |
| Wine bar | 50–60 | 45–55 | 12–22 |

family, and being say 25 per cent of total revenue in an operation which hires staff on the open market. Small family businesses like restaurants and takeaways can have low barriers to entry, and because of the family interest family staff members are willing to work long hours at rates of pay below what is acceptable to others, resulting in much lower staff cost percentages.

In some sectors of the foodservice industry, the market is becoming much more competitive and more concentrated in the hands of the large operators. For example, in retail foodservice, prime high street sites have become prohibitively expensive to all but those who can significantly reduce costs and afford the highly expensive mass advertising campaigns and premium rents. The barriers to entry in this 'retail foodservice' market are becoming higher and therefore restricting the smaller and family-run operations.

This move towards an oligopolistic industry structure is also found in 'contract', 'outside' and 'transport foodservice operations', and cost percentage comparisons between them can be made. The chain, or group, food and beverage operations place great value on reducing costs and cost percentages as this is seen as leading to greater profits, and opportunities for a greater market share than their rivals through more competitive pricing. In this highly competitive market, economies of scale, especially in distribution, purchasing and marketing costs, provide advantages over the smaller operator. A greater investment in new technology also provides opportunities to develop more efficient and cheaper operating systems. These large operators see their actual survival as dependent upon their ability to reduce and control their costs, and therefore the value placed on cost comparisons between them is high.

## Apportioning costs

In order to understand the cost structure of a food and beverage operation it is necessary to know why the various costs are incurred, and which costs can, or should, be attributed to the various parts of the operation. As the product is made up from a number of variables comprising the meal experience,[2] and is therefore not homogeneous – because different customers purchase and value different parts of the experience – apportioning costs requires the identification of the component parts of the product.

Costs are often identified as being either direct or indirect. *Direct costs* can, by definition, be apportioned directly to the various parts of the menu and drinks list. The ingredient costs of a meal or drink may be calculated accurately and therefore the direct cost for each item on the food and drinks list identified. The use of standard recipes and tailor-made spreadsheets is common amongst large operators in identifying and measuring these direct costs.

---

[2] The 'meal experience' (see page 13) comprises the food and drink, the level of service, the cleanliness and hygiene and the price/value for money and the atmosphere.

*Indirect costs*, which comprise almost all the other costs beside the ingredient costs, are much more difficult to apportion. Examples of these indirect costs are: staff, linen, maintenance, cleaning materials, marketing, management, administration, rent, rates, fixtures, fittings, equipment, insurance, training and fuel. In order to overcome the problem of measuring how much of these costs should be apportioned to the individual menu and drinks list items, the costs are commonly apportioned as a percentage of the selling price. This proportion is usually identified as the proportion of the total individual cost to total revenue, for example:

| | |
|---|---|
| Total food revenue | = £1000.00 |
| Total staff costs | = £300.00 |
| Staff cost (%) | = 30% |
| Individual menu item selling price | = £1.25 |
| Apportioned staff cost at 30% | = £0.375 |

All other indirect costs are often calculated and apportioned in this way, or they can be formed into groups such as overheads (for example, rent and rates), or operational expenses (for example, linen and cleaning materials). Which costs are included in these different groupings can vary from operation to operation. Many operations will simply group all these indirect costs together under 'overheads'; such apportioning is calculated as follows:

| | |
|---|---|
| Total food and beverage sales | = £1000.00 |
| Total overheads | = £120.00 |
| Overhead cost | = 12% |
| Individual menu or drinks list item selling price | = £1.25 |
| Apportioned overhead cost at 12% | = £0.15 |

Although this is an uncomplicated way to apportion costs, it is clearly not accurate. If total staff costs are 30 per cent of total revenue, it does not necessarily follow that all menu and wine list items have a labour element of 30 per cent of their selling price. It is the processes that the various ingredients undergo which determine the labour cost, and as various ingredients undergo different processes – some highly skilled and time-consuming, others simple and quick – the labour costs for individual menu and drinks list items are quite different. The same inaccuracy is inherent in apportioning other indirect costs.

It is for these reasons that in foodservice operations only the material costs (food and drink) are directly related to revenue. This is the basis of a gross profit calculation for all foodservice operations. All other costs are treated as being incurred by the operation as a whole. This is the basis for determining net profit. The appraisal of profits is discussed further below.

## Key points of cost appraisal

■ The cost structures of food and beverage operations vary, and change over time.

■ Costs can be measured in absolute terms or as percentages of total costs and revenue.

■ Changes in the proportional relationship between costs can be measured, helping to identify opportunities for increased efficiency through changing the operating systems.

■ Proportional relationships between costs and inflation also need to be taken into account.

■ Cross-sectional and time-series analyses can be used to appraise costs.

■ Rolling twelve-month totals can provide a useful basis for determining true trends and performance.

■ Increased competition amongst food and beverage operators is leading towards an oligopoly market in some sectors, creating a situation where operators with the lowest costs are perceived as having an important advantage.

■ Allocating direct costs is uncomplicated, but methods of allocating indirect costs need to be considered carefully.

**APPRAISING PROFITS**

Profits (or losses) are the difference between revenue and costs, and appraising profit requires the identification of the relationship between the revenue and the costs. The profit and loss account of an operation summarises the result of this relationship. Table 7.4 gives an example of a simple profit and loss account.

In the example given in Table 7.4 the profit is £200, but this does not necessarily tell the whole story. Because profitability is expressed in many different ways, and as food and beverage operators use these ways differently, it is important to clarify which costs have, or have not, been included in the profit measure.

**Table 7.4  Example profit and loss account**

| Item | £ |
|---|---|
| Income/revenue | 1000 |
| Direct costs/ingredient costs | 300 |
| Staff costs | 250 |
| Operating costs | 100 |
| Overheads | 150 |
| Total costs | 800 |
| Profit | 200 |

**Table 7.5**  Comparison of gross profits

|  | Example | | | | | |
|---|---|---|---|---|---|---|
|  | 4 oz beefburger | £ | Bowl of soup | £ | Food and beverage operation | £ |
| Income | Selling price | 3.50 | Selling price | 1.75 | Food and beverage revenue | 1000 |
| Expenditure | 4 oz burger | 0.50 | Stock | 0.07 | Food costs | 170 |
|  | Lettuce | 0.07 | Onions | 0.18 | Drink costs | 130 |
|  | Dill | 0.05 | Oil | 0.05 |  |  |
|  | Mayonnaise | 0.09 | Croutons | 0.04 |  |  |
|  | Bun | 0.15 |  |  |  |  |
| Total cost |  | 1.49 |  | 0.34 |  | 300 |
| Gross profit |  | 2.01 |  | 1.41 |  | 700 |

## Profitability measures

The main profitability measures are explained below:

- *Gross profit* (GP) in food and beverage operations is the difference between the selling price or revenue, and the cost of the food or drink ingredients. Three examples are given in Table 7.5.

- *Gross profit percentage* (GP%) is the gross profit measured as a percentage of the selling price or revenue. The GP% of the beefburger example is 57.4, the GP% for the soup is 80.6, and the GP% for the operation example is 70. Food and beverage operations use this measure extensively but it is important to recognise that a higher GP% does not always mean a higher GP. The soup has a higher GP% at 80.6 than the beefburger at 57.4, but the soup is less profitable in absolute or cash terms with a lower GP – at £1.41 – than the beefburger at £2.01.

- *Operating profit* is measured in different ways by food and beverage operators, but its common usage would be that profit which has been derived solely from the operation, and excluding any profit that might have been made from selling land or buildings for example, which may have been owned by the business. Again, it is necessary to establish if any such 'non-operational' profits have been included in this measure before it can be appraised. It is also necessary to establish if overhead costs have been deducted.

- *Operating profit percentage* is the operating profit measured as a percentage of revenue. As with GP%, a higher operating profit percentage does not always mean a higher operating profit; Table 7.6 gives two examples. Operation A has a higher operating profit percentage at 20 per cent than operation B at 15 per cent, but operation B has made a higher operating profit at £300 than operation A at £200.

**Table 7.6** Comparison of operating profits

|  | Operation | |
|---|---|---|
|  | A | B |
| Revenue | £1000 | £2000 |
| Operating costs[a] | £ 800 | £1700 |
| Operating profit | £ 200 | £ 300 |
| Operating profit (%) | 20% | 15% |

[a] These costs would include ingredient costs and staff costs, but maybe not overheads, therefore the extent to which the other costs might have been included needs to be established

■ *Net profit* is usually the measure which has deducted all costs from the revenue, including the overheads. However, it is possible that not all costs have been deducted. Sometimes the cost of interest payments, loan repayments and dividends will not have been deducted, and again care must be taken to check this.

■ *Net profit percentage* is the net profit measured as a percentage of revenue. Again, a higher net profit percentage does not always mean a higher net profit. (See operating profit example above.)

■ *Net operating profit* net operating profit percentage, both before and after tax and/or dividends, are other measures which are used. Again, it is necessary to check which costs have or have not been deducted, and to appreciate the difference between a percentage measure and an absolute measure.

■ *Departmental and unit profit* are measures that are used to identify the profitability of individual departments or units within a food and beverage operation. Some costs can be directly attributed to a department or unit, such as the cost of staff who work only in that section, and food and drink costs, but other costs such as rates and rent may be more difficult to apportion accurately.

■ *Yield* profitability measures are used mainly to measure the profitability of the beverage side of a food and beverage operation, although it can also be applied to the food side. Table 7.7 shows how yield is calculated.

At the end of each period, usually a week or month, the amount of beverage stock consumed is identified for each beverage item held in stock. The selling price of each of the beverage items – taken from the price list/wine list – is multiplied by the units of that beverage item consumed, to produce the yield. This yield is then measured as a percentage of the actual revenue.

In operation A the yield was 104 per cent. This happens because:
- Drinks have been mixed, as in a cocktail, which realises a greater revenue than the sum of the parts that have been used to create the mixture.
- Customers have been overcharged or short-changed.

**Table 7.7  Yield comparisons**

|                                          | Operations |        |
| ---------------------------------------- | ---------- | ------ |
|                                          | A          | B      |
| Total beverage revenue or yield          | £1000      | £1000  |
| Total selling price of beverage consumed | £ 960      | £1050  |
| Yield percentage                         | 104%       | 95.2%  |

- Customers have been given short measures.
- The yield measure has been miscalculated.
- Wastage has not been as high as expected.

In operation B the yield was 95.2 per cent. This happens because:
- Wastage or ullage has occurred.
- Customers have been undercharged.
- Customers have been given a larger measure than necessary.
- All the revenue has not been received.
- The measure has been miscalculated.

Measuring the yield percentage therefore allows an appraisal of that operation's efficiency in (a) delivering the product and (b) receiving the correct revenue.

Whichever profitability measures are used it is critical to know which costs have been included in the calculations, how they were apportioned and which costs may have still to be deducted. When this has been established it is then possible to appraise profitability in both absolute and relative terms.

Before going on to consider the nature of profit in more detail, a summary of the relationship between revenue, costs and profits for foodservice operations is presented in Figure 7.1.

Thus in foodservice operations:

- *Revenue* (or sales) is most often counted as 100 per cent, and percentages for costs are always determined on this basis, i.e. as a percentage of sales.

- *Gross profit* is total sales less cost of sales (or material costs for food and beverages) and again the gross profit percentage[3] is determined as a percentage of sales.

- *Net profit* is revenue less cost of sales, overheads and labour costs. Again, net profit percentage and the percentage of overheads and labour is calculated as a percentage of sales.

---

[3] For kitchen operations the gross profit percentage is sometimes referred to as kitchen percentage or kitchen profit.

| Food and beverage costs | Cost of sales |
|---|---|
| Labour costs | |
| Overhead costs | Gross profit |
| Net profit | |
| **Sales** | **Revenue 100%** |

**Figure 7.1** Summary of the relationship between revenue, costs and profits in foodservice operations

Examples of operational calculations, which include an illustration of the relationship between revenue, costs and profits, based on the matrix shown in Figure 7.1, are given in Appendix B.

## Exploring gross profit

Gross profit percentage (GP%) is widely considered to be the most important profitability measure. In most food and beverage operations this is measured weekly, although it can be measured as often as is required as long as there are the resources available.

GP% is a simple measure of efficiency but it is important not to confuse efficiency with profitability. On many occasions an efficient operation is also a profitable one, but this is not always the case. Food and beverage operations purchase ingredients which are processed into a consumable meal or drink. This process is adding value to the raw ingredients, and the extent to which value is added is a measure of that operation's efficiency at achieving this conversion process.

An operation which converts a £2 ingredient cost into an £8 meal or drink might be said to be 400 per cent efficient (the price divided by the cost), and an operation which converts a £1 ingredient cost into a £5 meal or drink can be said to be 500 per cent efficient. The second example is more efficient (500 is greater than 400) but is less profitable (£4 compared to £6).

An operation that has poor purchasing resulting in higher ingredient costs, poor storage resulting in wastage, poor security resulting in pilferage, poor production resulting in high wastage, poor portioning resulting in larger portions than specified and poor pricing resulting in lower revenue, will have a lower GP% than the same operation which improves on these poor performances. In larger foodservice organisations the unit or departmental manager is seen to have an influence over how these activities are performed, and as such the GP% is thought to measure a particular manager's performance. However, it is not usually the case that the unit or departmental manager has any influence over the price, this being determined higher up the organisation, and on many occasions they will not have an influence over the purchasing because specified suppliers and negotiated prices are again determined higher up the organisation.

The actual GP% figure against which a manager's performance is measured will also be set higher up the organisation. In a chain operation, these GP%s will be set for each operation based on the sales mix of the menu and beverage lists. This sales mix – the amount sold of each menu and beverage list item – will vary from operation to operation depending on the customer profile and the selling techniques of the staff.

The manager can influence the selling techniques of the staff, but usually has little influence over the customer profile. Perhaps the most influential factor over customer profile, especially in chain operations, is location. Bearing in mind these factors, an operation will be allocated a 'suitable' GP% to obtain. Achieving this prescribed GP% is seen to be a good performance, whilst not achieving it is seen to be a poor performance.

One way in which to decide upon the prescribed GP% is to run a particular unit or department over a period of time and take an average of the GP%s achieved. In reality, GP%s are often set with reference to a desired efficiency level based on what is thought to be achievable (see also potential profitability, page 241). This GP% is also seen to change as new menus are introduced.

An important factor which influences the introduction of new menus is the opportunity to increase the operation's efficiency, and therefore new menus may often come with a higher required GP%. In these situations a chain operation usually pilots the new menus in selected units in order to obtain customer feedback and to establish the new efficiency and profitability measure. This measure is then applied to the rest of the group's operations with slight variations for different customer profiles, as these will affect the sales mix of the individual units.

Having established the required GP%, the departmental or unit manager is then measured against the ability to achieve it. The dilemma with this measurement is that it measures a percentage, not an absolute figure. Percentages cannot be banked. A higher than required GP% will not necessarily realise a higher than required cash GP if the required revenue is not achieved (see Table 7.8).

**Table 7.8**   Comparison of GP in relation to revenue

|  | Operation | |
|---|---|---|
|  | A | B |
| Required revenue | £1000 | £1000 |
| Actual revenue | £ 900 | £1100 |
| GP% required | 65 | 65 |
| GP% achieved | 66 | 64 |
| GP required | £ 650 | £ 650 |
| GP achieved | £ 594 | £ 704 |

Operation A has a higher GP% than required, at 66 (good management?) but achieves a GP of only £594 – £56 below that required – because sales have not achieved their target (perhaps out of the control of the operation).

Operation B achieves a GP% below that which is required, at 64 (bad management?), but achieves a GP of £704 – £54 above that required – because sales have exceeded the target (again, perhaps out of the control of the operation).

Operation A could be said to be more efficient than operation B, but operation B is more profitable than operation A.

The example given in Table 7.8 indicates the reason why GP% is often more highly valued than GP itself. The GP% as a measure of efficiency will allow for variations of revenue. If operation A had achieved its GP% of 65, its actual GP would have been £584, and although this is below the required GP of £650 the operation can still be viewed as adding value or operating efficiently. The fact that sales are £100 under that which is required may not be directly under the influence of the manager. Indeed it is normal for sales to fluctuate owing to the inaccuracies of budgeting and forecasting. Therefore, by measuring GP%, allowances for these sales fluctuations are made. The same reasoning is applied to operation B. Sales are above the required or budgeted amount, but if the operation were running as efficiently as required and achieved its GP% of 65, the actual GP would have been £715 – £11 more than actually achieved.

## The dominance of gross profit percentages

Many departmental and unit managers will perceive the achievement of the GP% as more important than the achievement of the budgeted revenue. As explained earlier in this chapter (page 222), revenue budgets may be seen as being too high for the unit to obtain, and that even if the revenue budgets are achieved this may only mean that they are set higher next year. However, if the GP% is regularly achieved, the manager can state that the operation is being run efficiently. This thinking takes place at all the operational levels within a food and beverage operation. Regional managers and directors should be more concerned with cash profits than with percentage profits, but at the operational level the percentage profits are more highly valued, often because more senior managers can also attach too much value to them.

The reason for this anomaly is because the GP% measure is seen as a measure for controlling the efficiency of the management and staff rather than addressing profitability. As it is used as a control method, opportunities exist to exploit the system to the detriment of cash profit. A study by Shortt (1992) asked managers at a chain operation which items on their menus and beverage lists were identified for positive selling. (These were the items that managers trained their staff to positively sell.) As it is understood that different menu and beverage items realise different GPs and GP%s, the items identified by the managers for positive selling were always items with a relatively high GP%. Table 7.9 gives an example.

**Table 7.9** Comparison of GP and GP%

| Menu items | GP (£) | GP% | Selling price (£) |
| --- | --- | --- | --- |
| Beef | 6.00 | 50 | 12.00 |
| Plaice | 3.50 | 70 | 5.00 |
| Chicken | 4.50 | 75 | 6.00 |
| Lamb | 5.20 | 65 | 8.00 |

In the theoretical situation in Table 7.9, the two menu items identified by the manager for positive selling would be the plaice and chicken because they yielded a higher GP% than the beef and lamb. By selling these items the manager was aiming to achieve as high a GP% as possible for the individual sale of a menu item, which would in turn contribute positively to the achievement of the required GP% for the whole operation. If, in this situation, the required GP% was 68, the plaice and the chicken sales would shift the balance of GP% achievement towards this goal, but any sales of beef and lamb would shift this balance away from the goal. The manager is motivated by an efficiency control mechanism towards achieving a required profit percentage.

However, a more profit-focused examination of Table 7.9 reveals that it is not the plaice and the chicken dishes that are the most profitable items in cash terms. With GPs of £3.50 and £4.50, respectively, they are considerably less profitable than the beef and the lamb dishes at £6.00 and £5.20, respectively. A positive selling policy promoting sales of beef and lamb dishes would realise greater cash gross profits than the one promoting plaice and chicken dishes. However, because GP% is the control measure, the operation is seen to place more value on percentage profitability than on cash profitability, with the result of a decrease in cash profit. The fact that a control measure, which is so widely used in the foodservice industry, should have this effect (or at least the possibility of this effect) should be of serious concern to all foodservice operators.

## Potential gross profit and potential gross profit percentage

Some food and beverage operations attempt to avoid the situation described above by the use of a further measure, which is termed potential profitability.

With the increasing introduction of computerised tills and control systems, some operators calculate the GP and GP% that an operation should have achieved in theory for a particular time period. The ingredient cost and price of each menu or beverage item have already been entered into the till system which then automatically records the number of sales of these particular items, and thus a theoretical GP and GP% are calculated.

Recording such data is not new – computerised stock control systems are the main application of such systems – but not all operators are aware that these data can be converted into meaningful sales mix analysis information, of which potential GP and GP% are but two examples. Table 7.10 shows how potential GP and GP% are calculated.

**Table 7.10   Sales mix example**

| Menu item | Cost (£) | Price (£) | No. sold | Revenue | GP | GP% |
|-----------|----------|-----------|----------|---------|------|-----|
| Beef | 6.00 | 12.00 | 100 | 1200 | 600 | 50 |
| Plaice | 1.50 | 5.00 | 150 | 750 | 525 | 70 |
| Chicken | 1.50 | 6.00 | 130 | 780 | 585 | 75 |
| Lamb | 2.80 | 8.00 | 70 | 560 | 364 | 65 |
| Total | | | 450 | 3290 | 2075 | 63 |

**Table 7.11   Effect of changed sales mix**

| Menu item | Cost (£) | Price (£) | No. sold | Revenue | GP | GP% |
|-----------|----------|-----------|----------|---------|------|-----|
| Beef | 6.00 | 12.00 | 50 | 600 | 300 | 50 |
| Plaice | 1.50 | 5.00 | 200 | 1000 | 700 | 70 |
| Chicken | 1.50 | 6.00 | 130 | 780 | 585 | 75 |
| Lamb | 2.80 | 8.00 | 70 | 560 | 364 | 65 |
| Total | | | 450 | 2940 | 1949 | 66 |

Each of the four items on the menu in Table 7.10 is seen to be achieving a different GP and GP%. After totalling the GP and revenue, the potential GP and GP% are calculated at £2075 and 63, respectively. This potential GP and GP% are what the operation should achieve with this particular sales mix. However, if the sales mix were to change from one period to another for any number of reasons (weather, party bookings, change in positive selling routine), then the potential GP and GP% may also change. Using the example of Table 7.10, an increase in the number of plaice sold and a decrease in the number of beef sold, while the total number of covers served remains the same, produce a lower potential (and hence achievable) GP and GP%. Table 7.11 shows the new potential measures to be £1949 and 66, respectively.

In operations where potential GP and GP% are calculated it is possible to measure the operation's performance against that which was achievable in relation to the sales mix for that particular period. In the two examples above it is seen that, although the operation in Table 7.11 produces a potential GP% of 66 (a potential GP of £1949), it is not as profitable as the operation in Table 7.10, which produces a potential GP% of only 63 (but a potential GP of £2075 – £126 more). Operations that calculate potential cash GP and GP% are therefore more able to measure the operation's efficiency in relation to a changing sales mix. This method of calculating potential cash GP and GP% continues to take account not only of changing sales levels but also of changes in the sales mix, and as such can be seen as a much fairer way of measuring an operation's performance. More importantly, however, is the change in emphasis of this control and performance measure away from measuring GP% and towards measuring actual GP (cash). Thus, taking potential GP% and cash GP into account shifts the appraisal of profit towards cash and away from percentages.

However, in operations where potential GP% is calculated, there is evidence that there is a third GP% which is used to measure and control performance, namely a desired GP%. This desired GP% is set at a level that the operator would like to achieve, in much the same way as the GP% is set in operations where they do not calculate potential GP%. An example of how this might work in practice for a particular time period is:

| | |
|---|---|
| Potential GP% | 69 |
| Actual GP% achieved | 68.5 |
| Desired GP% | 70 |

In this example the operator has set a desired GP% of 70. This is the GP% that the operator wants to achieve. From the actual sales mix for that period it was possible only to achieve a GP% of 69 – the potential GP% – and a GP% of 68.5 was actually obtained. The value placed on this performance might therefore be as follows:

The unit was unable to achieve the GP% desired by the operator. This is a result of the sales mix and may have happened because waiting staff were unable to sell the required high GP% menu and beverage list items. However, the unit was also unable to achieve the potential GP%, which is a measure of their inefficiency to add the required value.

Calculating potential GP% and GP, and using them to help appraise food and beverage operations, still allows for fluctuations of revenue – the reason why GP% is used as the main performance measure – but moves the consideration of value in the direction of GP cash and away from GP%. That many foodservice operators do not calculate potential GP% and GP, even though they already have the technology to do so, means that they are potentially reducing their ability to maximise cash profitability.

## Sales mix analysis

Sales mix analysis methods involve identifying the sales relationship between the various menu and beverage list items. By far the most common application of these analyses is to determine the relationship of item numbers sold, i.e. a popularity index. A simple beverage list example is shown in Table 7.12.

From the information shown in Table 7.12 it can be observed that Loire wines represent 35 per cent of the total wine sales and as such are the most popular customer purchase. Bordeaux wines are the next most popular at 30 per cent. Rhône wines at 25 per cent are the third most popular, and champagne at 10 per cent is the least popular customer purchase.

**Table 7.12   Sales mix example (beverages)**

| Item | No. sold | % of total |
|------|----------|------------|
| Champagne | 20 | 10 |
| Rhône wines | 50 | 25 |
| Loire wines | 70 | 35 |
| Bordeaux wines | 60 | 30 |
| Total | 200 | 100 |

**Table 7.13   Example of profitability calculations**

| Item | GP (£) | No. sold | % | Total GP (£) | % of total GP |
|------|--------|----------|---|--------------|---------------|
| Standard burger | 0.90 | 650 | 31.2 | 585.00 | 23.8 |
| 4 oz burger | 1.20 | 540 | 25.9 | 648.00 | 26.4 |
| Standard cheeseburger | 1.08 | 320 | 15.3 | 345.60 | 14.1 |
| 4 oz cheeseburger | 1.40 | 290 | 13.9 | 460.00 | 16.5 |
| Double superburger | 1.65 | 285 | 13.7 | 470.25 | 19.2 |
| Total | | 2085 | 100.0 | 2454.85 | 100 |

Many operators use the identification and ranking of item popularity to assist with the compilation of new menus and beverage lists. In its most simplistic form the least popular item or items are removed from the listing, although this is not always the case. In Table 7.12, champagne might be retained on the wine list because customers expect to be able to purchase it when required, albeit infrequently. Champagne on the wine list will also contribute to the operation's image.

However, popularity should not be confused with profitability. There is a relationship between popularity and profitability, but the most popular selling item is not necessarily the most profitable. In order to examine this relationship it is important to identify which type of profit should be measured. As this is a relationship between individual menu and wine list items, the requirement is that the profit measure must also relate to these individual items. Apportioning costs to individual food and beverage items is difficult. How much of the electricity expenses should be apportioned to each item for example? The same difficulty is experienced when attempting to apportion labour costs. However, direct ingredient costs can be apportioned, which will result in a measure of GP for each individual item. A relationship between popularity and GP is illustrated in Table 7.13.

From Table 7.13 it is possible to compare a popularity ranking with a profitability ranking, as shown in Table 7.14. The profitability ranking is clearly different from the popularity ranking, enabling a more focused valuation of the sales mix in relation to how much the individual menu items contribute, at a GP level, to operational profitability.

**Table 7.14**  Example of popularity and profitability ranking

| Popularity ranking | % of sales | Profitability ranking | % of GP |
|---|---|---|---|
| Standard burger | 31.2 | 4 oz burger | 26.4 |
| 4 oz burger | 25.9 | Standard burger | 23.8 |
| Standard cheeseburger | 15.3 | Double superburger | 19.2 |
| 4 oz cheeseburger | 13.9 | 4 oz cheeseburger | 16.5 |
| Double superburger | 13.7 | Standard cheeseburger | 14.1 |

It is unclear how many food and beverage operators rank their menu and beverage list items in such a way. It appears that most of the large chain operations are using and developing such analysis techniques, as they have marketing departments with the resources required. These techniques have an element of some sophistication; for example, linking with the amount of stock held relative to its profitability, and consideration of a new menu item also relative to its potential profitability. However, these individual company techniques and developments, and their relationship with appraising and improving profitability, are not identified in any literature beyond self-promoting material, which does not critically evaluate the techniques, and makes it difficult to identify their value objectively. However, it is fair to assume that there is some value assigned to these approaches given the extent to which they are resourced. Shortt (1992), in attempting to evaluate these sales mix analyses techniques, found that there was considerable evidence that profitability can be, and was being, improved through the use of such techniques, particularly by larger organisations.

All the various sales mix analysis techniques categorise the individual menu and wine list items and suggest strategies for each category. These strategies are designed to improve profitability, but there is considerable evidence that the techniques themselves can be too complex and unproven to be assigned any value by many operations in the foodservice industry.

## Menu engineering

One approach to sales analysis which had gained some popularity is the technique known as 'menu engineering'. This is a technique of menu analysis that uses two key factors of performance in the sales of individual menu items: the popularity and the GP cash contribution of each item. The analysis results in each menu item being assigned to one of four categories:

- Items of high popularity and high cash GP contributions. These are known as the *Stars*.
- Items of high popularity but with low cash GP contribution. There are known as the *Plowhorses*.

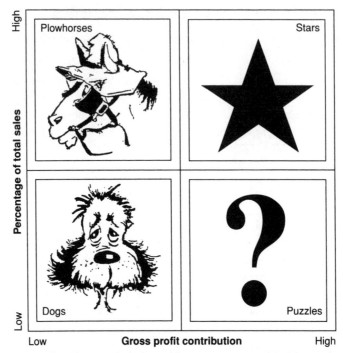

**Figure 7.2**   Menu engineering matrix (Adapted from Kasavana and Smith 1999)

- Items of low popularity but with high cash GP contributions. These are known as the *Puzzles*.
- Items of low popularity and low cash GP contribution. These are the worst items on the menu, and are known as the *Dogs*.

The advantage of this approach is that it provides a simple way of graphically indicating the relative cash contribution position of individual items on a matrix as in Figure 7.2.

There is a variety of computer-based packages which will automatically generate the categorisation, usually directly using data from electronic point-of-sale (EPOS) control systems. The basis for the calculations is as follows.

In order to determine the position of an item on the matrix, two things need to be calculated. These are:

- the cash GP category
- the sales percentage category.

The cash GP category for any menu item is calculated by reference to the weighted average cash GP. Menu items with a cash GP which is the same as or higher than the average are classified as high. Those with lower than the average are classified as low cash

GP items. The average also provides the axis separating Plowhorses and Dogs from Stars and Puzzles.

The sales percentage category for an item is determined in relation to the menu average taking into account an additional factor. With a menu consisting of ten items one might expect, all other things being equal, that each item would account for 10 per cent of the menu mix. Any item which reached at least 10 per cent of the total menu items sold would therefore be classified as enjoying high popularity. Similarly, any item which did not achieve the rightful share of 10 per cent would be categorised as having a low popularity. With this approach, half of the menu items would tend to be shown as being below average in terms of their popularity. This would potentially result in the frequent revision of the composition of the menu. It is for this reason that Kasavana and Smith (1999) have recommended the use of a 70 per cent formula. Under this approach, all items which reach at least 70 per cent of their rightful share of the menu mix are categorised as enjoying high popularity. For example, where a menu consists of, say, 20 items, any item which reached 3.5 per cent or more of the menu mix (70 per cent of 5 per cent) would be regarded as enjoying high popularity. Whilst there is no convincing theoretical support for choosing the 70 per cent figure rather than some other percentage, common sense and experience tend to suggest that there is some merit in this approach.

### Interpreting the categories
There is a different basic strategy which can be considered for items that fall into each of the four categories of the matrix.

- *Stars*  These are the most popular items, which may be able to yield even higher GP contributions by careful price increases or through cost reduction. High visibility is maintained on the menu, and standards for the dishes should be strictly controlled.

- *Plowhorses*  These again are solid sellers which may also be able to yield greater cash profit contributions through marginal cost reduction. Lower menu visibility than Stars is usually recommended.

- *Puzzles*  These are exactly that – puzzles. Items such as flambé dishes or a particular speciality can add an attraction in terms of drawing customers, even though the sales of these items may be low. Depending on the particular item, different strategies might be considered, ranging from accepting the current position because of the added attraction that they provide to increasing the price further.

- *Dogs*  These are the worst items on a menu and the first reaction is to remove them. An alternative, however, is to consider adding them to another item as part of a special deal. For instance, adding them in a meal package to a Star may have the effect of lifting the sales of the Dog item and may provide a relatively low-cost way of adding special promotions to the menu.

### Some potential limitations

■ *Elasticity of demand* One of the practical difficulties with price-level adjustment is not knowing enough about the elasticity of demand. The effect on demand (number of covers) of any one change in the general level of menu prices is usually uncertain. Also, what applies to one menu item applies equally to the menu as a whole. There is an additional problem of cross-elasticity of demand, where the change in demand for one commodity is directly affected by a change in price of another. Even less is known about the cross-elasticity of demand for individual menu items than is known about the elasticity of demand for the menu as a whole. Any benefit arising from an adjustment in the price of one item may therefore be offset by resultant changes in the demand for another item. Price-level adjustments must therefore be underpinned by a good deal of common sense, experience and knowledge of the particular circumstances of the operation.

■ *Labour intensity* In menu engineering the most critical element is cash gross profit. Whilst this may be important, the aspect of labour intensity cannot be ignored. The cash GP on a flambé dish, for example, may be higher than on a more simple sweet; however, when the costs of labour are taken into account – especially at peak periods – it may well be that the more simple sweet is the more profitable overall.

■ *Shelf-life* The food cost of an item used to determine the cash GP may not take account of cost increases which are the result of food wastage through spoilage, especially at slack times.

■ *Fluctuations in demand* Another factor is the consistency of the buying of the consumer. The approach assumes that changes can be made in the promotion of various items and that this will be reflected in the buying behaviour of the customer. The approach will work well where the potential buying pattern of the consumer is fairly similar over long periods. However, where the customers are continually changing, as for instance in the restaurant of an hotel, popularity and profitability can be affected more by changes in the nature of the customer and the resultant change in demand than as a result of the operation's attempting to manipulate the sales mix.

### Further applications

Whilst this technique is presented here related to menu food items, the same technique can also be applied to wine and drinks lists. It is interesting to note, for example, that in many instances the house wine, although having the highest gross profit percentage contribution, often makes a relatively low contribution to the cash gross profit. Additionally, the principles of the technique have also been applied to the selling of hotel rooms and the rates that may be charged, now known as 'yield management'.

It is clear, however, that although there are some difficulties, benefits can arise since the menu engineering approach requires the following:

■ Planning for continuous control of cash GP.

■ Giving prominence to, and controlling the determinants of, menu profitability, i.e. the number of items sold, the cash GP per item and the overall composition of the menu.

■ Application of an analytical approach recognising that menu items belong to distinctly dissimilar groups, which have different characteristics and which require different handling in the context of cash gross profit control.

## Exploring net profit and operating profit

These profitability measures are used to evaluate more fully the efficiency of a food and beverage operation in adding value because they take account of all or most of the costs incurred by the business. The relationship between costs and revenue to produce net and operating profit is not as directly proportional as the GP measure and it is more difficult therefore to identify the relationship between an individual menu and wine list item and total net/operating profit. This relationship has been researched by, amongst others, Pavesic (1989) but again the methods appear too complex to be adopted by much of the foodservice industry.

The main relationship for total net/operating profit appears to be with total sales revenue. This relationship is twofold. As a percentage measure it values an operation's efficiency at adding value. As an absolute measure it values a specific amount of residual utility – usually in cash – which has derived from an absolute revenue. As has already been examined, a high percentage measure may be of less residual utility – cash – than a lower percentage measure. However, as long as the measures are calculated using the same criteria, i.e. they use the same revenue and costs measures, they can be compared. This comparison can help appraise an operation's performance. Table 7.15 states some net/operating profit measures.

In the example in Table 7.15, all the measures have been made using the same criteria, year on year, and in both operations. An appraisal of the operation's performance, as individual one-off food and beverage operations, might be as follows.

### Operation A

■ Sales have increased by £100 000 year on year representing a percentage increase year on year of 6.67 per cent and 6.25 per cent, and overall of 13.3 per cent. Sales for 2000/01 are £100 000 (5.55 per cent) under budget.

■ Net operating profit increased 3.33 per cent by £5000 in year 2 and decreased 6.45 per cent by £10 000 in year 3. Net operating profit for year 3 is £35 000 (19.44 per cent) under budget. Net operating profit has declined by 3.33 per cent (£150 000 to £145 000) from 1998/99 to 2000/01; 2000/01 has seen a reversal of profitability.

■ Net operating profit as a percentage of sales has declined from 10 per cent to 9.7 per cent to 8.53 per cent compared with a required level of 10 per cent.

**Table 7.15**   Comparison of net operating profit measures

| | Financial year | | | | | | Budget for 2000/01 | |
|---|---|---|---|---|---|---|---|---|
| | 1998/99 | | 1999/2000 | | 2000/01 | | | |
| | £000 | % | £000 | % | £000 | % | £000 | % |
| **Operation A** | | | | | | | | |
| Sales | 1500 | | 1600 | | 1700 | | 1800 | |
| Net operating profit | 150 | 10 | 155 | 9.70 | 145 | 8.53 | 180 | 10 |
| **Operation B** | | | | | | | | |
| Sales | 700 | | 750 | | 800 | | 900 | |
| Net operating profit | 70 | 10 | 75 | 10 | 67.5 | 8.44 | 90 | 10 |

**Operation B**

■ Sales have increased by £50 000 year on year representing a percentage increase year on year of 7.14 per cent and 6.67 per cent, and overall of 14.3 per cent. Sales for 2000/01 are £100 000 (11.11 per cent) under budget.

■ Net operating profit increased 7.14 per cent by £5000 in year 2 and decreased 10 per cent by £7500 in year 3. Net operating profit for year 3 is £22 500 and (25 per cent) under budget. From 1998/99 to 2000/01, net operating profit declined by 3.57 per cent (£70 000 to £67 500); 2000/01 has seen a reversal of profitability.

■ Net operating profit as a percentage of sales (10 per cent) was maintained in 1999/2000 and has declined to 8.44 per cent in 2000/2001

The above evaluation identifies the differences between absolute figures and the differences between percentages. This may appear at times to be fairly tortuous, especially when all the changes are presented together. In reality, more value may be placed upon certain measurements than others, depending on the message to be communicated, and not all the measurements will be communicated at the same time.

Using the examples above it might be considered appropriate to say that sales have increased in operation A by over 6 per cent each year, and say nothing about net/operating profit's being almost 20 per cent under budget. This is why it is so important to question the presentation of the information that is provided. When it is stated that sales have increased by over 6 per cent each year, the immediate response should be to ask for other performance measures, in this case profit both in percentage and in cash terms. Questioning is crucial in order to fully appraise an operation. And it is important to remember that it is only cash, and not percentages, that can be banked.

## Industry norms

Many might argue that further value can be placed upon the information in Table 7.15 by comparing the performance of these operations with an industry norm, i.e. a measure which suggests a performance generally found and therefore expected within the industry. There are however two difficulties in this approach:

- Foodservice operations must be categorised into industry sectors before an average or mean net/operating profit can be calculated for that sector. It is possible to categorise foodservice operations but no two operations are the same (even chain operations differ), and each will probably have different objectives resulting in different values being placed upon their profitability.

- The environment in which food and beverage operations operate is dynamic. This environment relates to: consumer behaviour and social/cultural changes; the financial market; the national and international economic position; and political issues and legislation. Different operations will react to these continuing changes in different ways resulting in differing valuations of profitability. The norm therefore may be seen as an arbitrary measure.

However, if an operation's profitability is to be compared with other similar operations, care must be taken to establish the value of the norm in such a comparison. Shortt (1992) found that food and beverage operations taking part in the research had a required GP% in the range 68–72. There was no evidence however that certain operations were more likely to be at the top or the bottom of the range.

## The effects of inflation

Inflation is another consideration as it is a measure of the, usually upward, movement of prices across a range of commodities and services. For example, if net/operating profit had increased by 10 per cent over the past twelve months, and inflation had been 5 per cent over the past twelve months, it might be considered that in real terms profitability is up only 5 per cent (10 per cent profitability improvement minus 5 per cent inflation). This will be an important consideration for those managing, owning and directing food and beverage operations in the appraisal of profitability. In addition, company taxation and dividends are also an important consideration and will affect profitability.

## Stakeholder interests

As in any appraisal of performance, the important consideration in making any comparison is the value of the information to the stakeholders, i.e. those with a vested or invested interest in the business. An understanding of the stakeholder interests can make the appraisal of the operation more objective and of more value.

## Key points of profit appraisal

■ It is always necessary to be clear how any profit measure is contrived and ensure that any comparisons made are like with like.

■ Profitability measures themselves have no value, it is only when they are appraised against an objective that they may have some value attached to them.

■ Setting the objective, norm and/or budget is difficult and sometimes results in subjective judgements.

■ Sales mix analysis is important in determining the difference between the popularity and profitability of items.

■ Gross profit percentages are used as a measure of efficiency but this is not the same as measuring profitability.

■ Profit percentages are often used as the basis for comparison, but cash profit contribution is what the operation should be seeking to achieve.

■ Comparison with industry norms can be useful, if applied with caution, especially to chain operations.

■ Comparison over time can be useful with rolling twelve-month totals providing a useful basis for determining true trends and performance.

■ Considering profitability must take account of the needs and interests of the operation's various stakeholders.

### APPRAISING THE PRODUCT

It is clearly good business sense to monitor the level of satisfaction that customers have with the current customer service specification. This is especially important in relation to changing customer needs. Objective product appraisal will help in determining the extent to which the customer service specification is matching, and continuing to match, both the operator's and the customers' expectations.

We saw in Chapter 1 a six-stage process for an *integrated approach to service quality management* (pages 31–3). This process was summarised in Figure 1.8 (page 32). Stages 4 and 5 of the process require the monitoring of the operational aspects (technical and procedural standards) and the monitoring of customer satisfaction. The undertaking of these two stages in tandem will provide information on the product of the operation, which will identify the changes that might be necessary to the customer service specification.

Single unit and/or owner-operated food and beverage operations often adopt a fairly subjective and intuitive approach to product appraisal. However, this does not mean that it cannot be as effective as a structured and objective one. This subjective and intuitive approach may be more efficient for a single operation that does not have to appraise and control its product over a multi-unit structure. Also, although it is highly dependent on the integrity and skills of its management and staff, there is really no problem if the customers also have the same subjective values and perceptions. It is this intuitive response to customer needs that enables some single food and beverage operations to be highly successful.

Chain operations usually lead the field in this area. With their branded products it is necessary to effect tight control over the customer service specification. Appraising and controlling revenue and costs are systemised through budgeting and standardised procedures. Appraising and controlling the product are also effected through standardised procedures, including the use of standards manuals. Many of these approaches are also adaptable and useful to a single foodservice operation. These include:

- *Customer satisfaction questionnaires*  Customer satisfaction questionnaires are often found in hospitality operations or sent to customers after they have experienced the product. The forms usually ask for some rating of the experience, with details ranging from factors such as warmth of greeting to value for money and also likelihood of recommending the operation to someone else. Whilst these types of form can be very useful from a public relations point of view, they often provide little in the way of useful objective measurement of the achievement of the customer service specification.

- *Complaint monitoring*  The monitoring of complaints (and compliments) can assist in measuring the achievement of customer satisfaction and the achievement of various aspects of the customer service specification. The effectiveness of this process, though, is dependent on being able to determine if the complaint is a result of not meeting the customer service specification. It is quite possible that complaints will come from those whose expectations are higher than the intended customer service specification or that the complaints are unjustified or the result of some other dissatisfaction which is not under the control of the operation.

- *Staff focus group sessions*  The running of staff focus groups can provide a valuable review process for operations, especially when independent people lead these sessions. Opportunities can be taken to review the customer service specification against the experience of the staff who have to operate as part of it. Reports from the service staff can provide a springboard from which to go back through the design of the original customer service specification and to identify where changes can and need to be made.

- *Mystery shopper*  A mystery shopper is an unidentified customer who tests the services of the organisation. This individual will check that standards are maintained. The mystery shopper will work to a brief and checklist (basically a diagnostic tool). Some mystery shoppers will also be involved in benchmarking competitors. Mystery shoppers are not expert; they need by necessity to remain customers. The individual shoppers tend, then, not to be professionals, although the companies behind them are professional.

- *Process reviewer*   The process reviewer differs from a mystery shopper in that the process review is employed to identify problems and also opportunities for improvement. This approach can also be adapted for use in making comparisons with competitors. The process reviewer will more than likely be an internal reviewer (a member of staff) who will also signal training needs. Reviews are primarily concerned with checking if the right things are being done.

- *Quality auditor*   Quality auditors are usually independent people who are concerned with checking on the standards at every stage in order to ensure conformance to procedures. An audit can also test hypotheses or substantiate hunches about organisational service efficiency and effectiveness. The auditor offers independent evaluation of facility and service quality to determine fitness for use and conformance to customer service specifications. The auditor will both observe and participate in the guest experience. Audits tend to be consumer orientated and usually provide a wealth of detail on the operation as well as comparisons with competitor achievement.

- *Quality standards analyst*   The quality standards analyst (QSA) is a professional, often with over twenty years' hospitality industry experience (usually at a minimum standard of four-star hotels). A QSA has in-depth knowledge of interpersonal skills, communication and selling skills, classical cuisine and contemporary international cuisines. They also have in-depth knowledge of beverages and excellent observational skills and memory. They are, in short, expected to have a sound knowledge of all aspects of hotel and restaurant operations. This type of analyst is generally brought in by senior management. The analyst will undertake a planned and systematic examination of the quality system and its implementation and determine the adequacy of the system and conformance to it. This individual will also look at all quality-related aspects of the business. As well as producing a standard report, the analyst will ensure that the report is more qualitative in nature than a quality auditor's report, which is usually more quantitative. The analyst offers independent, expert and articulate evaluation of the experience through observation and participation. Comparisons can also be undertaken with competitor operations. The data collected by QSAs is actionable. Decisions can be made on correcting below-standard performance, rewarding outstanding performance and on what changes are needed to the customer service specification.

The basis of many of these approaches is often a checklist of aspects, with some operations having identified and specified over 150 of these. This list will contain aspects covering such areas as:

- The words, demeanour and body language of the welcome.
- The information and selling routine.
- The time taken to deliver each menu and beverage list item ordered.

- The taste, colour, texture, temperature and presentation of menu and beverage items.
- The presentation of the bill and concluding routine.

Appendix C gives an example of a fine dining audit checklist and an example of a beverage audit checklist.

Once the customer service specification has been evaluated in terms of both the operational aspects (technical and procedural standards) and the level of customer satisfaction, an appraisal can take place in non-customer areas. This part of the appraisal can cover such areas as:

- Temperature and stocking levels in the fridges and freezers.
- Cleanliness, security and safety of all areas.
- Current data collection and collation up to date.

Once this product audit has been completed the results are often calculated as a percentage of the possible achievement. Each operation will, or should, have already determined the level of achievement required. If the level of achievement is unacceptable then resources are concentrated to rectify specific areas of underperformance (or non-compliance with the customer service specification). This process is dynamic, and as changes are made to the product, so the customer service specification is modified.

## Using product appraisal data

The various processes outlined above will produce a variety of data about the operation. This can be used to review, and alter where necessary, the customer service specification. However, within the data there will also be information that may provide for a broader range of possibilities. Better use of the data can provide for a far more qualitative, and therefore richer, analysis of the information, which leads to a better understanding of the operation.

The data can be used to generate information on what is important to the customer and how the operation is achieving those things, is capable of achieving those things and also if the staff share the same view on what is important. Considering these various aspects is the basis of some of the thinking behind the SERVQUAL approaches as discussed in, for instance, Kasper *et al.* (1999). Three examples of useful comparison matrices, which apply and extend some of the approaches, are presented below.

### Customer importance/operation achievement

This two-by-two matrix considers all the aspects of the customer service specification and is used to indicate the level of importance the customer attaches to them, against the level of the achievement of the operation in meeting these requirements. Placing the various aspects on the matrix can be useful in determining and planning what action should be taken. The matrix, which has four positions, is shown in Figure 7.3.

**Achievement by operation**

| | | Low | High |
|---|---|---|---|
| **Importance to customer** | High | Position 2<br><br>Priority to improve | Position 1<br><br>Priority to maintain |
| | Low | Position 4<br><br>Low priority but monitor<br>over time | Position 3<br><br>Puzzle<br>Action not to waste<br>achievement |

**Figure 7.3** Customer importance/operation achievement matrix

- *Position 1: High importance and high achievement* The first priority of any operation is to maintain these aspects. This is always true as taking action on other positions before these are attended to could endanger achievements in this position. Action should be taken in the remaining three positions only if the operation can be sure that aspects already in this position can be maintained.

- *Position 2: High importance and low achievement* The second priority is to examine and take action on these aspects. It is clear that these aspects are of high importance to the customer and therefore action taken on them can lead to quick returns in improved customer satisfaction levels. Action to be taken here can be a mixture of reviewing equipment appropriateness and stock levels as well as staff training and development.

- *Position 3: Low importance and high achievement* Aspects that appear in this position are always a puzzle. There is something being achieved but it is not of great importance to the customer. Aspects here can be combined with aspects in position 2 so that possible trade-offs can be achieved. Offering the customer high achievement in something else could in some way compensate for things which are of high importance but which are not currently being fully achieved. Offering a fast business lunch option could, for instance, potentially compensate for a limited menu.

- *Position 4: Low importance and low achievement* The initial response to aspects that appear here is to leave them. Yes, they are of low priority but customer needs change and these factors do need to be monitored. Long-term lack of achievement could lead to possible future customer dissatisfaction with another aspect of the service.

**Capability of operation**

|  | | Low | High |
|---|---|---|---|
| High | | **Position 2**<br><br>Priority to improve | **Position 1**<br><br>Priority to maintain |
| Low | | **Position 4**<br><br>Low priority but monitor<br>over time | **Position 3**<br><br>Puzzle<br>Action to apply<br>capability |

*Importance to customer*

**Figure 7.4** Customer importance/operation capability matrix

### Customer importance/operation capability

This two-by-two matrix considers aspects of the customer service specification and is used to indicate the level of importance that the customers attach to them against the extent to which the operation is capable of achieving them. Placing the various aspects on the matrix can be useful in determining and planning what action should be taken. The matrix, which has four positions, is shown in Figure 7.4.

- *Position 1: High importance and high capability* Again the first priority for action in any operation is to maintain these aspects. This is always true. Taking action to improve capability elsewhere could endanger achievements in this position. Action should be taken in the remaining three positions only if the operation can be sure that aspects already in this position can be maintained.

- *Position 2: High importance and low capability* The second priority is to examine and take action on these aspects. It is clear that these aspects are of high importance to the customer and therefore action taken on them will lead to quick returns in improved customer satisfaction levels. The action taken, however, may also mean that the customer service specification is changed and that the customer is advised more clearly that the operation is not able to offer a particular aspect.

- *Position 3: Low importance and high capability* Aspects that appear in this position are a puzzle. There is something that the operation is capable of achieving but it is not currently of great importance to the customer. Again, aspects here can be combined with aspects in position 2 so that possible trade-offs can be achieved. Additionally, a feature and benefit can be made of this particular aspect so that customer satisfaction can be improved through an impression being given of greater added value.

- *Position 4: Low importance and low capability* The initial response to aspects that appear here is to leave them. The priority for action planning may be low, but again customer needs change and these factors do need to be monitored. Long-term lack of capability could lead to possible future customer dissatisfaction either with another aspect of the service or with the operation's not being able to respond to future priorities that customers may have.

### *Customer importance/staff importance*

This matrix considers aspects of the customer service specification and the level of importance the customer attaches to them against the extent to which the same aspects are important to the staff. Again, placing the various aspects on the matrix can be useful in determining and planning what action should be taken. The matrix has four positions and is shown in Figure 7.5.

- *Position 1: High customer importance and high staff importance* The first priority again of any operation is to maintain these aspects. This is again always true. Strengthening the capability of staff and rewarding their achievement of these aspects will reinforce their importance for staff and the operation as a whole. Again it is important to focus on these aspects first, as taking action to balance things up elsewhere could potentially endanger achievements in this position. Again action should be taken in the remaining three positions only if the operation can be sure that aspects already in position 1 can be maintained.
- *Position 2: High customer importance and low staff importance* The second priority is to examine and take action on these aspects. It is clear that these aspects are of high importance to the customer and therefore action taken on them will lead to quick returns in improved customer satisfaction levels. However, there could be a variety of reasons why staff may not consider these aspects important. These reasons may range from difficulties that the staff encounter in providing a particular type of service, such

| Importance to customer | Importance to staff: Low | Importance to staff: High |
|---|---|---|
| High | Position 2<br>Priority to improve | Position 1<br>Priority to value and maintain |
| Low | Position 4<br>Low priority but ensure skills available to monitor over time | Position 3<br>Puzzle<br>Action to resolve |

**Figure 7.5** Customer importance/staff importance matrix

as equipment shortages, to a lack of competence or confidence. Action taken here, then, should be well considered, although clearly the intention is that the staff should attach the same value as the customers to the level of importance of a particular aspect of the customer service specification.

- *Position 3: Low customer importance and high staff importance*   Aspects that appear in this position are again a puzzle. These are things that the staff think are important to achieve but which are not currently of great importance to the customer. This can have serious consequences for an operation. If the members of staff believe that they have capabilities that the customer and the establishment do not value, or that they do not in effect share the same values as the customer in relation to the customer service specification, then it does raise questions about the suitability of the staff in the first place. Difficulties here can also be affecting the problems being identified by aspects in position 2. Trade-offs are not really possible. The aspects that are of importance to the customers must be reflected in the importance attached to them by staff, otherwise the customer service specification cannot be achieved.

- *Position 4: Low customer importance and low staff importance*   The initial response to aspects that appear here is again to leave them. The priority, for action planning purposes, may be low but again customer needs change and these factors do need to be monitored. Therefore there is some merit in increasing the awareness of staff about these aspects so that they are able to monitor possible changes over time in the customers' priorities.

The use of these three approaches can be complex and sophisticated using well-designed questionnaires and external consultants to provide greater objectivity. However, these approaches can also be used simply and productively as, for example, a basis for conducting staff focus groups or as a basis for team development sessions.

## APPRAISING THE WHOLE OPERATION

When appraising the whole of the food and beverage operation it is useful to consider the enterprise at three levels. These levels are:

- *Operational*, which includes day-to-day sales and the way the product is provided and promoted.
- *Business*, which is considering the performance of the enterprise in terms of profitability, competitiveness and other business measures.
- *Corporate*, which is considering the strategic direction of the operation and how this is being achieved.

In a single business unit these three levels are operating together. In a larger enterprise, different members of staff and management may undertake the responsibilities for each of these levels separately.

It can be useful to consider any enterprise as having these three levels as it enables any matter, at whatever level, to be considered within the context of the organisation as a whole, rather than as an independent issue. Thus operational issues and decisions made about them are set within the business requirements and also then within the contribution that is being made to the corporate direction of the enterprise.

Operations are not an end in themselves. Decisions made to correct underperformance or overperformance at the operational level have to take account of the business implications and the strategic direction required. It may well be that operational underperformance or overperformance is a result of changes in the business environment, and this should be identified before any corrective action is taken, otherwise such action can lead, at best, to an effort potentially frustrated and, at worst, to resources wasted. Equally, corporate and business decisions must take account of the capability of the operation to achieve the revised performance levels.

## When and how

Decisions need to be made on when the appraisal of the whole operation should take place and how such an appraisal should be performed.

*When* the appraisal takes place will be dependent upon the constraints and opportunities perceived by the enterprise, and the rate of change in these issues. Although formal performance appraisal can normally be undertaken half-yearly or yearly, it is often the case, especially within a fast-changing business environment, that the process is organic, with the formal processes being used to confirm the action, which may have already been taken.

*How* such an appraisal is structured will affect the outcome of the appraisal process and the value placed upon it. It can be helpful to separate the appraisal of the whole operation into three main activities:

- quantitative analysis
- business environment appraisal
- qualitative evaluation.

These three areas are interdependent, but it can be useful to consider them separately before considering the interrelationship between them and subsequently the processes for making strategic decisions.

### 1 Quantitative analysis

An analysis of financial and other quantitative data relating to a specific foodservice organisation is useful because undertaking it can:

- Enable a study of trends and progress over a number of years.
- Enable comparisons with the competition and the industry as a whole.
- Reveal lost profit and growth potential.

■ Point the way forward by identifying areas needing improvement. This is especially the case when the organisation is not performing well compared with major competitors or within the industry as a whole.

■ Identify and emphasise possible danger areas.

Much of the first part of this chapter has been concerned with identifying techniques for quantitative operational appraisal. Alongside the operational ratios, other financial ratios should also be considered. Ratio analysis is used extensively to assess the financial position of a company. It is aimed at characterising the company in a few basic areas affecting its financial standing.

There are many ways of grouping operational and financial ratios and formulae. The following are the main categories for most of the common formulae:

■ operational ratios

■ activity ratios

■ profitability ratios

■ liquidity ratio

■ gearing ratios

■ stock market ratios.

Each of the common ratios, the formulae and explanations of what the individual ratio can indicate are detailed under these six headings in Appendix D. As there are a number of formulae in each of the categories, this type of analysis can seem complicated. However, the operational ratios summarised in Appendix D have already been considered in some detail in the early part of this chapter. Many of the rest of these ratios are calculated at either the business or the corporate level in the organisation.

In order to interpret fully the meaning of a ratio, it is necessary to have some basis of comparison. For operational ratios, there will usually be internal budgets and objectives against which to measure them. To illustrate this further, an example of budget and trading results comparison and evaluation is detailed in Appendix E.

Operational ratios can also have more general values based on traditional experience and industry norms. Many of the rest of the ratios also have such values. For instance, generally desirable figures for liquidity are a liquidity ratio of 2 and an acid test ratio of 1. Such absolute figures are difficult to justify completely and relative figures are therefore often used with respect to the industry average or close competitors. When considering the share price of a company, for example, it is usual to compare the company's share price with other companies' share prices within the sector and to compare it against the FTSE 100.

No single figure provides sufficient information for evaluating the operational and business performance and also the financial health of the enterprise. Reasoned judgements as to the financial standing of the company will involve groups of calculations being undertaken. The important point is that this analysis taken as a whole is what needs to be considered, not any particular figure.

Skills in quantitative analysis and evaluation are an essential part of food and beverage management. This is because quantitative analysis and evaluation of the operation:

■ are essential parts of performance appraisal, alongside other analytical tools, and

■ need to be considered over time in order to compare how they vary year on year and, where possible, how they compare with the average for the industry.

Generating quantitative data provides a useful background for appraising the performance of the organisation, but care needs to be taken when the results are being interpreted:

■ The view that is being provided is based on historical data. It does not automatically imply that the trend identified will continue into the future.

■ At best, average ratios provide a guideline to existing proportions that are representative in a given industry.

Additionally, a number of different ratios need to be calculated before any conclusions should be drawn:

■ Ratios should be used as an additional tool to back up issues identified in another area of analysis.

■ The evaluation of the ratios is more important than the figures themselves.

The further reading at the end of the chapter lists several useful texts for the reader wishing to explore financial ratios more deeply.

## 2 Business environment appraisal

Appraising the business environment enables a food and beverage operation to understand how it relates to the current business environment, how the business environment is changing, and facilitates an objective view of the future. Appraising the business environment also includes an examination of the competition and the threats to the operation which competitors may pose.

The range of resources apportioned to this activity can vary, with large operators employing economists and strategic directors, and small operators often relying on instinct and intuition. For the hospitality industry there is a range of professional sources of information which regularly provide opportunities for sharing information and gaining insights into changes in the business environment. These include the professional and trade bodies and the trade press.

There are also several techniques available to assist in the appraisal of the business environments, which are covered in detail in a variety of texts and publications. We have previously considered two of these in Chapter 1: PESTLE analysis (pages 15–18) for considering primarily the macro-environment, and Porter's five forces (pages 18–21) for considering primarily the industry environment. In Chapter 2, we have also considered how the food and beverage product can be developed to ensure a consumer–product relationship as a dynamic process.

The PESTLE analysis, when carried out well, is a sophisticated approach which provides for a fairly wide and deep evaluation of the current and potential business environment.

- *Political* influences might include issues such as the availability of grants and subsidies, and the intervention of the Monopolies and Mergers Commission.
- *Economic* influences might include exchange rates (as they affect tourism), inflation and taxation.
- *Social* issues might concern changing market needs, demographic changes and changing patterns of employment.
- *Technological* issues might concern the operating systems of a business, channels of distribution (how a business communicates with its customers) and data- and information-gathering.
- *Legal* issues might mean changes in legislation, for example hygiene and food safety, opening hours, employment contracts and responsibilities, trade descriptions, licensing.
- *Ecological* might mean the increasing requirements for energy conservation or the acceptability of genetically modified foods.

Porter's five forces model helps in considering the competitiveness of a particular industry. The approach takes account of the *rivalry amongst existing firms* competing in the industry, the threat of *new entrants*, the strength of *buyers*, the strength of industry *suppliers* and the extent to which *substitute products* can affect the demand for particular foodservice products.

Using these, and other, analysis techniques is a learning process, which will strengthen the organisation by making possible a more focused appraisal of how the food and beverage operation complements and matches the business environment in which it operates.

The value placed upon any of the analysis tools by foodservice operators will be dependent upon the operators' skills and objectives. To ignore these approaches is unwise; to include them in appraising an operation's performance, no matter how modestly, is good business sense.

### 3 Qualitative evaluation

In many ways the qualitative evaluation of an operation is on the one hand the hardest to achieve well, but on the other hand potentially the most rewarding. It is about getting to the heart of the reasons for the success of the operation and for considering how to maintain and develop it further.

The previous section in this chapter, 'Appraising the product', details various approaches to qualitative analysis on which to make judgements about the extent to which the organisation is achieving its customer service specification. We have also considered the various approaches to quantitative analysis (pages 260–2 above) and approaches to appraising the business environment. In all cases, any qualitative evaluation needs to be considered taking account of the current and future business needs as well as being supported by data.

We have already identified that:

■ Quantitative assessment should be used as an additional tool to back up issues identified in another area of analysis.

■ The evaluation of the quantitative analysis is more important than the figures themselves.

Qualitative evaluation takes account of the quantitative analysis and also the appraisal of the external business environment. The outcomes of qualitative evaluation are informed views being taken on, for example, the extent to which:

■ The customer service specification is appropriate to meet the current and intended customer demand, or are some parts of the specification higher than required and others insufficient?

■ The customer service specification can be simplified to make it easier to provide, or to make it more cost effective and reliable.

■ The service is consistent and reliable and whether that is a major selling point.

■ Processes and procedures are competitive with those of competitors. If not, why not?

■ All the aspects of quality control and quality assurance of the food and beverages being sold and the service of them are being controlled.

■ The equipment is at the standard required (both in capability and stock level terms) to meet the customer service specification and what equipment will have to be improved or replaced.

■ Members of staff are well selected, up to the job and supported by sufficient training.

■ Members of staff are paid well enough and are motivated to contribute to the fulfilment of the customer service specification.

■ Staff suggestions are listened to in order to consider changes to the range of products on offer.

■ The organisation has the ability to maintain the current customer service specification and the ability to respond to change.

Attempting to develop views on these types of issue can illuminate other issues such as the effectiveness of the customer service specification in meeting what the customer wants, and also what staff and managers understand the competitors are about to do.

The data that will be generated from the quantitative analysis and the appraisal of the business environment will have already generated a variety of possible actions to be taken. Action will be as much dependent on the needs of the operation as it will on determining the effectiveness of the operation in meeting current and future business demands.

### Using the catering cycle as an analysis tool

A systematic way of approaching the appraisal of the operation is to use the catering cycle as an analysis tool. The cycle can be used as a dynamic model. Figure 7.6 gives the eight stages of the cycle (which we first saw in Chapter 1, page 2) and indicates the issues that could be considered under each stage.

There are two dimensions to using the catering cycle in this way:

- Using the catering cycle to present the information that has been generated will help to organise what is known about the operation and its performance, but more importantly it will also help to identify where there are gaps in the information and where additional information might be required to make the evaluation more complete.

- Viewing the operation as a cycle will help to identify operational strengths and weaknesses. Within the cycle, any difficulties which are identified in one area of the cycle will cause difficulties in the elements of the cycle that follow. For instance, difficulties with

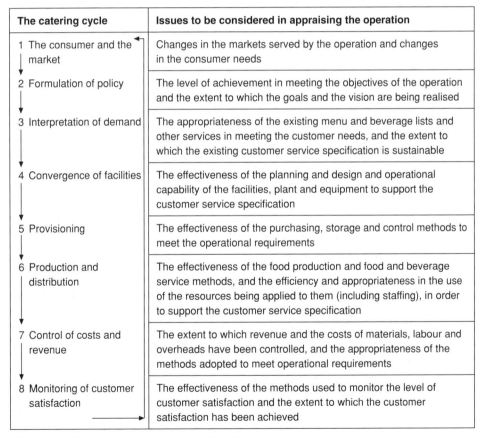

| The catering cycle | Issues to be considered in appraising the operation |
|---|---|
| 1 The consumer and the market | Changes in the markets served by the operation and changes in the consumer needs |
| 2 Formulation of policy | The level of achievement in meeting the objectives of the operation and the extent to which the goals and the vision are being realised |
| 3 Interpretation of demand | The appropriateness of the existing menu and beverage lists and other services in meeting the customer needs, and the extent to which the existing customer service specification is sustainable |
| 4 Convergence of facilities | The effectiveness of the planning and design and operational capability of the facilities, plant and equipment to support the customer service specification |
| 5 Provisioning | The effectiveness of the purchasing, storage and control methods to meet the operational requirements |
| 6 Production and distribution | The effectiveness of the food production and food and beverage service methods, and the efficiency and appropriateness in the use of the resources being applied to them (including staffing), in order to support the customer service specification |
| 7 Control of costs and revenue | The extent to which revenue and the costs of materials, labour and overheads have been controlled, and the appropriateness of the methods adopted to meet operational requirements |
| 8 Monitoring of customer satisfaction | The effectiveness of the methods used to monitor the level of customer satisfaction and the extent to which the customer satisfaction has been achieved |

**Figure 7.6** The catering cycle as an analysis tool

purchasing will have effects on production and service, and control. Similarly, the difficulties experienced under one stage of the cycle will often have their causes in the stages
that precede it.

The catering cycle helps in considering the operation as a whole, i.e. as an operating
system. Approaching the analysis and evaluation of the operation using the catering cycle
will help to determine the limitations of the information that is known, which will then
lead to better evaluation of the operation and its performance.

The true causes of difficulties in any of the eight stages, and their implications, are more
easily and accurately identified using the catering cycle model. In operations, the causes
of difficulties in one stage are often to be found in the one or two preceding rather than
in that stage itself. For instance, difficulties with food and beverage service can often be due
to equipment shortages, stockouts, or incorrect pricing information rather than as a result
of difficulties directly associated with the service. Similarly, difficulties identified in one stage
will also have knock-on effects on the stages that follow. Being able to identify and understand these various interrelationships will mean that decisions on operational changes will
only be considered after finding the true cause of any difficulties, and taking account of
the effects that any proposed changes might have throughout the operation as a whole.

### External comparison
The current performance of the operation will have been compared with performance
in the past and also against the current goals and objectives of the organisation. This can
then also be extended to making comparisons with other organisations. This is sometimes called *benchmarking*.

Benchmarking is a process of making comparisons with the performance indicators of
other foodservice operations, and then also making comparisons with the performance
indicators of organisations in similar types of operation, but in different industries, to see
how the organisation compares with best practice. This process could involve undertaking comparisons using many of the ratios which are given in Appendix D as well as, for
instance, complaint levels, or stock handling, or energy saving, or staff turnover in other
service operations. There can be useful lessons to be learnt if the organisation does not
compare well.

In the same way as the catering cycle can be used as a basis for investigating the internal operation (see Figure 7.6 above), it can also be used as a basis for comparison with
other operations. Information gathered about competitors' operations can be organised
and examined in a similar way to information gathered about the internal operation. This
helps to make the comparison more systematic and objective.

Additionally, in recent years there has been an increased interest in *performance
indicators* in both the public and private sectors. These are often fairly simple quantitative
measures such as:

- time to answer the telephone
- time to respond to a 999 call

- percentage of trains arriving on time
- percentage of patients on a hospital waiting list for more than two years.

They might also be more specific or detailed, such as those widely used in the hospitality industry. The industry uses quantitative measures such as:

- average sales per sales person
- gross profit percentages
- occupancy levels
- energy efficiency measures.

Although few people would disagree with the need to try to improve efficiency whilst maintaining standards, or with the need to assess efficiency and effectiveness, the use of performance indicators can have drawbacks:

- The concentration on quantitative measures tends to draw too much attention to that which can easily be measured, rather than considering the much richer concepts of service and quality, which are much more difficult to measure.
- Performance indicators measure behaviour, but they also have a tendency to change behaviour: people start to work to satisfy the indicator rather than the requirements of the customers.
- Some of the indicators are prone to being manipulated in order to give the impression of a higher quality than is actually being achieved.

In any case, the question always needs to be asked as to whether any organisation should actually be doing the things that the performance indicators measure. Many people work extremely hard doing jobs that either do not need doing or do not need doing in that way. Instead of asking questions such as, how can things be done better, at lower cost or faster, it is often better to first ask, why do we do what we do at all?

Effective qualitative evaluation is the essence of successful food and beverage management. It is systematic, in that it is supported by data, but it also allows for professional judgement to be applied. Done well, it can ensure that valuable resources are not wasted on making the operation comply with a customer service specification that either is no longer relevant to customer demand or no longer able to be achieved by the physical capabilities of the operation, by its staff or both. Overall, the food and beverage manager's job is to ensure that the right questions are being asked, not to provide all the right answers.

## MAKING STRATEGIC DECISIONS

Assessing the achievement of an organisation against its aims and within the business environment leads to the requirement to consider making strategic decisions about the current operation and the future of the organisation.

## The origins of strategy

Strategy is the means by which organisations attempt to achieve their goals. In most organisations there is likely to be a complex set of stakeholders concerned to influence the policies and hence the strategy of the organisation.

Mintzberg *et al.* (1998) identify *five Ps for strategy*. They reference instances of strategy meaning each of the following:

| | |
|---|---|
| Plan | A consciously intended course of action. |
| Ploy | A specific 'manoeuvre' intended to outwit an opponent or competitor. |
| Pattern | In a stream of actions. |
| Position | A means of locating an organisation in an 'environment'. |
| Perspective | An ingrained way of perceiving the world. |

These are only five of many uses of the word 'strategy'. Mintzberg *et al.* see links between these five uses and encourage readers to explore the different perspectives on an organisation and its activities that each use gives. The key to the matter is not to get the *right* definition but to achieve a better understanding of what different writers or speakers mean by strategy, i.e. what the underlying concepts are that they are trying to get across.

As a working definition for the purposes of this book, let us propose that strategic decisions are:

■ Major decisions that affect the direction that an organisation, or part of an organisation, is committed to for the next few years.

■ Decisions which involve a commitment of resources.

■ Decisions which involve complex situations at corporate, business unit and operational level which may affect and be affected by many parts of the organisation.

Within this context there are then a number of terms often used in relation to strategic decision-making. These include:

| | |
|---|---|
| Vision | A conceptual or imagined view of the organisation as it might be in the future. |
| Mission | The fundamental purpose of an organisation, which is intended to lead it towards its vision. |
| Policy | A set of ground rules and criteria to be applied when making decisions. |
| Goals/aims | The broad intentions of the organisation. |
| Strategy | The means by which the organisation tries to fulfil its goals/aims. |
| Objectives | Measurable statements of what must be achieved as part of the strategy in order for the goals/aims to be realised. |
| Tactics | Decisions and actions intended to achieve short-term objectives. |

These terms are presented here in a hierarchy. Thus *policies* are derived from thinking about the *vision* and the *mission* of the organisation, and *objectives* are determined in order to ensure that the *goals/aims* of the organisation are achieved. (Goals and objectives have been discussed in Chapter 1, pages 23–6). The interpretation of these terms can, however, vary depending on where and how they are being used.

## Levels of strategy

It is now widely recognised that strategy-making should take place at different levels of the organisation. In the same way as we identified three levels for the appraisal of the whole operation (page 259), it is also common practice to identify three levels of strategy: corporate, business unit and operational levels.

- *Corporate strategy* includes the plans for the strategic direction of the enterprise and how this is to be achieved.
- *Business strategy* is developed for the business unit, whether this be a single establishment or a division of a company.
- *Operations strategy* includes the product, market, and functional and departmental plans.

The part of the organisation where the responsibility will lie for these different levels will vary from organisation to organisation. In a small company the business unit will also be the corporate level and operational level; in a larger organisation the levels can be separated, with different managers at each level. How the three levels of strategy relate can be illustrated as in Figure 7.7.

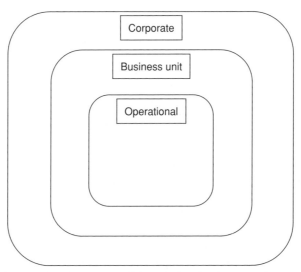

**Figure 7.7** The three levels of strategy and the relationship between them

The strategies at the various levels in an organisation clearly need to be consistent. However, this does not mean that they have to be common or the same. The appropriate business and operational strategies for a national foodservice company may not need to be the same in each of the locations it is operating in (for example, resort, city centre, tourist area, transportation). It is also worth reminding ourselves that any foodservice operation is not necessarily in one market. The same unit could, for instance, be in the restaurant, licensed trade, banqueting, conference, business and leisure markets. In short, different approaches may be required for different customer groups, or more appropriately the different types of demand, which the operation is designed to satisfy.

## Assessing organisational capability

Any foodservice organisation should be in a position to assess its strengths and weaknesses and determine what it sees as its core competences. Many of the existing strengths and weaknesses, which already exist within the operation, are as result of linkages between different activities and the consistency of the operational strategies. It can therefore often be shown that:

■ Better training of staff tends to result in better service.

■ Early attention to problems may avoid expensive compensation later.

■ Greater prevention of problems reduces unexpected demands.

■ Better design leads to lower service costs.

■ Liaison between departments allows for better planning, reduced costs and improved customer service.

One way of exploring these issues further is to consider *resource analysis*. This is concerned with:

■ Identifying the strengths and weaknesses of the organisation's resources in meeting the requirements of the current strategies.

■ Identifying how the current resources could meet the needs of possible changes in the business environment and therefore customer demand.

■ Identifying what changes would need to be made to the current resources in order for the organisation to meet future and competitive demands.

There are various methods for carrying out a resource analysis. Some organisations go through very formal processes, whilst others have a more informal approach. Whichever way it is done, it is important that, once carried out, it is continuously updated. One approach to resources analysis (based on approaches to resource audit described by Johnson and Scholes (1999)) is:

1 Carry out a value chain analysis:
  **(a)** to look at how effectively and efficiently all the resources are being used in each stage of the operation;
  **(b)** to look at how effectively the resources are contributing to meeting the objectives and goals of the organisation;
  **(c)** to develop and use measures for the control of resources.
  (The value chain includes all the stages of the operation. For foodservice operations the various stages are indicated in Figure 1.3, page 6.)

2 Draw comparisons:
  **(a)** with past performance of the organisation;
  **(b)** with norms in the industry;
  **(c)** with best practice in similar activities in other types of organisation.

3 Assess balance within the organisation:
  **(a)** analyse the range of products which are offered and make decisions about their ability to meeting current demand;
  **(b)** analyse the skills/personalities of the staff involved in order to determine the extent to which they complement the requirements of the customer service specification;
  **(c)** analyse the flexibility of the organisation in meeting the range of current demand;
  **(d)** analyse the capability of the resources of the operation in order to determine the extent to which the operation is able to meet potential future demand.

Undertaking these activities should lead to the identification of key issues which will enable the identification of the:

■ Strengths and weaknesses of the operation.

■ Core competences of the operation (What do we do and how good at it are we? And then, what could we do and how good at it could we be?)

Such an audit should enable the organisation to assess its current and potential strategic capability.

The development of the strategies for the organisation can then take into account:

■ The current and potential strategic capability of the organisation.

■ The opportunities and threats it faces.

■ An identification of the future resources and capabilities required to implement an adopted strategy.

Strategic analysis, planning and implementation are a continuum, but not a sequence. Therefore, equally there may need to be modifications to the existing strategies to take account of the strengths and weaknesses of the existing resources, as well as ensuring that plans are considered which will develop the resources so as to be able to implement future strategies.

## Strategic analysis and planning

Strategic analysis of the organisation is concerned with attempting to identify:

- Its strengths and weaknesses.
- The opportunities and threats facing it at the time.

Most writers on strategic management argue that the task of managers is to develop strategies which:

- Use the organisation's strengths to capitalise on external opportunities or counter threats.
- Seek to alleviate the organisation's weaknesses.

This is in an effort to achieve the organisation's objectives and goals and hence satisfy its stakeholders. Strategy formulation is thus an interplay between internal strengths and weaknesses, external opportunities and threats, and stakeholders' expectations.

SWOT (strengths, weaknesses, opportunities, threats) analysis is useful to the food and beverage operator because it allows a focused identification and evaluation of the issues which affect the operation. Strengths and weaknesses are usually internal to the operation and might include such items as the product, staffing, management and the effectiveness of the operating systems. Opportunities and threats are usually external to the business and might include such items as the existing and potential customer needs, interest rates, demographic changes, infrastructure developments and national and local economic outlooks.

Strategic management, then, can be considered to be a process aimed at managing the interface between the external environment (the opportunities and threats) and the internal capabilities (the strengths and weaknesses) of the organisation.

### Using SWOT analysis

SWOT analysis can be used in considering the organisation and the business environment in which it operates and as a basis for developing strategy in line with its mission. It can be a very powerful and effective tool because it has the great benefit of conceptual simplicity. The idea of identifying what you are good at, and where you are weak, is very simple. But in practice different managers have different perceptions of the strengths and weaknesses of the same organisation. The same is true of opportunities and threats.

However, the conceptual simplicity of SWOT allows it to be used creatively. It can bring into the open conflicts of perception and test assumptions. Used well, it can cut through internal politics and its use and application need not be threatening.

### Using SWOT analysis in practice

Strategy should be related to the external environment and the internal resources and capabilities of the organisation, not made in a vacuum. Similarly, the separate components

|  | | **Strengths** | **Weaknesses** |
|---|---|---|---|
|  | | List of strengths | List of weaknesses |
| **Opportunities** | List of opportunities | Strengths to make use of opportunities | Weaknesses which prevent you from exploiting opportunities |
| **Threats** | List of threats | Strengths to counter threats | Weaknesses which prevent you from countering threats |

**Figure 7.8**   SWOT matrix

of a SWOT analysis should not be considered in isolation, as can be seen in the extended SWOT matrix shown in Figure 7.8, sometimes referred to as a TOWS matrix.

To use this as a process tool, specific opportunities and threats need to be listed to see how each of these links to the strengths and weaknesses of the organisation. This helps in making decisions on the actions that need to be taken. Similarly, an organisation can list individual strengths and weaknesses and see how these relate to the potential opportunities and threats. It is also useful to match these against the needs of the existing markets, the potential markets and also to those of competitors.

An organisation may have resources that give it strengths to take advantage of opportunities in the external environment (box 1) or that can be used to reduce the effect of the threats (box 3). Alternatively, external opportunities and threats may cause an organisation to examine current weaknesses (boxes 2 and 4) and eradicate these so that it can take advantage of opportunities or counter threats. In some situations, an organisation can use existing or newly developed strengths to benefit from new opportunities (box 1).

### The need for constant monitoring
Business generally is going through a period of rapid change, which is turbulent and uncertain, not developmental or evolutionary. In this situation, it is not enough simply to monitor periodically the factors that in the past have indicated opportunities and threats. Rather, foodservice organisations need to be constantly on the lookout for new issues and new developments, which may have a radical effect on the business environment and on the actions of competitors, both of which may have an effect on the business that the foodservice organisation is in.

The annual event of monitoring 'key variables' in readiness for an update of the annual plan, or budget, may be too infrequent: an important opportunity may be missed or a dangerous threat may become a reality. Even if a threat is recognised, the organisation may not be able to adapt in time.

Monitoring can also be more difficult because many opportunities and threats are not easily recognisable. A development in an obscure area of technology may have effects on a wide variety of sectors of the economy that few, if any, people recognise at the outset. The developments, which may ultimately have a high impact on a business, do not often happen in an area that directly affects a particular organisation, but to businesses three or four positions up- or downstream. For example, changes in the use of specific packaging materials affect not only the manufacturers of the packaging materials but also the wholesalers and then the foodservice operation, which subsequently retails the products.

In such a situation there can be an in-built pressure to collect more and more data on an ever-increasing number of factors to try to make the future more certain. This can be counterproductive and cause data overload – 'paralysis by analysis'. There is more data available but less information than before.

### Assessing for now and the future

The assessment of strengths and weaknesses cannot stand still. It is a continuous process. Strategic capability needs to be assessed, not just for now but also for the future. As time passes, the current strategy will have developed and been modified and also the external business environment is likely to have changed. This in turn will lead to the need to modify strategies in the light of these changes.

There is then a continuous interplay between formulation, implementation and assessment of SWOTs now and in the future. The process of assessing current strengths and weaknesses should be part of this process. They should be assessed in terms of their appropriateness not only now but also for the future. It works in many ways:

- What possible external changes might make a current strength into a weakness or vice versa?
- How can a current strength be used to explore a future opportunity?
- How can strength be developed further to be of greater benefit in the future?

The other issue that needs to be faced is where changes are required and where the resource capabilities of the operation are unable to meet them.

As the market, competition and the business environment change over time, so there will need to be changes in the core competences of the organisation. A current core competence that gives a foodservice operation an edge over competitors may become commonplace amongst competitors in a few years. Thus any organisation needs to be continually developing its core competences so as to be better prepared to face the future.

## The basis of strategy

One of the most influential concepts in the development of strategic thinking has been that of generic strategies. Michael Porter (1980, 1985) claims that there are three basic ways by which organisations can achieve a 'sustainable competitive advantage' over its rivals. These are the 'generic strategies' of:

- *Cost leadership*  A strategy whereby the organisation sets out to be the lowest-cost producer in its industry.

- *Differentiation*  A strategy based on enhancements to products which are valued by customers and for which the customer will be prepared to pay higher prices in order to obtain unique benefits.

- *Focus*  A strategy where the organisation chooses a narrow competitive scope, that is it selects a particular segment or group of segments of the market that it can serve exclusively well. There are two variants of this strategy:
  - a focus based on cost, whereby the organisation seeks a cost advantage in its chosen segment;
  - a focus which is based on achieving differentiation in that segment.

Porter argues that, for an organisation to be successful over the long term it must be clear which of the generic strategies it is following. Such a choice then informs all strategic decisions that must be made.

A development of Porter's approaches has been the *strategy clock* of Johnson and Scholes (1999). This has eight different strategy options (rather than Porter's four) based on combinations of price (low to high) and perceived added value (low to high). It attempts to ensure coherence of strategy across different resources in the organisation, and links the use of resources to customer requirements.

The strategy clock takes a customer perspective on strategy by plotting perceived added value against price. These are both factors external to the organisation that relate to how customers make their purchasing decisions. However, a modification to this model is proposed here in that the horizontal axis should more appropriately be the 'cost to the customer' rather than simply being the price (in cash terms), as in the Johnson and Scholes model. We have discussed this issue in Chapter 2 (page 41), where we indicated that *value* in a food service operation is more likely to be measured by the customer as the relationship between *worth* and the *total cost to the customer*. This 'cost to the customer' included, for instance, the lost opportunity of being somewhere else, travel costs, the possibility of disagreeable company, poor service or poor food.

Taking account of this modification, the strategy clock, as shown in Figure 7.9, illustrates that the strategic routes indicated by the positions 1 to 5 can be sustainable strategies, and that the strategic routes indicated by positions 6, 7 and 8 are destined for failure.

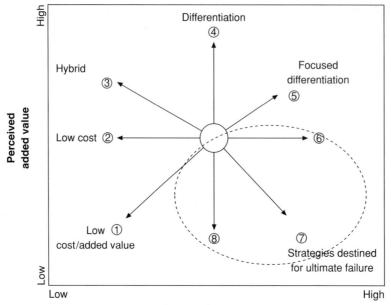

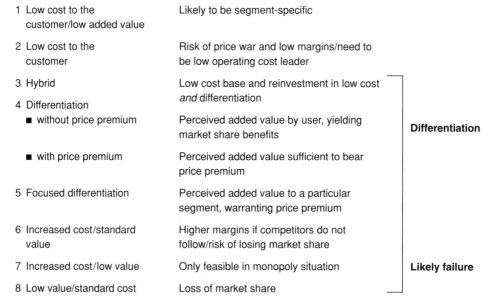

**Figure 7.9**   The strategy clock (Adapted from Johnson and Scholes 1999)

Developing this further, the strategic basis of each of the eight routes may be summarised as in Figure 7.10. From this figure it can be seen that:

■ *Strategic routes 1 and 2* are strategies that are aimed at achieving sales through being of low cost to the customer.

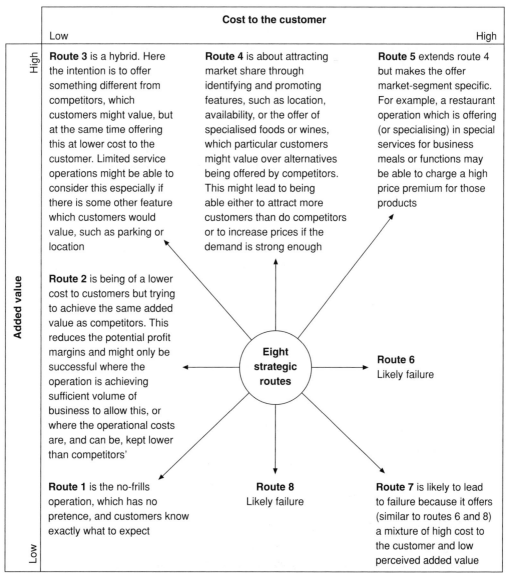

**Figure 7.10**   Eight possible strategic routes for foodservice operations (Adapted from Johnson and Scholes' strategy clock)

■ *Strategic route 3* is a hybrid.

■ *Strategic routes 4 and 5* are about being different from competitors.

■ *Strategic routes 6, 7 and 8* offer a mixture of high cost to the customer and low perceived added value and therefore all of these are likely to be unsuccessful strategies,
which will ultimately lead to the failure of the business.

Using this application of the strategy clock for considering the strategic route for foodservice operations may at first appear simple. However, the nature of any food and beverage
product is that it may be aimed at simultaneously meeting a wide variety of different types
of demand. This is both in terms of the types of demand being met by one particular part of
the product and in terms of the nature of a foodservice operation offering, for instance, a
range of products – breakfast service, morning coffee, business lunches, afternoon teas, family
meals, special diet provision, pre-theatre meals, evenings out, post-theatre meals, special
parties, functions and also retail merchandise and parking services. It is therefore quite
likely that any operation will need to split the product(s) down and consider the types of
demand being met and then place each of these products separately on the strategy clock.

## Strategic direction

Ansoff (1988), suggested an approach to strategy selection as he believed that a number
of links or strands, in a 'common thread', exist between an organisation's current and
'possible' new strategies. He suggested that there are four components that, if carefully
considered, will give specific guidance as to the most appropriate strategies. The four
components are:

■ *Product-market scope*  The scope within which the business currently operates, the
type of activity currently undertaken and the markets to which products are offered.

■ *Growth-vector components*  The possible direction of growth starting from the current
product market position.

■ *Competitive advantage*  The characteristics that should be looked for in potential
growth opportunities, in order to achieve a strong competitive position.

■ *Synergy*  The 2 + 2 = 5 phenomenon. The combining of two companies should produce greater returns than the two can achieve on their own.

### Ansoff's growth matrix
The growth matrix (shown in Figure 7.11) takes the process a step further by interrelat-
ing the product and market areas, each of which will vary depending upon whether we
are dealing with 'new' or 'old' products or markets, or both. For example, if the current
product range is being provided within existing markets, the organisation needs to have
a clear 'market penetration strategy'. If the products are current, but are being offered
within the new markets, then a market development strategy will be required. If the

**Products**

| | | Present | New |
|---|---|---|---|
| **Markets** | Present | Do nothing<br>Withdrawal<br>Consolidate<br>Market penetration | Product development |
| | New | Market development | Related diversification<br>Unrelated diversification |

**Figure 7.11**  Ansoff's growth matrix with alternative strategies/directions

organisation has developed new products that it aims to sell within a new market, the strategy needed will be 'diversification' orientated.

The strategic options Ansoff proposes are explained below:

■ *Do nothing*  A 'no change' strategy can be wrongly perceived as 'no strategy'. If there are no foreseen internal and external environmental changes, the organisation may deliberately choose to continue with the strategies currently being undertaken. A positive decision to retain the business in its present market is a perfectly logical one. To stand still in a dynamic environment, however, is to move backwards, but changing strategies in an unchanging environment may be quite inappropriate. Generally though, unless an organisation's environment is very stable, 'do nothing' is unlikely to be a viable option, but it can serve as a useful comparison when considering other options.

■ *Withdrawal*  There may be circumstances in which it makes sense to withdraw from a particular activity in a particular market, especially if continuation is no longer profitable or viable. For a single foodservice operator this is often that hardest decision to have to make.

■ *Consolidate*  This implies taking action to retain existing market shares. In growth markets this will lead to increased sales. In mature or declining markets, actions such as improved service or quality, or reduced costs may be required.

■ *Market penetration*  This is a strategy of attempting to increase market share. This is likely to be easier in growth markets. In mature or declining markets, competitors are likely to react to competitive moves (for example, lowering prices, increasing advertising, improving quality) to steal their business.

■ *Product development*  This involves offering new products to existing markets. A decision to develop new products may be based on an identified customer need which is not being met, or be derived from technological advancements. New product development always carries an element of risk as many new products do not achieve required levels of profitability and may lose money.

■ *Market development* This involves taking existing products into new markets. These may be new market segments, new uses of existing products, or new geographic markets. Penetrating new markets is risky as it represents a move into the unknown.

■ *Diversification* Although this term is often used fairly loosely, here it is used in the sense of offering new products to new markets. There are two types of diversification:

  – *related*, where the development is broadly within the same industry. This can further be classified as:

    ■ *backward integration*, which is a move into an activity that is already an input into the foodservice organisation's existing operations, i.e. backwards in the supply chain, further away from the customers, such as a restaurant's having interests in a farm;

    ■ *forward integration*, which is a move into an activity which is an output of the organisation's existing operations, i.e. forwards in the supply chain, nearer to the consumer. This is difficult as many foodservice operations are already at the end of the supply chain. However, it can include activities such as joining marketing consortia;

    ■ *horizontal integration*, which is a move into a competitive or complementary activity, such as a restaurant's linking with leisure attraction or being located within an hotel;

  – *unrelated*, where the development is outside of the industry in which the organisation currently operates. This can be, for instance, a foodservice operation's also being in the car trade.

Diversification in any form is doubly risky as it involves both products and markets of which the organisation has no experience. Nonetheless, the attraction of diversification is often irresistible for organisations, apparently offering possible opportunities to control supply (backward integration), control markets (forward integration), spread risk (particularly in unrelated diversification), utilise underemployed capacity or cash, and so on. Particularly attractive is the prospect of synergy whereby two or more activities complement each other to the extent that the whole is greater than the sum of the parts. This simple concept that $2 + 2 = 5$ is often put forward as the reason for diversification, but in many cases it has proved very difficult to achieve.

When applying Ansoff's matrix – or more importantly the thinking behind it – an organisation can consider possible options it could adopt in each of the four segments of the alternative strategies matrix in Figure 7.11 and then appraise each of these for suitability.

This approach requires the process to be undertaken systematically in order to answer a variety of questions as follows:

■ *Present market, present products* What would be the implications of doing nothing? Is withdrawal feasible? What would consolidation or market penetration mean for the organisation?

■ *Present market, new product*   This presents much scope for creative powers. What sort of new product could be developed for the present market? The business environmental analysis (see page 262) and SWOT analysis (see page 272) could give some clues here.

■ *New market, present products*   This requires a reassessment of the strengths of the products. Has the organisation considered fully the scope for entering into new markets?

■ *New markets, new products*   Here there is a need to control imagination. Diversification may look attractive, but there are a host of potential dangers and risks. Decisions of this nature tend to involve a considerable outlay. This is particularly true of unrelated diversification. What special skills can the organisation bring which will promise success in new and unfamiliar markets? Unless these can be identified then it would be better to forget it.

### Life cycle analysis

Life cycle analysis is an approach that attempts to consider what strategies might be appropriate, taking account of the position of the product in the product life cycle and also the competitive position of an organisation. The life cycle analysis, or product-market evolution analysis, considers two dimensions: the market situation, described in four stages from embryonic to ageing, and the competitive position described in five stages from weak to dominant.

In order to identify the operation's position within the life cycle, eight external factors or descriptors of the evolutionary stage of the industry are considered. These are:

1 market growth

2 growth potential

3 range of product lines

4 number of competitors

5 spread of market share between these competitors

6 customer loyalty

7 entry barriers

8 technology.

The balance of these factors determines the position of the organisation within the life cycle. The competitive position of the firm within the industry can also be established by looking at these characteristics in relation to its industry life cycle.

The approach can be used to identify possible strategies that might be considered where each of the four stages of industry maturity cross with each of the four competitive position stages. Thus, for instance, a strong competitive position in a mature market shows that the possible strategies might be to aim to attain cost leadership, to renew the product, to aim for a focused strategy or to seek to differentiate the product.

This approach does provide a useful way of thinking about the appropriateness of particular strategies and also enables existing strategies to be compared against those identified in the model. Knowles (1996) suggests that the main virtue of this approach is that it can be used to establish the suitability of particular strategies in relation to the stage of industry maturity and the organisation's competitive position. Johnson and Scholes (1999), whilst recognising that such an approach can be helpful in guiding strategic choice, warn that because the matrix which is used is so detailed it might wrongly lead to the belief that strategic choice is a simplistic affair. It is not.

***Determining the stage in a product life cycle*** The hospitality industry provides products that are already well established alongside some products that are newly launched and others that are at the end of their life cycle.

In the life cycle analysis, as in other approaches, determining the stage in the product life cycle of the particular foodservice product is necessary in order to consider the appropriateness of current strategies or to consider future ones. However, identifying the position of the various foodservice products can be difficult.

Buttle (1996) identifies four stages of the product life cycle: introduction, growth, maturity and decline. As well as presenting this classic view of the product life cycle he also identifies two specific and, for the foodservice industry, very important, variants:

■ The first is the *fad product* life cycle, which is characterised by rapid growth matched by equally dramatic collapse. Certain types of restaurant or disco might fall into this type of life cycle.

■ The second variant is the *extended product* life cycle. This cycle is characterised by an extended maturity phase, which implies high consumer repurchase levels, with little loss of sales to other competitors. Some products of the hospitality industry can fall into this type of life cycle. Examples are some fashionable luxury restaurants and five star hotels, essential function food service outlets, lifestyle products such as holidays and a wide variety of other products that have been revamped and relaunched.

When considering the complexity of the foodservice product and endeavouring to determine the position of a particular product in the product life cycle, it is worth taking account of these two variants in particular, as these will change the interpretation of some of the more standard life-cycle-based models. In many cases the foodservice product being considered will be positioned in the extended life cycle phase. Therefore the main strategies required are those that are aimed at developing and extending existing sales through repackaging and relaunching the product.

## Strategic means

Through the use of the approaches put forward by Johnson and Scholes (1999) and Ansoff (1988), various strategic options can be identified. Johnson and Scholes (1999) argue that strategic direction can be implemented through three basic means: internal development, acquisition (external) development and through joint ventures. Each of these three options is considered below:

### Internal development

Internal development is also referred to as organic growth. It depends on the organisation using its own competences and resources to put its strategy into effect. The advantages are that the organisation can build and develop the required skills and knowledge without encountering the cultural problems often associated with developments involving other organisations. Internal development also enables developmental costs to be spread over a longer period. In many foodservice operations, internal development is the only realistic option. Its major disadvantage is the length of time that may be required to develop new products, acquire new skills and gain access to the new markets which a particular strategic direction might imply.

### Mergers and acquisitions

Acquisition has proved a particularly attractive means of moving quickly in a chosen strategic direction although this has mainly been related to larger organisations. The ownership structures of UK and American companies have made this a common means of achieving fast and very visible strategic action for many organisations.

The reasons for acquisition vary. Rapid entry to particular markets, immediately increased market share, cost savings through rationalisation, balance sheet improvements or other financial reasons including more favourable tax treatment, may all play a part. Potential problems for acquiring firms usually arise from not knowing exactly what is being bought. Many factors do not emerge until after acquisition.

Mergers differ from acquisitions only in the sense that the coming together is voluntary, although it may be under (business) environmental pressures.

Mergers and acquisitions are often justified on grounds of potential synergies, although these often prove difficult to realise. However, the biggest problems usually arise post merger or acquisition when cultural differences between the two organisations emerge. When combined with internal political activity these often cost more in terms of time and resource to resolve than originally envisaged.

### Joint development

Joint developments are becoming both increasingly varied and popular. They arise where an organisation recognises the need to work with one or more outside organisations to achieve its strategy. It may be a need to share costs or scarce resources, knowledge or skills, or regulatory or legal constraints, which lead to the need for joint development. Such arrangements include joint ventures, marketing consortia, franchising, business networks, strategic alliances, subcontracting. Issues to be considered include how to manage relationships between the organisations, and identifying when the arrangement should be ended and how.

## Evaluation criteria

Clearly it is possible to think of many different options for any foodservice organisation given its position in the business environment at a particular point in time. Making choices about which of these alternatives will best help the organisation to achieve its strategic objectives requires some criteria against which to evaluate the alternatives. What criteria to use will depend on how success is measured in the organisation. However, Johnson and Scholes (1999) suggest that it can be helpful to consider the *suitability*, *feasibility* and *acceptability* of any given option.

### Assessing suitability

Consideration of suitability can be based on assessments of whether the option:

- Exploits the core competences of the foodservice organisation.
- Seizes opportunities presented to the foodservice organisation by changes in the business environment and counters any threats which the organisation may be facing.
- Meets the expectations of key organisational stakeholders.

These considerations are not necessarily mutually exclusive but there may be conflict within and between them. It may therefore be useful to consider the issues which can arise, using three different approaches. Again, these are not mutually exclusive, and each one may offer new insights into the options being evaluated:

- *Strategic logic* This is the rational/economic approach concerned primarily with matching an organisation's core competences with the business environment (and in particular the market) it faces. Such an approach draws heavily on the various models of strategic analysis mentioned here and elsewhere (for example, PESTLE, SWOT, Porter's competitive advantage concepts, Johnson and Scholes' strategy clock, Ansoff's matrix, life cycle analysis, and so on).

- *Cultural fit* This approach attempts to assess the extent to which an option fits the prevailing culture and the political realities in the organisation. If a proposed strategy is likely to be rejected by key players in the organisation or runs counter to the prevalent organisational thinking, it is likely to encounter difficulties during implementation no matter how logical it may appear from an economic perspective. This raises the issue of whether an organisational culture can be changed to suit an apparently desirable strategy or whether strategy should be driven from the existing culture.

- *Research evidence* It may be quite reasonable to ask why, with so much research being carried out by businesses and academics over many years, it is necessary to approach each strategic decision as if it were unique. It can be argued that any such decision will indeed be unique, but any decision-making can be usefully informed by experience of other, similar decisions. Monitoring the trade and business press, networking through professional trade bodies and associations, taking the advice of consultants and generally reading the business literature can prove very rewarding.

### Assessing feasibility

Feasibility is concerned with whether the foodservice organisation can put the strategy into operation. In other words, does it have the resources such as finance, skills, equipment and the technology to support the strategic choices being made? Of particular concern should be the assessment of:

- *Funding* Any strategy is likely to require capital investment. A cash flow forecast is vital to assess both the amounts and timing of the investment and the returns from the project.

- *Break-even* It is essential to assess the volume of sales required to achieve the desired return from any strategy. It is then possible to assess the resource implications of such a volume and whether it is possible to achieve such a level of sales.

- *Resource implications* This is a detailed assessment of the physical and human resources required to achieve the strategy. If there is a shortfall between existing and required resources the organisation will need to determine how this can be met in the timescales and within the costs assumed by the proposal.

### Assessing acceptability

The key issue in assessing acceptability is an understanding of stakeholder expectations. These may well vary between different stakeholder groups. Of particular interest to many key stakeholders (particularly managers, owners and providers of finance) will be an assessment of the potential financial returns and risks from any particular proposal.

Financial return can be assessed using payback or discounted cash flow (DCF) investment appraisal methods. Cost/benefit analysis is widely used in the public sector, where the analysis of profit is inappropriate or too narrow a measure. Cost/benefit analysis attempts to put a financial value on all costs and benefits, including intangibles.

Financial risk can be assessed by calculating the projected financial ratios that a strategy implies. Important factors are gearing ratios (increased gearing through increased borrowing exposes a company to greater risk) and liquidity ratios (lowering the liquidity ratios increases financial risk). (See Appendix D for a listing of key financial ratios.) Another useful approach is to use sensitivity analysis, particularly by using spreadsheet packages, to pose 'what if?' questions. These approaches enable owners and managers to assess the impact of changes in interest rates, capacity, utilisation, market shares, and so on, on the financial projection for a possible strategy.

## Strategy and organisational types

If the approaches to strategic management were (or could be) undertaken in a wholly scientific way, decisions would only be rational and objective. But organisations are complex and the culture and power that exists in and around an organisation will substantially affect the decisions that are made. Some of this will be reflected in, and thus determined by, the nature of the goals of the organisation.

We saw in Chapter 1 (page 26) that organisational goals will tend to be derived from a mixture of economic, managerial and social factors. It can also be useful to consider the type of organisation that the foodservice operation might be, as this will substantially affect the specific approaches that will be adopted and the nature of the strategic decisions that will be made.

The nature of any organisation is created through a complex interplay between the various stakeholders involved and the level of power that they can exert. Individual owner-operated foodservice businesses will often predominately reflect the nature of the owner, as the owner is likely to hold the most power. In larger organisations the number of stakeholders involved will increase, and with this the predominance of power may shift to, for instance, shareholders or strong groups of customers.

Considering organisations from this perspective can help to indicate why, for instance, similar foodservice businesses facing similar business environments, might make quite different strategic decisions. The actual decisions about the strategic approaches adopted, the strategic direction of an organisation, the basis of strategy and the ways in which strategies will be achieved, are likely to be largely dependent on the predominant organisational characteristics of the enterprise.

## The reality of strategic decision-making

In this latter part of Chapter 7 we have considered some essential elements of the process of strategic decision-making. The intention has been to encourage the consideration of strategic issues in a systematic way through the application of a range of approaches, only some of which have been identified here. However, although it may appear from this presentation of the material that strategic management is a linear process starting with the establishment of a mission and ending with implementation, these elements in fact have to run in parallel. Any operation will fail if it attempts to sets out its mission without knowing what its resources are or without considering the practicalities of implementation.

Strategic management is largely organic in nature and affected by a range of factors, such as organisational culture, which will mitigate against viewing the process as being simply scientific. The process of strategy that enables successful strategic management to be achieved certainly includes the need for some formal planning, but there is also a need for all managers to be involved in the continuous strategic management of the enterprise. In addition, no matter how well planned a strategy may seem to be, there will be many forces that will affect the extent to which the planned course of action will be achieved, and the possibility of this must also be taken into account in the strategy process. Strategic management therefore needs to:

- Be recognised as being complex and judgemental.
- Be a continuous, rather than a once-a-year process.
- Combine a variety of different approaches and techniques.
- Be done by managers not planners.
- Be based on a continuum of formulation and implementation.
- Be flexible enough to cope with an uncertain future.

## SUMMARY

This chapter has first identified the component parts of a food and beverage operation and examined how their performance may be appraised. Issues concerning the objectives of a food and beverage operation have been addressed, as has the importance of being able to carry out any appraisal or performance objectively. Although highly interrelated in practice, we have considered separately the appraisal of the product and the appraisal of the operation as a whole. This has allowed for a detailed examination of the methods by which these can be achieved. Additionally, appraising the whole operation has been further separated into considering the quantitative performance, the business environment in which the organisation exists and making qualitative judgements on the performance of the operation, including assessing performance by comparison. The chapter has then gone on to consider strategic decision-making through exploring the origins and levels of strategy and strategic analysis tools, including determining the organisational capability. Finally, the basis for strategy, the direction, the means of achieving it and the evaluation criteria that might be used to make decisions about the choices, have also been highlighted. The chapter has concluded with a word of caution about the realities of strategic decision-making.

## REFERENCES

Ansoff, H. I. (1988) *Corporate Strategy*, London: Penguin.

Buttle, F. (1996) *Hotel and Food Service Marketing*, London: Cassell.

Johnson, G. and Scholes, K. (1999) *Exploring Corporate Strategy: Text and Cases*, 5th edition, Hemel Hempstead: Prentice Hall.

Kasavana, M. and Smith, D. (1999) *Menu Engineering: A Practical Guide to Menu Analysis*, Okemos, MI: Hospitality Publications, Inc.

Kasper, H., van Helsdingen, P. and deVries, W. (1999) *Services Marketing Management: An International Perspective*, New York: Wiley.

Knowles, T. (1996) *Corporate Strategy for Hospitality*, Harlow: Longman.

Mintzberg, H., Quinn, J. B. and Ghoshal, S. (1998) *The Strategy Process*, revised European edition, Hemel Hempstead: Prentice Hall Europe.

Pavesic, D. V. (1989) 'Psychological aspects of menu pricing' *International Journal of Hospitality Management* vol. 8, issue 1.

Porter, M. (1980) *Competitive Strategy*, New York: Free Press.

Porter, M. (1985) *Competitive Advantage*, New York: Free Press.

Shortt, D. P. J. (1992) 'Pricing and profitability in the restaurant industry', MBA dissertation, Brunel University, Middlesex.

## FURTHER READING

For examples of financial analysis applied specifically to hospitality industry enterprises see Knowles, T. (1996) *Corporate Strategy for Hospitality*, Harlow: Longman.

For a variety of approaches to applications see Harris, P. (1999) *Profit Planning*, Oxford: Butterworth Heinemann.

Also, reference can be made to Johnson, G. and Scholes, K. (1999) *Exploring Corporate Strategy, Text and Cases*, 5th edition, Hemel Hempstead: Prentice Hall.

# LEARNING ABOUT FOOD AND BEVERAGE MANAGEMENT

This book has been developed to support learning either as part of a formal college or employer-based programme or as part of a self-study programme. The objectives of each of the chapters have been written to reflect learning outcomes, i.e. to identify what you might be seeking to learn about or wanting to do within the workplace.

This book can be approached in two main ways: either by working through the various chapters in order, or by selecting what parts of the book are relevant to a particular learning programme or your job. To help you in using this book the aims and objectives of each chapter are listed below. This listing can be used to identify what parts of the book might be relevant at particular points in time.

Whatever approach is adopted it is recommended that all of Chapter 1 be covered. This chapter lays the foundations for much of the text and also places the consideration of food and beverage (or foodservice) operations and management within context. The structure of the book is detailed, the systems approach explained and food and beverage operations are set within a business framework from the start.

## CHAPTER 1    FOOD AND BEVERAGE OPERATIONS AND MANAGEMENT

### Aim

This chapter aims to set the scene for the rest of the text.

### Objectives

This chapter is intended to support you in:

- setting the contents of this book in context
- identifying and applying a systems approach to foodservice operations

- developing ways of categorising the industry sectors
- exploring the nature of the foodservice product
- identifying the nature of customer demand
- analysing the business environment in order to identify factors which may affect the success of a foodservice organisation
- identifying the legal framework in which the foodservice industry operates
- setting organisational goals and objectives
- gaining an insight into service quality and quality management issues
- setting standards for food and beverage operations
- balancing customers' service requirements with resource productivity
- developing an integrated approach to service quality management.

## CHAPTER 2    DEVELOPING THE CONSUMER–PRODUCT RELATIONSHIP

## Aim

This chapter aims to further explore the nature of demand for food and beverage products through the application of a systematic approach to the development of the consumer–product relationship.

## Objectives

This chapter is intended to support you in:

- adopting a systematic approach to the development of a consumer–product relationship
- further identifying and appraising key issues associated with the nature of demand for food and beverage products
- identifying key stages of product development
- identifying and applying various approaches to the development of a consumer–product relationship
- determining the usefulness and limitations of various techniques and their application to the development of the consumer–product relationship
- developing the consumer–product relationship as a dynamic process.

## CHAPTER 3   FOOD PRODUCTION

### Aim

This chapter aims to demonstrate the importance of sound menu planning and emphasise its importance in the planning, implementation and management of food production systems.

### Objectives

This chapter is intended to support you in:

- planning menus
- ensuring that hygiene management is an implicit function in the food production process
- managing food production as an operating system
- knowing details of the main centralised production systems available to the foodservice operator and the advantages and disadvantages of each
- managing volume within food production systems
- developing and managing the purchasing function and its relationship with the total operational process
- developing and applying operational control procedures.

## CHAPTER 4   BEVERAGE PROVISION

### Aim

This chapter considers beverage provision within foodservice operations.

### Objectives

This chapter is intended to support you in:

- working within the licensing framework for the sale of alcoholic beverages
- developing wine, drink and other beverage lists
- developing specific skills in managing the purchasing, storage and control of wine stocks
- pricing of wine and drink lists
- developing sales and increasing profits
- operating purchasing, storage and control systems for wine and drinks.

## CHAPTER 5 OPERATIONAL AREAS, EQUIPMENT AND STAFFING

### Aim

This chapter aims to outline the broad and some detailed considerations in the planning, design, equipping and staffing of foodservice operations.

### Objectives

The chapter is intended to support you in:

- developing a systematic approach to the planning, designing, equipping and staffing of foodservice operations
- making operational choices which contribute to meeting both customer and operational needs.

## CHAPTER 6 FOOD AND BEVERAGE SERVICE

### Aim

This chapter considers various aspects in the management of food and beverage service.

### Objectives

This chapter is intended to support you in:

- developing your understanding of the service sequence and the service process
- identifying and categorising food and beverage service methods
- exploring the relationship between operational choices in food and beverage service and resource productivity
- developing approaches to the maintenance of good customer relations
- dealing with the management of the volume in food and beverage service
- identifying and applying sales promotion principles
- managing the seven stages of the service sequence
- controlling revenue.

**CHAPTER 7   APPRAISING PERFORMANCE AND MAKING STRATEGIC DECISIONS**

## Aim

This chapter aims to identify and evaluate the techniques of measuring and appraising the performance of food and beverage operations and to consider and apply approaches to strategic decision-making.

## Objectives

This chapter is intended to support you in:

- considering the basis for performance appraisal
- identifying the aspects of foodservice operations which are commonly appraised
- developing skills in the application of a range of performance measures and appraisal techniques to individual aspects of food and beverage operations, the product and the whole operation
- determining the usefulness and limitations in the various quantitative and qualitative appraisal techniques and their application to food and beverage operations
- identifying the components of strategic planning as a systematic process
- identifying and applying approaches to business analysis and evaluation
- selecting and applying strategic planning models and approaches appropriate to food-service operations.

# OPERATIONAL CALCULATIONS

Chapter 7 details the appraisal of revenue (page 224), costs (page 228) and profits (page 234). This appendix provides examples of operational figures and calculations.

Being able to interpret operational data is an essential skill for the food and beverage manager. In order to be able to do that well it is necessary to have a sound understanding of the basis for operational calculations.

Below are examples of the figures that can be generated in a foodservice operation and how these can be used to create operational data.

## EXAMPLE FIGURES

The following information is based on a 120-seat café restaurant:

*Operational hours*
The restaurant is open six days a week all year

*Opening hours*
Lunch service    12 noon to 2 p.m.
Dinner service   7 p.m. to 10 p.m.

*Average customer numbers*
Lunch    40
Dinner   75

*Average customer spending*

| Food | Beverage |
|------|----------|
| Lunch £6 per head | £3 per head |
| Dinner £10 per head | £5 per head |

*Staffing establishment*
Lunch    One member of staff per 10 customers
Dinner   One member of staff per 15 customers

All staff are employed for the entire service period plus one hour prior to the service and one hour after the service

*Costs*
The food costs are 40 per cent of the annual food revenue.
The beverage costs are 50 per cent of the annual beverage revenue.
The staff (labour) costs are averaged at £5.50 per hour per member of staff.
The total overhead cost for one year is estimated at 20 per cent of the total annual revenue (food and beverage).

Using this information it is possible to calculate all of the following:

1 **(a)** The annual food revenue
  **(b)** The annual beverage revenue
  **(c)** The annual lunch revenue
  **(d)** The annual dinner revenue
  **(e)** The total annual revenue.

2 The total average number of staff needed each day for the service of:
  **(a)** Lunch
  **(b)** Dinner.

3 The total annual labour costs.

4 The percentage of labour costs in relation to the total annual revenue.

5 The average daily percentage seat occupancy during the year for:
  **(a)** Lunch
  **(b)** Dinner.

6 The average daily overhead costs for each day of operation.

7 The gross profit cash and percentage for the year for:
  **(a)** Food
  **(b)** Beverage
  **(c)** Total (food and beverage).

8 The total amount of money left over at the end of the year (net profit) after all costs have been deducted and its percentage of the total revenue.

## EXAMPLE CALCULATIONS

The calculations are as follows:

**1 (a)** The annual food revenue:

Lunch food revenue = Spend per head × No. of covers × No. of days
× No. of weeks
= £6 × 40 covers × 6 days × 52 weeks
= £74 880

Dinner food revenue = Spend per head × No. of covers × No. of days
× No. of weeks
= £10 × 75 covers × 6 days × 52 weeks
= £234 000

Total annual food revenue = Lunch food revenue + Dinner food revenue
= £74 880 + £234 000
= £308 880

**(b)** The annual beverage revenue:

Lunch beverage revenue = Spend per head × No. of covers × No. of days
× No. of weeks
= £3 × 40 covers × 6 days × 52 weeks
= £37 440

Dinner beverage revenue = Spend per head × No. of covers × No. of days
× No. of weeks
= £5 × 75 covers × 6 days × 52 weeks
= £117 000

Total annual beverage revenue = Lunch beverage revenue + Dinner beverage
revenue
= £37 440 + £117 000
= £154 440

**(c)** Total annual lunch revenue = Annual lunch food revenue
+ Annual lunch beverage revenue
= £74 880 + £37 440
= £112 320

**(d)** Total annual dinner revenue = Annual dinner food revenue
+ Annual dinner beverage revenue
= £234 000 + £117 000
= £351 000

**(e)** Total annual revenue = Annual lunch revenue + Annual dinner revenue
= £112 320 + £351 000
= £463 320

*or*

$$= \text{Annual food revenue} + \text{Annual beverage revenue}$$
$$= £308\,880 + £154\,440$$
$$= £463\,320$$

2  The total average number of staff needed for each day for the service of:

(a)  Lunch

One member of staff is required for 10 customers. The average number of customers per day is 40. Therefore:

$$\text{Average number of staff for lunch} = \frac{40}{10}$$
$$= 4$$

(b)  Dinner

One member of staff is required for 15 customers. The average number of customers per day is 75. Therefore:

$$\text{Average number of staff for dinner} = \frac{75}{10}$$
$$= 5$$

3  Total annual labour costs:

$$\text{Lunch labour costs per day} = \text{No. of staff} \times \text{Working hours} \times \text{Rate per hour}$$
$$= 4 \text{ staff} \times 4 \text{ hours} \times £5.50$$
$$= £88$$

$$\text{Dinner labour costs per day} = \text{No. of staff} \times \text{Working hours} \times \text{Rate per hour}$$
$$= 5 \text{ staff} \times 5 \text{ hours} \times £5.50$$
$$= £137.50$$

$$\text{Total labour costs per day} = \text{Lunch labour costs} + \text{Dinner labour costs}$$
$$= £88 + £137.50$$
$$= £225.50$$

$$\text{Total annual labour costs} = \text{Total labour costs per day} \times \text{No. of days} \times \text{No. of weeks}$$
$$= £225.50 \times 6 \times 52$$
$$= £70\,356$$

4  Percentage of labour costs in relation to total annual revenue:

$$\text{Labour cost percentage} = \frac{\text{Labour costs}}{\text{Revenue}} \times 100$$
$$= \frac{£70\,356}{£463\,320} \times 100$$
$$= 15.18\%$$

5 The average daily percentage seat occupancy during the year for:
  (a) Lunch

$$\text{Lunch percentage seat occupancy} = \frac{\text{Covers actual}}{\text{Covers available}} \times 100$$

$$= \frac{40}{120} \times 100$$

$$= 33.34\%$$

  (b) Dinner

$$\text{Dinner percentage seat occupancy} = \frac{\text{Covers actual}}{\text{Covers available}} \times 100$$

$$= \frac{75}{120} \times 100$$

$$= 62.50\%$$

6 The average daily overhead cost:
  Overheads are 20 per cent of revenue. Therefore:

$$\text{Total annual overheads} = \frac{20}{100} \times £463\,320$$

$$= £92\,664$$

$$\text{Daily overheads costs} = \frac{\text{Annual cost}}{6 \text{ days} \times 52 \text{ weeks}}$$

$$= \frac{£92\,664}{312}$$

$$= £297 \text{ per day}$$

7 The gross profit cash and percentage for the year for:
  (a) Food cash gross profit and percentage
     Food cost is 40 per cent of total food revenue. Therefore gross profit is 60 per cent of total food revenue.

$$\text{Gross profit on food} = \frac{60}{100} \times £308\,880$$

$$= £185\,328 \text{ cash (GP\% = 60)}$$

  (b) Beverage cash gross profit and percentage
     Beverage cost is 50 per cent of total beverage revenue. Therefore gross profit is 50 per cent of total beverage revenue.

$$\text{Gross profit on beverage} = \frac{50}{100} \times £154\,440$$

$$= £77\,220 \text{ cash (GP\% = 50)}$$

(c) Total cash gross profit and percentage

Total cash gross profit = Food gross profit + Beverage gross profit

$$= £185\ 328 + £77\ 220$$
$$= £262\ 548$$

$$\text{Percentage gross profit} = \frac{\text{Cash gross profit}}{\text{Revenue}} \times 100$$

$$= \frac{£262\ 548}{£463\ 320} \times 100$$

$$= 56.67\%$$

**8** The total amount of money left over at the end of the year after all costs have been deducted and its percentage of total revenue (net profit).

Net profit = Gross profit − (Labour costs + Overhead costs)
$$= £262\ 548 - (£70\ 356 + £92\ 664)$$
$$= £99\ 528$$

$$\text{Net profit as a percentage of revenue} = \frac{\text{Net profit}}{\text{Revenue}} \times 100$$

$$= \frac{£99\ 528}{£463\ 320} \times 100$$

$$= 21.48\%$$

## CHECK MATRIX

In foodservice operations there is an established relationship between revenue, costs and profits. In order to check that all the cash and percentages figures are correct, a matrix can be constructed. This matrix is based on Figure 7.1 (page 238), which summarised the relationship between revenue, costs and profits. The check matrix for the figures used in the example above is given in Table B.1.

**Table B.1**  Calculations check matrix

|  | £ | % |  | £ | % |
|---|---|---|---|---|---|
| Material costs[a] | 200 772 | 43.34 | Cost of sales[a] | 200 772 | 43.34 |
| Labour cost | 70 356 | 15.18 ⎫ |  |  |  |
| Overheads | 92 664 | 20.00 ⎬ | Gross profit | 262 548 | 56.66 |
| Net profit | 99 528 | 21.48 ⎭ |  |  |  |
| Revenue/Sales | 463 320 | 100.00 | Revenue/Sales | 463 320 | 100.00 |

[a] Cost of sales = costs of food and beverages

# PRODUCT APPRAISAL – AUDIT FACTOR LISTINGS

Appraising of the product for a foodservice operation can include audits. This is discussed in Chapter 7, page 254.

Two example checklists are given below. The first is for a fine dining restaurant and the second is for the beverage operation of a fine dining restaurant.

## EXAMPLE CHECKLIST FOR THE AUDIT OF A FINE DINING RESTAURANT

1 If reservation made, table ready on time?

2 How was reservation handled?

3 Guests greeted within 30 seconds of arrival?

4 If reservation made, guest surname used?

5 Welcome/reception (guest recognition) personnel make and maintain eye contact with pleasant facial expression?

6 Guest(s) seated within 1 minute of arrival?

7 First impression?

8 Interior design and ambience?

9 Guest(s) seated at table for appropriate number of guests?

10 Greeter exhibits professional demeanour?

11 Guest(s) offered beverage within 2 minutes of seating – 3 minutes for a party of four guests?

12 Guest(s) served ordered beverage within 4 minutes of seating – 6 minutes for a party of four guests?

13 Literature (the menu, wine list, other)?

14 Alternatives shown/offered?

15 Post-ordering, food served within:
   **(a)** appetiser 10 minutes lunch
   **(b)** appetiser 15 minutes dinner
   **(c)** (not applicable if amuse-bouche served)

16 Pace of meal is appropriate and convenient?

17 Server exhibits professional demeanour and is viewed as 'reading' the guest(s)?

18 Server makes eye contact with pleasant facial expression?

19 Server comments are clearly enunciated and modulated?

20 Server is knowledgeable about the menu?

21 Sommelier is knowledgeable about beverages and wines and offers range of wines from the list?

22 Staff are calm and well organised?

23 Staff maintain attentive posture nearby?

24 Another drink is suggested within two minutes of being empty?

25 Server suggests accompaniments such as appetisers and desserts?

26 Sommelier suggests other wines, beverages and digestifs?

27 Service staff attitude/style/communication skills, customer handling/selling skills?

28 All orders complete and condiments appropriate?

29 Was water served automatically?

30 Extra place settings have been removed?

31 Table/dishes promptly cleared and reset?

32 Comfort?

33 Pricing?

34 Choice?

35 Cooking?

36 Quality of aliments?

37 Seasonality of aliments?

38 Embellishments?

39 Assessment?

40 Formality?

41 Lighting?

42 Bill provided within 1 minute of request?

43 Bill presented with pen in folder?

44  Bill complete and totalled?

45  Bill or verbal payment request is correctly itemised and/or priced?

46  Prompt collection of payment made?

47  If cash, correct change returned?

48  If cash, receipt offered?

49  If cash, money properly reported (not applicable if no audit)?

50  Check has been neatly prepared and is easy to read?

51  Were checks presented in a clean quality folder, or silver tray, with pen?

52  If charged, properly posted to room account?

53  Cash/charge transactions appear normal?

54  Timestamp and date correct?

55  Staff uniform/attire in good condition?

56  Staff uniform/attire clean?

57  Staff uniform well fitting?

58  Staff neatly groomed?

59  Staff do not engage in excessive talk/horseplay?

60  No employee is smoking in view?

61  No employee consuming food or drinking in view?

62  Staff are unobtrusive?

63  Was supervisor apparent?

64  Was supervisor managing staff?

65  Was supervisor positively interacting with guests?

66  Were food and beverages attractively arranged?

67  Did aliments/beverages correspond to the menu (trades) descriptions or requests?

68  Were hot items served hot? Cold items served cold? Frozen items served frozen?

69  Were white wines opened and served from an ice-bucket?

70  Were aliments served fresh in colour and texture?

71  Did aliments have a good flavour?

72  Were portions adequate and consistent?

73  China and glassware not chipped, scratched, pitted or faded?

74  Was china and glassware clean?

75  Was flatware in good condition – not dented, worn or tarnished?

76  Was flatware clean?

77 Is the cutlery of quality? Is it clean?

78 Is the crockery of quality? Is it clean?

79 Were paper goods neat and clean?

80 Was linen clean, French-folded and in good condition?

81 Was the temperature in the room comfortable?

82 Was a sound system in use? Comment.

83 Was the sound quality and volume suitable?

84 Was there live music?

85 Was the live music good? Comment.

86 Was the floor/carpet clean?

87 Was the floor/carpet worn, damaged or permanently stained?

88 Were the ceiling, walls and doors clean?

89 Were the ceiling, walls and doors worn, damaged or permanently stained?

90 Were there any lights which were burned out or dusty?

91 Were counters/tables clean?

92 Were counters/tables worn, chipped or damaged?

93 Were service stations/sideboards clean and orderly?

94 Were service stations/sideboards worn, chipped or damaged?

95 Were chairs/booths clean?

96 Were chairs/booths worn, damaged or permanently stained?

97 Were the windows, drapes and window treatments clean?

98 Did window treatments acceptably moderate the natural flood of light into the restaurant area?

99 Did all furniture, fixtures and equipment appear mechanically sound and in good repair?

100 Were plants, flowers and table decorations appropriate, attractive and healthy? Were their containers clean?

101 Were menus, wine lists, and posters descriptive, neat and clean? Comment on copy.

102 Were diet/fitness items available?

103 Were vegetarian alternatives available?

104 Were regional, ethnic or fusion items available?

105 If specials were available, were they adequately promoted in the outlet?

106 If buffets or trolleys were used, were they mentioned or promoted widely?

107 What was the policy on smoking? Non-smoking? Were there isolated areas for both?

108 Was the table crumbed after the main course?

109 Was hot food brought to the table or to the waiters' stations under cloches?

110 Was a restaurant menu displayed and priced at the front of the restaurant (entrance)? Was the copy easy to read?

111 Were vacated table-tops reset within 5 minutes of the guest's departure?

112 Were tables level and padded?

113 Were mirrors and glass clean and polished and free from dust, food and wear marks?

114 Were rest rooms clean and fresh smelling?

115 Was there considerable noise stemming from the kitchen?

116 Sensory evaluation (five sensing)?

117 Skill/dexterity?

118 Is the cutlery of quality? Is it clean?

119 Is the crockery of quality? Is it clean?

120 Are staff knowledgeable about extended information; the locale, the hotel etc.?

121 Were odour hedonics considered?

122 Was there evidence of empathetic merchandising taking place?

123 How was the exit handled from the restaurant, in terms of staff communication/ recognition?

124 Where did you excel?

125 Holistic impression?

## EXAMPLE CHECKLIST FOR THE AUDIT OF THE BEVERAGE PROVISION OF A FINE DINING RESTAURANT

1 Guests to be greeted within 1 minute?

2 Staff uniform/attire in good condition?

3 Staff uniform/attire clean and fit for purpose?

4 Staff neatly groomed?

5 Server exhibits professional demeanour?

6 Server makes eye contact with pleasant facial expression?

7 Staff are calm and well organised?

8 Server comments are clearly enunciated and suitably modulated?

9 Special promotion lists (if any) are presented?

10 First drink(s) served within 5 minutes of arrival?

11 Fresh complimentary snacks served and replenished with clean napkins/serviettes if appropriate?

12 Another drink suggested within 1 minute of being empty?

13 Ashtrays cleaned after 1 cigarette?

14 Appropriate hygienic method employed to secure contents during this process? or,

15 No smoking policy adhered?

16 Bill presented with pen in folder?

17 Bill or verbal payment request accurate?

18 Timely collection of payment?

19 If cash, correct change given?

20 If cash, clearly itemised, easy-to-read receipt offered?

21 If cash, money properly reported?

22 If charged, properly posted to account?

23 Check, if any, properly posted to account?

24 Check, if any, neatly prepared and easy to read?

25 Cash/charge transactions appear normal?

26 No employee smoking in view?

27 No employee eating or drinking in view?

28 No product seen given away or unaccounted for?

29 Anything else untoward happening?

30 Employees do not engage in excessive talk/horseplay?

31 Was supervisor present?

32 Was supervisor positively interacting with guests?

33 Was the beverage portion correct? Was the flavour good?

34 Was a shot measure/dispenser being used and other weights and measures issues brought to light (for example, notice on measures)?

35 Was the drink adequately iced, chilled or heated?

36 Stirrers, straws as appropriate?

37 Garnishes fresh and appropriate?

38 Coaster and napkins appropriate and fresh?

39 Coasters and side-tables promptly cleaned?

40 Was glassware used of quality?

41 Appropriate glassware clean, not pitted or chipped?

42 Tables promptly cleared and cleaned?

43 Was room temperature comfortable?

44 Was there a sound system in use? Were the sound quality and volume good?

45 Was live music being played?

46 Was sound quality and volume adequate?

47 Were both floor and carpets clean?

48 Were either floor or carpets worn, damaged or permanently stained?

49 Were ceiling, walls and doors clean?

50 Were chairs/booths clean?

51 Were chairs/booths worn, damaged or permanently stained?

52 Were windows, drapes and window treatments clean?

53 Did window treatments acceptably moderate the natural flood of light into the restaurant area?

54 Drapes and window treatments in good repair?

55 Did all furniture/fixtures and equipment appear mechanically sound and in good repair?

56 Were plants, flowers and table arrangements attractive, appropriate and healthy, with clean containers?

57 Was the back-bar clean and neat?

58 Were menus, cards and posters descriptive, clean and neat?

59 Does the environment seem secure and comfortable?

60 Fixtures and light bulbs in good working order, polished and free of cloudy film?

61 Walls and doors are free of dust, stains, splatters, wear-and-tear marks?

62 Chair joints are tight?

63 Tables are level and clean, with table bases free from scratches and wear-marks?

64 Has space management been considered?

65 Is poor space management/layout impacting negatively upon purchasing behaviour?

66 How enthusiastic are personnel to please guests?

# OPERATIONAL AND FINANCIAL RATIOS

The most of the common quantitative performance measures for a foodservice operation (as identified in Chapter 7) are the operational ratios and financial ratios. These may be grouped under six main categories:

- operational ratios
- activity ratios
- profitability ratios
- liquidity ratio
- gearing ratios
- stock market ratios.

The most common operational and financial ratios, the formulae for them and explanations of what the individual ratio can indicate are grouped under these six headings below

| Ratio | Formula | Meaning |
|---|---|---|
| **Operational ratios** | | |
| Gross profit % | $\dfrac{\text{Sales revenue} - \text{Cost of sales} \times 100}{\text{Sales}}$ | A measure of operational efficiency (not profitability). Shows the gross profit, i.e. the sales less the costs of materials (food or beverage) as a percentage of sales. Conversely, can be used to indicate the percentage of material costs. Can be used over time for budgeting and comparison purposes and for comparison with industry norms |

| Ratio | Formula | Meaning |
|---|---|---|
| Net profit % | $$\frac{\text{Sales revenue} - \text{Total costs} \times 100}{\text{Sales}}$$ | Shows overall net profit percentage, i.e. the sales less the total costs as a percentage of sales. Conversely, can be used to indicate the percentage of costs. Can also be used over time for budgeting and comparison purposes and for comparison with industry norms |
| Average check | $$\frac{\text{Sales}}{\text{No. of bill transactions}}$$ | Measures the average amount spent per bill transaction. Usually calculated for a specific service period in order to compare spending power of customers and average customer group sizes over time. Useful when interpreting and comparing sales figures |
| Spend per head | $$\frac{\text{Sales}}{\text{No. of customers}}$$ | Measures the average amount spent per person served. Usually calculated for a specific service period in order to compare spending power of individual customers. Can be broken down further to indicate spend on food or beverages. Useful when interpreting and comparing sales figures over time |
| Material costs % | $$\frac{\text{Sales} \times 100}{\text{Cost of materials}}$$ | Identifies the cost of materials (either food or beverage) as a percentage of the sales revenue. Usually calculated separately for food and beverages and also then down to individual or groups of menu or beverage items. Useful for comparison over different service periods and for comparison against industry norms |

| Ratio | Formula | Meaning |
|---|---|---|
| Labour costs % | $\dfrac{\text{Sales} \times 100}{\text{Cost of labour}}$ | Identifies the cost of labour as a percentage of the sales revenue. Useful for comparison over different periods and for comparison against industry norms |
| Productivity index | $\dfrac{\text{Sales}}{\text{Cost of labour}}$ | Alternative method for showing labour costs in relation to sales. Low index would be where there is a high labour cost in relation to sales. Can be used as budget measure and also for comparison with industry norms |
| Revenue per employee | $\dfrac{\text{Total sales}}{\text{No. of staff employed}}$ | Gives sales revenue per member of staff. Can also be calculated for full-time equivalent. Used as a measure of efficiency. Usually calculated for specific service periods and comparison made over time |
| Sales per seat available | $\dfrac{\text{Sales}}{\text{No. of seats available}}$ | Indicates the amount of sales that are generated per seat available. Usually calculated for given service periods and compared over time. Can also be calculated on the sales per seat used. Comparison between these two figures can indicate efficiency of operation |
| Seat turnover | $\dfrac{\text{No. of seats used}}{\text{No. of seats available}}$ | Indicates the occupancy efficiency of the seating in a foodservice area. Usually calculated for specific service periods and compared over time |
| Sales per square metre | $\dfrac{\text{Sales}}{\text{Total area of operation in square metres}}$ | Can also be calculated per square foot. Commonly also used in retail operations. Can be useful in bar areas or for takeaway operations where earnings per seat cannot be calculated |

| Ratio | Formula | Meaning |
|---|---|---|
| **Activity ratios** | | |
| Net asset turnover | $\dfrac{\text{Sales}}{\text{Net assets}}$ | Measures how effectively the net assets are used to generate sales; measures how many sales are generated by each pound sterling of net assets |
| Fixed asset turnover | $\dfrac{\text{Sales}}{\text{Fixed assets}}$ | Measures the utilisation of the company's fixed assets (i.e. plant and equipment); measures how many sales are generated by each pound sterling of fixed assets |
| Stock turnover (rate) | $\dfrac{\text{Cost of sales}}{\text{Average value of stock}}$ | Measures the number of times the stocks of food or beverage items were turned over during the year. Indicates management's ability to control investment in stocks |
| Stock turnover (period) | $\dfrac{\text{Average value of stocks}}{\text{Cost of sales}} \times 365$ | Indicates the stock level being held as shown by the number of days it takes to use and replace it |
| Debt turnover | $\dfrac{\text{Sales}}{\text{Debtors}}$ | Indicates the number of times that debtors are cycled during the year |
| Average collection period | $\dfrac{\text{Debtors} \times 365}{\text{Sales}}$ | The number of days' credit the firm gives to customers. The longer the period the more cost to the firm in outstanding debts |
| **Profitability ratios** | | |
| Return on capital employed | $\dfrac{\text{Profit before interest and tax} \times 100}{\text{Capital employed}}$ | Measures the performance of the firm regardless of the method of financing |
| Return on equity | $\dfrac{\text{Profit after tax} \times 100}{\text{Shareholder funds}}$ | Measures the rate of return or profitability of the shareholders' investment in the company |
| Gross profit margin | $\dfrac{\text{Profit before interest and tax}}{\text{Sales}}$ | Shows the total margin available to cover operating expenses and still yield a profit. Useful for comparison over time and with industry norms |

| Ratio | Formula | Meaning |
|---|---|---|
| Net profit margin | $\dfrac{\text{Net profit after tax}}{\text{Sales}}$ | Shows how much after-tax profit is generated by each pound of sales. Also useful for comparison over time and with industry norms |
| **Liquidity ratios** | | |
| Current ratio | $\dfrac{\text{Current assets}}{\text{Current liabilities}}$ | Indicates the extent to which a firm can meet its short-term liabilities from short-term assets. This should be in the region of 2:1 or 1:1 to reflect a healthy proportion of current assets (stock, debtors and cash) to current liabilities (overdraft, creditors) |
| Acid test or quick ratio | $\dfrac{\text{Current assets} - \text{stocks}}{\text{Current liabilities}}$ | Measures the firm's ability to pay off short-term liabilities from current assets without relying upon the sale of its stock. A stricter test of liquidity because it compares only money assets (cash and debtors) to current liabilities |
| **Gearing ratios** | | |
| Debt ratio | $\dfrac{\text{Long-term debt}}{\text{Capital employed (net assets)}}$ | Measures the extent to which borrowed funds have been used to finance the company's net assets. The more long-term debt the higher is the gearing and the greater the risk incurred. Gearing is generally considered to be high above 1:1 |
| Debt-to-equity ratio | $\dfrac{\text{Long-term debt}}{\text{Share capital}}$ | Measures the funds provided by long-term creditors against the funds provided by shareholders |
| Interest cover | $\dfrac{\text{Profit before interest and tax}}{\text{Interest payable}}$ | Indicates the ability of the company to meet its annual interest costs. The higher the ratio the less risk is involved, as the interest being paid becomes a smaller proportion of the profit generated |

| Ratio | Formula | Meaning |
|---|---|---|
| **Stock market ratios** | | |
| Earnings per share | $$\frac{\text{Profit after tax}}{\text{No. of ordinary shares in issue}}$$ | Shows the after-tax earnings generated for each ordinary share. High earnings per share can encourage new investors and promote investor loyalty |
| Price/earnings | $$\frac{\text{Market price per share}}{\text{Earnings per share}}$$ | Shows the esteem in which the market holds the company; the higher the ratio the more popular the share |
| Net dividend yield | $$\frac{\text{Dividend per share}}{\text{Market price per share}}$$ | Indicates the dividend rate of return to ordinary shareholders |
| Dividend cover | $$\frac{\text{Earnings per share}}{\text{Dividend per share}}$$ or $$\frac{\text{Profit to pay ordinary dividends}}{\text{Ordinary dividends}}$$ | Measures the extent to which the company pays dividends from earnings. High dividend cover is healthy provided that investors judge the gross dividend on ordinary shares to be adequate. Low dividend cover may indicate that gross dividends to ordinary shares have been set too high |

# BUDGET AND TRADING RESULTS COMPARISON AND EVALUATION

Chapter 7 identifies that in order to interpret fully the meaning of operational ratios, it is necessary to have some basis of comparison. For operational ratios, there will usually be internal budgets and objectives against which they can be measured.

Being able to interpret trading results is an essential skill for the food and beverage manager. In order to do that well it is necessary to have a sound understanding of the basis of operational ratios and of their interpretation.

Below is an example of the budget and trading results for a foodservice operation followed by an analysis and evaluation of the data.

## THE BUDGET AND TRADING FIGURES

The figures presented in Table E.1 are for a 62-seat, plated table service, café-style restaurant. The restaurant holds a restaurant licence and is open from 8.30 a.m. to 9.30 p.m., Monday to Saturday.

## ANALYSIS

For the data provided in Table E.1, operational ratios can be calculated as the basis for comparison. Table E.2 gives the trading figures together with a variety of performance measures. Table E.3 looks at the percentage variance against budget.

Table E.4 gives the percentage for food and drink sales of the total sales; Table E.5 shows the average spend per head on food and drink; and Table E.6 shows the average seat turnover.

**Table E.1** Budget and trading results for three months

|  | Budget | | 1st month | | 2nd month | | 3rd month | |
|---|---|---|---|---|---|---|---|---|
|  | £ | £ | £ | £ | £ | £ | £ | £ |
| **Food** | | | | | | | | |
| Sales | 21 600 | | 21 525 | | 21 750 | | 21 375 | |
| Food costs | 7 560 | | 7 800 | | 8 220 | | 7 920 | |
| Gross profit | | 14 040 | | 13 725 | | 13 530 | | 13 455 |
| **Beverages** | | | | | | | | |
| Sales | 3 090 | | 3 300 | | 3 345 | | 3 180 | |
| Liquor costs | 1 230 | | 1 290 | | 1 305 | | 1 253 | |
| Gross profit | | 1 860 | | 2 010 | | 2 040 | | 1 927 |
| **Total sales** | 24 690 | | 24 825 | | 25 095 | | 24 555 | |
| **Total cost of sales** | 8 790 | | 9 090 | | 9 525 | | 9 173 | |
| **Total gross profit** | | 15 900 | | 15 735 | | 15 570 | | 15 382 |
| **Unallocated costs** | | | | | | | | |
| Labour costs | 6 420 | | 7 275 | | 7 335 | | 7 515 | |
| Overheads | 4 440 | | 4 500 | | 4 575 | | 4 650 | |
| **Total costs** | 10 860 | | 11 775 | | 11 910 | | 12 165 | |
| **Net profit** | | 5 040 | | 3 960 | | 3 660 | | 3 217 |
| **Stockholding** | | | | | | | | |
| Food | 3 750 | | 4 125 | | 4 020 | | 4 110 | |
| Beverages | 750 | | 795 | | 810 | | 780 | |
| No. of customers | 5 410 | | 5 340 | | 5 420 | | 5 430 | |

**Table E.2** Analysis of the budget and trading results for three months

| | Budget | | | 1st month | | | 2nd month | | | 3rd month | | |
|---|---|---|---|---|---|---|---|---|---|---|---|---|
| | £ | £ | % | £ | £ | % | £ | £ | % | £ | £ | % |
| **Food** | | | | | | | | | | | | |
| Sales | 21 600 | | | 21 525 | | | 21 750 | | | 21 375 | | |
| Food costs | | 7 560 | 35 | | 7 800 | 36 | | 8 220 | 38 | | 7 920 | 37 |
| Gross profit | 14 040 | | 65 | 13 725 | | 64 | 13 530 | | 62 | 13 455 | | 63 |
| **Beverages** | | | | | | | | | | | | |
| Sales | 3 090 | | | 3 300 | | | 3 345 | | | 3 180 | | |
| Liquor costs | 1 230 | | 40 | 1 290 | | 39 | 1 305 | | 39 | 1 253 | | 39 |
| Gross profit | 1 860 | | 60 | 2 010 | | 61 | 2 040 | | 61 | 1 927 | | 61 |
| **Total sales** | 24 690 | | | 24 825 | | | 25 095 | | | 24 555 | | |
| **Total cost of sales** | 8 790 | | | 9 090 | | | 9 525 | | | 9 173 | | |
| **Total gross profit** | 15 900 | | 64 | 15 735 | | 63 | 15 570 | | 62 | 15 382 | | 63 |
| **Unallocated costs** | | | | | | | | | | | | |
| Labour costs | 6 420 | | 26 | 7 275 | | 29 | 7 335 | | 29 | 7 515 | | 31 |
| Overheads | 4 440 | | 18 | 4 500 | | 18 | 4 575 | | 19 | 4 650 | | 19 |
| **Total costs** | 10 860 | | 44 | 11 775 | | 47 | 11 910 | | 47 | 12 165 | | 50 |
| **Net profit** | 5 040 | | 20 | 3 960 | | 16 | 3 660 | | 15 | 3 217 | | 13 |
| **Stockholding** | | | STO[a] | | | STO | | | STO | | | STO |
| Food | 3 750 | | 2.01 | 4 125 | | 1.89 | 4 020 | | 2.04 | 4 110 | | 1.92 |
| Beverages | 750 | | 1.64 | 795 | | 1.62 | 810 | | 1.61 | 780 | | 1.61 |

[a] STO = stock turnover

**Table E.3**  Variance percentage against budget

|  | 1st month | 2nd month | 3rd month | To date |
|---|---|---|---|---|
| Food sales | −0.34 | 0.69 | −1.04 | −0.08 |
| Food costs | 3.17 | 8.73 | 4.76 | +5.56 |
| Gross profit | −2.24 | −3.63 | −4.20 | −3.35 |
| Liquor sales | 6.80 | 8.25 | 2.91 | +5.99 |
| Liquor costs | 4.80 | 6.09 | 1.87 | +4.28 |
| Gross profit | 8.06 | 9.67 | 3.60 | +7.11 |
| Total sales | 0.55 | 1.64 | −0.54 | +0.55 |
| Total cost of sales | 3.41 | 8.36 | 0.94 | +5.38 |
| Total gross profit | −1.03 | −2.07 | −3.25 | −2.12 |
| Wage and staff | 13.31 | 14.25 | 17.00 | +14.88 |
| Overheads | 1.35 | 3.04 | 4.73 | +3.04 |
| Total costs | 8.43 | 9.67 | 12.02 | 10.03 |
| Net profit | −21.42 | −27.38 | −36.15 | −28.33 |
| Net profit under budget | −£1 080 | −£1 380 | −£1 822 | −£4 282 |

*Note*: Variance percentage = [(Actual − Budget)/Budget] × 100

Variance percentage to date = [(Actual to date − Budget to date)/Budget to date] × 100

**Table E.4**  Percentage food/drink sales of total sales

|  | Budget | | 1st month | | 2nd month | | 3rd month | |
|---|---|---|---|---|---|---|---|---|
|  | £ | % | £ | % | £ | % | £ | % |
| Food | 21 600 | 87.5 | 21 525 | 86.8 | 21 750 | 86.6 | 21 375 | 87 |
| Beverage | 3 090 | 12.5 | 3 300 | 13.2 | 3 345 | 13.4 | 3 180 | 13 |
| Total | 24 690 | 100.0 | 24 825 | 100.0 | 25 095 | 100.0 | 24 555 | 100.0 |

**Table E.5**  Average spend per head

|  | Budget (£) | 1st month (£) | 2nd month (£) | 3rd month (£) |
|---|---|---|---|---|
| Food | 3.99 | 4.03 | 4.01 | 3.94 |
| Beverage | 0.57 | 0.62 | 0.62 | 0.59 |
| Total | 4.56 | 4.64 | 4.63 | 4.52 |

*Note*: Average spend per head = Sales (food and/or beverages)/No. of customers

**Table E.6  Average seat turnover**

| Budget | 1st month | 2nd month | 3rd month |
|--------|-----------|-----------|-----------|
| 3.64 | 3.58 | 3.62 | 3.64 |

*Note*:  Seat turnover = No. of customers served/No. of seats available

Figures assume that establishment is open for 24 trading days per month (4 × 6 days)

## EVALUATION

Evaluation of the operational data which has been generated might be as follows.

### Apparent strengths

■ Conservative budget (given the number of seats) and targets for sales are being met.

■ Reasonable match between spend and number of customers and budget with principal problem being costs.

### Areas for concern

■ Food costs are higher in variance than sales resulting in the gross profit running under budget at £1410 to date (−3.35 per cent).

■ Liquor costs are lower in variance than sales, with sales being over budget between 2.91 and 8.25 per cent, £555 for the three months to date (+5.99 per cent). This has also resulted in drink being a slightly higher proportion of total sales (food sales have varied only −0.08 per cent to date).

■ Stock turnover in food is slightly lower than budgeted possibly suggesting a problem with purchasing not matching usage.

■ Wage costs are between 13.31 and 17.0 per cent over budget (+14.88 per cent or £2865 to date) with upward trend indicating possible overstaffing.

■ Overheads are increasing from 1.35 to 4.73 per cent over budget, again with upward trend (£405, or +3.04 per cent to date).

■ Overall performance of restaurant is poor against budget. Net profit is between −21.42 and −36.17 per cent under budget with overall downward trend and −28.33 per cent under budget to date (£4282). The reduction in the net profit is mainly as a result of increasing labour costs but there are also increases in the food cost and overhead costs, which are contributing to this reduction in the net profit.

### General overview

■ Sales on food are more-or-less static on budget whilst drink sales are slightly over budget. Also the main problems are seen to be staff costs along with food cost being over budget along with increasing overhead costs.

- Overall there is a need to reduce costs to budget or increase sales to achieve targeted net profit.

- Assuming the budget to be accurate, and that costs can be brought under control, there may be little need for change. However, without information on the nature of the customer demand being met, and the business environment in which this restaurant is operating, no further judgement can be made.

Additional information required to make evaluation more complete will include:

- Basis of budget formulation including investigation of budgeting procedures to identify their appropriateness and accuracy.

- Previous trading information for comparison and to consider trends over the longer term.

- Analysis of sales mix and service period breakdown to show types of customer demand being met and popularity of menu and beverage items.

- Examination of food costs, purchasing and control system including pricing of food items. As well as possible problems with the relationship between demand and purchasing, which may lead to waste, there may also be difficulties with increases in prices of food.

- Identification of reason for drink sales increase and higher gross profit in order to determine cause (overages can indicate problems as much as shortages).

- Staffing information and breakdown of wage costs including investigation of staffing costs with a view to reducing them in line with budget.

- Examination of reasons for the high variance in actual overhead costs against budget.

- Assessment of the business environment.

# INDEX